EVERYTHING I NEEDED TO KNOW ABOUT BUSINESS...
I LEARNED FROM
A CANADIAN

Leonard Brody and David Raffa

SECOND EDITION

WILEY

John Wiley & Sons Canada, Ltd.

Library and Archives Canada Cataloguing in Publication Data

Brody, Leonard
    Everything I needed to know about business...I learned
from a Canadian / Leonard Brody, David Raffa. — 2nd ed.
Includes index.
ISBN 978-0-470-15975-0
    1. Success in business. 2. Management. 3. Success in
business—Canada. 4. Management—Canada. 5. Entrepreneurship—
Canada. 6. Businesspeople—Canada—Biography. I. Raffa, David
II. Title.
HF5386.B842 2008   658.4   C2008-906495-X

Production Credits

Cover design: Graham Dobson
Interior text design: Natalia Burobina
Printer: Tri-Graphic Printing

John Wiley & Sons Canada, Ltd.
6045 Freemont Blvd.
Mississauga, Ontario
L5R 4J3

Printed in Canada

1 2 3 4 5 TRI 13 12 11 10 09

I dedicate this book to the teachers in my life who have always pushed me to be a better student:

To my mother Esther for showing me what it truly means to be an entrepreneur.

To my father Irwin for teaching me the fine art of resiliency.

To my sister Lisa for her fortitude and courage.

To my niece Natalie for finally showing me the meaning of the word 'love'.

To my grandparents, Yona-Moshe, Manya & Lajos for watching over me and making me desperately want to be a better person in preparation for that special day when I get the chance to meet them.

To my step brother & sister Noel and Moira for reminding me that family is more than blood.

To my cousins Randy, Cara, Shauna, Mark, Brian, Marilyn, Didi, Wendy, Leslie, Karen and Marla for showing me what it means to cherish and forgive your parents.

To my Aunty Cecile & Uncle Aaron for giving me the gift of a Jewish education when it truly wasn't in my reach.

To my brothers from another mother: Morty, Harry, Lance, Ben, Nathan, Yuck, Phil and Mitch for constantly reminding me how truly meaningless this all is and that hanging out is really all that matters.

To the cities of Tokmak, Odessa, Melitopol & Tel-Aviv for the gift of knowing where I came from and for the stark reminder of just how lucky I am to be a Canadian.

Finally and sadly, I dedicate this book to the memory of:

My Aunty Betty Shapiro, you were always like a mother to me. You are so missed.

My cousin Israel Asper, thank you for believing in me. I carry your words with me everyday.

Leonard Brody

I would like to dedicate this book to the women in my life.

To the loving memory of my mother, Anne Raffa, who taught me so many valuable lessons, which I carry with me to this day, and who encouraged me to go above and beyond. I miss you Mom.

To my wife, Louise, my best friend and soul mate. Mama Gator, you continue to inspire me, thrill me, surprise me, love me and support me. Without you, none of it would have been possible, and none of it would matter. I so look forward to our continuing our excellent adventure together.

To my three incredible, spirited, adventurous daughters, Lindsay, Rachel and Carmen. You are the greatest gifts I have ever received. Go do crazy things that inspire you, excite you, thrill you and scare you. You girls rock.

You are the fuel that feeds my fire.

David J. Raffa

Contents

Foreword

BY ANGUS REID

I've spent a good part of the last thirty years engaged in that quintessentially Canadian passion: trying to figure out what makes us unique as Canadians, especially in relation to our cousins in the USA. Oh, I've looked at a lot of surveys, polls and statistics that more or less conform with the established CBC definition of Canadians as a caring, community-minded people who, so far at least, put programs like health care ahead of tax cuts. And I've seen some questionable characterizations of Canadian culture when it comes to social issues— contrary to some thinking, we're not all social welfare cases who want the government to intervene in every aspect of our lives. But if there's one stereotype about Canadians that's dead wrong, it's that we're a bunch of economic morons who approach the bustling world economy with the acumen of someone who recently fell off a turnip truck.

When I was asked to write the foreword to this book on Canadian entrepreneurs, I jumped at the opportunity for two reasons—one political and the other personal. With respect to the first, my motivation was to challenge several myths about the source of Canada's economic success. We don't put nearly enough emphasis on the importance of entrepreneurship as a fundamental driver of the Canadian economy. A lot of words have been used over the years to describe Canadians' national character but here's one I'll bet you haven't heard very often: *enterprising*. That's right. Canadians are entrepreneurial, business-minded, resourceful, venturesome—in short, we've become a nation of hustlers. And as stories like those presented in this book attest, it turns out we're pretty good at it.

Before I examine the broader issue of entrepreneurship in Canada, a brief note is in order on my personal interest in this subject and my second reason for writing this foreword. Maybe it's just the company I keep, but I seem to be increasingly surrounded by friends and relatives starting new ventures or at least beginning to tilt their creativity and energy in the direction of new opportunities. Forget about the *Survivor* series on TV or even Donald Trump's popular *Apprentice* program; the biggest entertainment in my house (at least for me!) is the many hours spent listening and learning about the latest small business capers of my son Andrew (market research software for the Internet), son-in-law Grant (small ticket leasing), brother Mark (cell phones and business equipment) or any of several budding entrepreneurs who care to darken my door.

There's no adrenaline rush quite like starting your own business. And nothing is more likely to give you long sleepless nights or turn you into a chronic user of Tums. I've had plenty of personal experience in all these departments. In 1979, I made a life-changing decision that I've never regretted. I took a big gamble and left my privileged (and tenured) position as a university professor to start my own market research and polling company. And I did this in Winnipeg, probably the toughest market in the country to sell those services (because everyone knows each other in Winnipeg and doesn't need a poll to figure out what the community is thinking!).

I didn't know what a balance sheet was, thought the smiling guy in the corner office at my bank was actually my friend (his name really was Mr. Coffin!) and believed that the best way to bring partners and senior colleagues into my business was to have a lawyer do the negotiation. I survived a couple dozen cash flow crises, had my share of personnel problems and dealt with attacks (mostly unfair, but sometimes deserved) from competitors and the odd journalist.

But with a lot of hard work, a bit of luck and some fortunate timing, I was able to grow this business from nearly zilch in year one to about $50 million in sales twenty years later. By 1999, the Angus Reid Group had become the largest research company in Canada with offices across North America and an annual growth rate of 30 percent. We had a portfolio of blue chip clients and contracts with the likes of London's *The Economist* and Atlanta-based CNN. Not bad for a company that was started above a 7-11 in Winnipeg by a kid with a degree in sociology.

It turns out that in 1979 I wasn't the only Canadian starting his own business. Indeed, according to Stats Canada, the country as a whole was experiencing the start of a revolution of sorts—beginning around the time that I was shifting from the ivory towers of academia to the private sector.

Throughout most of the 1960s and '70s, the Canadian and American labour forces were very similar, with about ten percent of workers in each country self-employed. But starting in 1979 and gaining momentum as the new millennium approached, self employment levels in Canada zoomed ahead of those in the USA. Through the 1990s, self-employment growth was responsible for an astounding 80 percent of all new jobs in Canada compared with the US, where self-employment growth hardly made any difference to net new jobs. When the dust started to settle in 2000, US self-employment levels were still at about ten percent of all jobs while in Canada these levels had practically doubled to almost 20 percent. Almost one in five Canadian workers were self-employed and, in some provinces, such as BC, this figure approached 25 percent.

Based on these figures one might be excused for assuming that matters like small business, entrepreneurship and new ventures would be at the top of the government's economic agenda. But think again. Until recently, small business was combined with tourism in most provinces as an area of ministerial responsibility.

During the 1990s Canada was engaged in what Paul Martin, then finance minister and later our Prime Minister, called a battle for economic survival. But who really won this battle? Looking back almost a decade some would have us believe that tough economic medicine deserves much of the credit. But what about the literally hundreds of thousands of Canadians who started new ventures after jumping (or being pushed) from the towers of the Canadian business establishment? Where's their monument?

During the first decade of the twenty-first century, the Canadian economy has been remarkably resilient. Our captains of industry and politicians of all stripes have been eager to claim credit for Canada's recent economic successes; but for me, the real story has to do with all those who started new ventures, especially during the 1990s. For those who care to connect the dots it should come as no surprise that a workforce made up of increasing numbers of self-employed is also a workforce where people work harder and smarter in the face of adversity and change and aren't likely to lay themselves off.

If Canada's entrepreneurial revolution has played such a key role in producing a vibrant economy, it follows that public policy must focus on how to nurture and sustain it. Doing so will require attention on two fronts: firstly, recognizing and reinforcing those elements of our society that have helped produce this remarkable transformation; and, secondly, identifying ways to facilitate the further growth and development of our home-grown enterprises.

The reasons for the fairly recent, yet remarkable differences between Canada and the US in the area of self-employment are matters of vigorous debate. But at least two of the unique features of Canadian society that may play a strong role in producing our special entrepreneurial landscape may come as a surprise to those who prefer ideological purity in all matters pertaining to business. They're our strong commitment to both public education and universal health care. The former has produced a level of education that's the highest in the Americas and towards the top of the list around the world. This is key because becoming an entrepreneur in the new economy requires strong analytical skills to tackle the opportunities that exist in the burgeoning services sector where most new businesses are started.

As for health care, the kind of publicly supported, universal system that exists in Canada is far more conducive to new business startups than the system in the US. Part of this is simply a matter of economics—this is one expense that new and growing business in Canada need not incur. But more importantly, under the Canadian system there is full portability, which means that workers, even those with existing health conditions, can switch jobs and even start their own businesses without fear of crushing health insurance costs, or, even worse, no insurance at all.

The examples of education and health care underscore important links between public programs and private initiative in Canada. That both health care and education have been suffering from inadequate funding and growing problems of access and quality should be a concern not just for Canada's liberal-left, but also for our business community.

And finally there's the matter of how to provide a more fertile environment for the many new ventures in Canada to grow and prosper after they've passed through the formative stage. I know there are a lot of issues that get discussed in this context, including access to foreign markets, the availability of skilled labour, support for research and development and those perennial favourites—cutting taxes and red tape. But for me and a great many other company founders that I know, the inefficiency of Canada's capital markets is the most important determent.

Consider my own experience. By the time the new millennium arrived, the Angus Reid Group was on the cusp of being transformed from a Canadian leader to a global player. At just that moment, we met the fate of most other rapidly growing Canadian companies—we got gobbled up by a bigger fish. A French-based company with the unlikely name of Ipsos offered us almost $100 million in cash. How could we refuse?

In the summer and fall of 1999, we had tried to tap Canadian financial markets with a $5 million offering priced at less than half the deal we did with Ipsos in early 2000. But there were virtually no takers (we ended up raising the money through a pre-existing group of external shareholders). The experience of trying to raise money in Canada for an existing small cap player left me cold. Without added capital, my dream of building a global operation was brought to ground. But fortunately there was a silver lining—the significant premium paid by our acquisitor provided balm for any wounds.

Heard this story before? You bet. Every day the business pages report another Canadian company being gobbled up by an international player. Sometimes we even hear about it going the other way where a Canadian company is the acquirer. But lately, that seems to be the exception. In the Canadian market research industry, most of the large firms are now part of foreign companies and none are themselves global players. This seems to be increasingly the case for most sectors of the Canadian economy. Unless action is taken soon on this front, we may find ourselves confined to serving as an incubator of new ventures; a nursery to feed global businesses hungry for energy and creativity.

This book tells the story of twenty-four of Canada's most successful entrepreneurs. Some are household names and others are barely known outside their business categories; some started with nothing and others grabbed the reins of already successful companies founded by others; some made their stake in Canada, others abroad. But all share the common passion of entrepreneurs around the world: the courage and sensibility to appreciate risk, a sense for innovation and the ability to lead others in pursuit of common goals. And all have demonstrated what can be accomplished on the global stage by Canadians in business.

Over the last decade, Canada has made huge strides as an enterprising society. If we can get it right over the next twenty-five years, we'll see the list of internationally recognized businesses from Canada grow dramatically. The leaders are already out there—we just have to make sure we're prepared to support them.

And, by the way, I'm now one of "them"—again. A couple of years after I sold my original business I got involved in a start up with my son Andrew. We're peddling polling and related software through a dozen offices from Sydney to Paris. We're already bigger than the company we sold in 2000 and in no hurry to sell. Like most entrepreneurs across this great country, we're addicted to chasing dreams, even at the risk of confronting the odd nightmare.

Acknowledgements

Leonard and David would like to show their sincerest gratitude to the following people who, in their own special way, pitched in and made this book a reality:

We owe you…big time.

Jinny Addesa, Debra Amador, Andrew Atkins, Kelly Beck, Mikki Brunner, Maureen Chant, Denis Connor, Wiliam Fox, Ray Matthews, Jim Heppell, Frank Holler, Tanner Philp and all of the staff at Lions Capital, Neil Huff, Angel Marino, Candace Moakler, Terry Nagel, Penny Nightingale, Joseph Nostor, Rich Simons, Faith Strecker-Nemish, Sophie Tsementzis, Victor Webb, Kelly Will, Michael Adams, Ron Bernbaum, Michael Binder, Ian Burchett, Mark Busse and Industrial Brand Creative, Jim Charlton, Sherry Cooper, Linda Davidson, Alan Edwards, Leonard Edwards, Harvey Enchin, Pat Fera, Rob Fonberg, Marcel Gaumond, Ann Gibbons, Michele Goshulak, Marcy Grossman, Peter Harder, Val Jackson, Paul Kedrosky, John Klassen, Paul Laberge, Debbie Landa, Thierry LeVasseur, Michael Levine, Jaime Pitfield, Arnie Pollard, George Reznik, Thane Stenner, John Tennant, Chaim Wigoda and The Team at Wiley Canada.

Most importantly, we want to thank the subjects of this book for giving us their valuable time and insight…for allowing us into their world and giving us all the gift of their wisdom.

A Very Heartfelt Thank You

This book would not have happened without the work ethic, dedication and spirit of:

Tony Wanless (twanless@knowpreneur.net). You are a true gentleman and it was a pleasure to call you a team mate.

An enormous thank you to Bonnie Irving and Tracy Mabone who collectively made this book more meaningful than we could have every accomplished without them.

Without the hard work and dedication of Rahaf Harfoush, this second edition would have never seen the light of day….thank you.

Introduction

Every journey starts with an elemental spark—a decision. Regardless of the path taken or its outcome, choosing to move forward is the essence of business. But while sparks are necessary, they will not sustain a fire. In 2003, this book was nothing more than an idea, an ember we floated about over coffee from time to time. But as we discussed some of the themes we might cover and people we might interview, the spark soon grew into a small flame. As the writing process got underway, the stories and insights we had the good fortune of hearing fanned that flame, and before we knew it—a fire. As the final parts of the book came together in the fall of 2004, we came to believe that the themes and lessons in this book were not just something for us as authors to be proud of, but critical for our nation to stand up and pay attention to.

Our goal was to follow up on the success of the book that Leonard had written two years earlier, *Innovation Nation: Canadian Leadership from Java to Jurassic Park*, by giving it a sibling. However, we believed that this kin, although younger in age, would have to be more mature and advanced than its older counterpart—sibling rivalry at its finest. We wanted a linear book that was easy to read and touched the four corners of management/entrepreneurial issues. And while we wanted to include some of the usual suspects, we also wanted to secure the thoughts of successful Canadians who were off the radar screen and had made their mark in something other than a traditional business.

Upon closer inspection, it was amazing to discover how many candidates fit this bill, and just how far their reach spread throughout the globe. To ensure that the book was more than just mere profiles, we adopted a rule that if a chapter was too focused on the person and did not provide a valuable take-away, it was scrapped. Moreover, if the lesson did not provide new and incisive ideas, we interviewed and re-interviewed until it got there.

While passing along the advice of these thought-leaders was a primary motivation behind this project, we also had a much higher purpose in mind—to inspire our fellow Canadians. There is no doubt that we have, as a country, lacked anecdotal nourishment when searching for business icons we could call our own. Yet Canadians should appreciate, as we think this book demonstrates, that they belong to a breed that is truly the best in the world. In fact, we believe strongly that if this book doesn't, at a minimum, strike that chord, we have failed.

In conversations around boardrooms throughout the globe, when businesspeople are opining on the great entrepreneurial nations of our time, it is nothing short of a travesty that Canada's name is too often overlooked. We are, as a people, some of the most savvy, shrewd and innovative players of the new millennium. The good news is that we are almost always referred to in the way that you would want to hear others speaking about your own children. We are thought of as kind, good-natured, thoughtful and easy to get along with. To be sure, these are all great attributes. We are, however, much more than that. If you take these attributes and layer the truth about our corporate prowess on top, Canadians are simply the best business partners you could ever hope for.

Why are we so strong? This could easily be the subject of another book altogether (a challenge of which we hope the likes of an Angus Reid or Michael Adams might some day undertake). For our purposes here, let us just say that it is our history, geography and political culture that have brought us to pole position. We believe that Canadians have three fundamental characteristics that make us champions in the business sphere:

- We are a nation of listeners and observers.
- Innovation has been at the core of our soul since before Confederation.

- We understand the fine art of compromise.

Canada is one of the few liberal democracies in the world that was created without the hand of conflict pushing at its back. We experienced no revolution, suffered through no civil war. Rather, our ancestors were people who listened and observed the environment and pressures around them. Out of this methodology, a nation was born. When looked at from a business perspective, the Canadian heritage is rooted in our profound ability to deeply understand market forces and to produce results based on that comprehension: we listen, observe, and then respond. You can't open a management book these days without hearing the praises and importance of both. In fact, many would argue these are the most important skills in business today. We, as a country, have mastered them.

Due to the geographic constraints that Canada has faced from day one, innovation has consistently been one of the most critical elements of our national fabric. The country could not have survived without its preoccupation with research and development. Whenever technological advances could be used to unite the country—radio, satellite, mobile phones—it was embraced at the federal level and Canadians consistently led the global adoption curve in usage. The construction of our national railway (very different in purpose than similar efforts in the U.S.) is an example of this exercise in technological nation building. Quietly, innovation became a part of our everyday lives; Canada is one of few nations where technology was required to physically conjoin its citizens.

And finally, most observers would agree that, as a generalization, Canadians are a compromising bunch. It makes us easy to work with, likable and masters at bringing people together. Whether it was years of growing up playing shinny in the backyard, or learning how to interact creatively when snowed in for days on end, we are great at getting along with everyone. Try this little test: ask Americans who have worked with a Canadian whether or not they liked that individual. The answer is a resounding yes 99 percent of the time. (Of course, we are neither statisticians nor pollsters, so forgive our crude methodology.) Simply put, Canadians make great team mates.

So, where has this gotten us? In a word—results. The Global Entrepreneurship Monitor has consistently ranked Canada as one of the top 10 entrepreneurial nations in the world. We are fourth in the world in business efficiency, according to the World Competitiveness Yearbook (WCY), and that same report rated Canada as the third most competitive economy on the planet in 2004. Not bad for a nation that makes up less than three percent of global production. The WCY also dispelled a classic Canadian self-deprecation—that we are not as experienced as business managers as our neighbours to the south. Well, according to the WCY, we are one of the best there is when it comes to management practices. And finally, *The Economist* predicted Canada would be the most competitive economic engine globally from 2004 to 2009.

Much of this success has come at the behest of private sector efforts to ensure we brought up our game considerably from what was a very difficult period for this country during the early 1990s. However, most macroeconomists understand that entrepreneurialism in its purest form, without policy nurturing it and providing a level playing field, leads to the kind of disaster that saw Roosevelt forcibly bring in the New Deal in 1929. So, kudos to the Canadian government for putting innovation and entrepreneurialism on their agenda. Whether right or wrong, agree or disagree, a thank you is in order to our captains in Ottawa for at least putting the ball in play. They listened to industry and reacted. From lowering taxes to boosting R&D spending and venture capital output, this country is a very different place today than it was in 1994. These steps have helped us rise from the ashes of a crippling deficit to be the only nation in the G-8 to produce a surplus budget eight years running.

That is not to say that all is rosy. We still have a significant amount of work to do if we are to earn our rightful seat at the global table. We don't have the time to consider all of the necessary fixes in this book, nor do we, the humble authors, have the knowledge or experience to propose all of the specific measures. However, we do believe that there is one thing that must be in place in order for us to continue moving forward. We require a change in our attitude toward ourselves—a fundamental shift in our spirit. This thought is nothing new and was espoused by the late Israel ("Izzy") Asper, the like of whom as a character and entrepreneur we will not see for a very long time. We are rightly accused of having a national preoccupation with being "Lords of the Middle Kingdom" (sorry, Frodo). Izzy used to say that the difference between the person who owns a single cable station and someone who owns an international network is that the latter chose to think big. So, the best way to remember one of our greatest entrepreneurs is to live up to his words: reach for the stars or don't bother. We have the prowess, the culture, the temperament, and now, after this last great decade in our history, the experience. Forward march.

What you'll find in these pages are some of the greatest management thinkers of our era opining on the great mysteries of business today. The subjects are varied—from the captain of one of the most famous writing teams in Hollywood, Joel Cohen of *The Simpsons*, teaching you about lessons on teamwork, to world-renowned architect Moshe Safdie, who advocates building community into an organization. All of these individuals have two threads tying them together— they are the thought leaders in their respective fields, and they all happen to be Canadian.

As both of us are active in the venture and entrepreneurial community on a daily basis, we thought it might be fitting to end off with a thought or two of our own. After much debate over many coffees, we realized that that best advice we could offer doesn't come from the business sphere at all. It comes instead from the famous playwright and philosopher, George Bernard Shaw, and may be the best summary of the many messages contained in the pages to come:

People are always blaming their circumstances for what they are. I don't believe in circumstances. The people who get on in this world are the people who get up and look for the circumstances they want, and, if they can't find them, make them.

(George Bernard Shaw, *Mrs. Warren's Profession*, 1893)

After telling people about this book over the last year, we have both been accused of being shameless flag wavers. Well, we couldn't agree more. We hope this book inspires you to grab one and join us.

Leonard Brody & David Raffa
Fall, 2004

PART ONE

First Period

Learning to Skate

CHAPTER ONE

Within These Walls

Place, Harmony and Organizational Design

FEATURING THE WISDOM OF MOSHE SAFDIE

Most new ventures begin with a loose organizational structure to accommodate flexibility and uncertainty. In fact, at the outset, many companies don't put much thought into the subject at all. At some point, however, organizational design becomes necessary in order for a company to function effectively as a mature entity.

Where better to look for inspiration about that structure than among architects, who design the spaces where people live and work every day? Their creations—which foster harmony, inspire creativity and, most important, build community—reflect design principles that also apply to companies.

Moshe Safdie is a world-renowned architect, and has spent his life developing his body of work. In 1967 his student thesis became the Habitat building at the World Exposition in Montreal. The tiered and stacked structure of living spaces, which still holds iconic status, included in its landscape a series of open spaces where residents could gather and talk. Evoking images of the plazas and bazaars of the ancient cities of the Middle East, Habitat shook the architecture world and set Safdie on a course that would see him design many of the world's foremost structures.

In his career, Moshe Sadfie has designed everything from houses to office buildings, libraries to giant scientific laboratories, even entire cities. In all his designs, he has incorporated the "linear centre"—his signature theme—a place where people can meet and feel comfortable enough to exchange ideas. It is the architectural form of home.

To Safdie, a linear centre is a must-have for every community. Since busi-nesses are, in essence, communities, Safdie's linear centre concept can also be applied to the building of organizations. Safdie's emphasis on individuals' needs for positive interaction—whether in buildings, cities or companies— is essential thinking for all business managers who wish to maximize their human resources.

—⁓—

Update: *Moshe is currently working on several projects that will be com-pleted in 2009. These include the Marina Bay Sands project in Singapore, the Asian University for Women in Bangladesh, and the United States Institute for Peace headquarters in Washington D.C.*

When a painter begins to design a work of art, he or she usually starts by applying a group of design principles to the piece and then favours one or two to fulfill its purpose. In Rembrandt's case, for example, it was a balance of light and dark to evoke a sense of mystery. When Beethoven composed a symphony, he favoured repetition of a signa-ture refrain to create a series of aural crescendos.

In fact, when they begin their works, designers from all disciplines apply a standard set of principles that have been recognized for cen-turies. Invariably they take some combination of the seven design ele-ments—balance, repetition, gradation, contrast, harmony, dominance and unity—to form a finished work emphasizing one or two of the elements to give it a unique signature.

While they may not consider themselves artists in the traditional sense, entrepreneurs and managers alike are designers of a sort when it comes to the composition of their businesses. Like artistic design, organizational design involves the combination of several elements to form a cohesive and powerful whole—in this case a company. The dif-ference between entrepreneurs and designers, however, is that entre-preneurs rarely recognize the greater purpose their design serves.

This failure is the downfall of most organizational architects. En-veloped in examining revenues, profit and loss, and other metrics, managers tend to take a structural, instead of a holistic, point of view. A business, however, is not just an organization geared toward financial gain; it is a medium built around the people who are its sum.

Many businesses survive as small entrepreneurial entities without any forethought into organizational planning. But as an enterprise grows, functions demand an increasingly intricate structure to correlate and harness those diverse tasks and division of labour. Companies must be purposely designed, instead of merely being roughly structured, before they can be trusted to grow organically.

Unfortunately, once systems are required, they might morph into bureaucracies that force compartmentalization in order to operate "efficiently." But this can result in smothering human interaction and stifling the creativity that was the reason for the organization's existence in the first place. (Often what is done to create efficiency is itself inefficient.) Further, badly designed enterprises can subvert the ongoing work. Organizational design must be planned for so that managers can control it. The injection of design into the creation of an enterprise has led many theorists to refer to it by another term—"organizational architecture."

This name was coined by authors David A. Nadler and Marc S. Gerstein. Their article "What Is Organizational Architecture?" advanced the premise that "the design of social systems such as organizations is fundamentally similar to the design of physical artifacts such as buildings. If architecture is the art of shaping physical space to meet human needs and aspirations, then organizational architecture is the art of shaping 'behavioural' space to meet the needs and aspirations of a business."[1]

Architecture, they explained, involves four components that must fit together to make an effective building. They defined these as purpose, structural materials, style and collateral technology. This same component fit could be applied to organizational design, they added. "Just as designing buildings presents architects with fundamental questions about purpose, structural materials, style and collateral technologies, designing organizations poses a parallel set of questions for senior managers.

"The chief role of the CEO in the corporation of the future will be to imbue a company's design with clarity of purpose, to ensure that the design can fulfill the strategic requirements of the business (since even flawless execution cannot compensate for limitations of basic architecture) and to utilize the most appropriate organizational building materials."[2]

1   David A. Nadler and Marc S. Gerstein, What is Organizational Architecture? *Harvard Business Review*, 1992.
2   "What is Organizational Architecture?" *Harvard Business Review*.

While the authors were pioneers in advancing this theory, some critics were quick to point out flaws in their thinking: buildings cannot be metaphors for organizations because buildings are static and organizations are dynamic. However, this challenge does not destroy the theory in principle; it merely requires a better understanding of what an architect actually does.

Certainly, architecture, at its root, is the design of buildings. But if the task is broken down, architecture also involves the design of physical spaces as they relate to people. In short, it is a design schema that relates to people's collective physical senses, much as a painting is a design scenario that relates to people's visual senses. Architecture therefore involves the design not only of buildings but also of communities, which are collectives of individual people who come together for a common purpose. That is why many architects are now designing not only buildings, but also entire villages, towns and other urban settings—the physical spaces in which communities are contained and thrive.

The encyclopedia Wikipedia defines a community as a "set of people with some shared element. The origin of the word community comes from the Latin *munus*, which means the gift, and *cum*, which means together, among each other, so community could be defined as a group of people who share gifts which they provide to all. When there is a clearly shared interest (economic or otherwise) among a set of people, the people collectively might be called community."[3]

According to social psychologists, there are four elements that contribute to a sense of community:

- membership;
- influence;
- integration and fulfillment of needs;
- shared emotional connection.[4]

Communities defined by physical space or shared interests exhibit all of these attributes and, interestingly, so do most healthy businesses.

---

3 Wikipedia.org.
4 Steven Wright, *Exploring Psychological Sense of Community in Living-learning Programs and in the University as a Whole*, University of Maryland, 2004.

From an architectural point of view, every floor and room creates a smaller community within a larger community of buildings. From an organizational point of view, a business is a community that is often composed of several smaller communities, or departments. In both cases, people come together in groups to share interests and exchange ideas in a form of cross-fertilization, thereby helping each other in the pursuit of those interests.

Organizational design theory has been changing to encompass this view, just as architectural and artistic theory is beginning to filter into the study of organizational behaviour. In particular, some architects are now specializing in the organizational design of communities, physical and corporate. It is in this body of knowledge that companies can learn how to better structure themselves. This has been increasingly recognized by corporate North America, most notably in the technology sector, where traditional boxy closed-door floor plans have often given way to open and individualized workspaces that beget creative interaction.

One such individual who has turned his mind to the organizational design of communities is world-renowned architect Moshe Safdie. A Canadian, Israeli and U.S. citizen, Safdie turned his student thesis into the revolutionary Habitat housing project at Expo 67 in Montreal. Habitat launched a distinguished career of designing some of the most impressive structures in the world. The list includes the National Gallery of Canada in Ottawa, Vancouver's Library Square, the Skirball Cultural Center in Los Angeles and the Eleanor Roosevelt College at the University of California in San Diego. Safdie was also deeply involved with the rebuilding of sections of Jerusalem, taking responsibility for major segments of the restoration of the Old City and the reconstruction of the new centre, thereby linking the Old and New Cities. Also in Israel, where he maintains an office (as he does in Toronto), Safdie was involved in the design of the new city of Modi'in, the Yad Vashem Holocaust Museum and the Rabin Memorial Center.

Safdie, 67, has also been active with projects in the developing world and has designed two airports, the Lester B. Pearson International Airport in Toronto (in a joint venture with Canada's Adamson Associates and New York architects Skidmore, Owings & Merrill) and the Ben Gurion International Airport in Israel. Safdie has served as Director of Urban Design and Ian Woodner Professor of Architecture and

Urban Design at the Harvard Graduate School of Design, in addition
to teaching at various other universities.

In his work Safdie has shown a marked desire to apply modern
architectural thought to historical structures, and to design spaces that
reflect change while preserving the values of community, particularly
citizen interaction. Many of his large-scale projects, such as his first
work, Habitat, and the rebuilding of sections of Jerusalem, involve
stacking living spaces around central plazas to encourage public interaction—in his mind, the heart of community life. Similarly, his public
buildings, such as libraries in Vancouver and Salt Lake City, promi-
nently feature public squares where people can assemble.

Safdie advocates the need to recognize the requirements of community in urban design. He is the author of several books on architecture and urban planning, especially *The City After the Automobile*,
which introduced his concept of a "linear centre"—a central area of
concentrated development that serves as a public arena and gathering
place. This public arena, or plaza—a place where people can interact
and exchange ideas—is central to almost all of Safdie's work. He believes public interaction is essential to urban life if people are to thrive.
This explains why crowded city centres often have a sense of kinship
while (largely suburban) areas ruled by the automobile do not.

Similarly, Safdie feels that just as urban areas and buildings should
be constructed around linear centres, every organization that wants
to thrive must incorporate this concept of community into their day-
to-day affairs. The overarching principle that governs Safdie's designs
strongly applies to the architecture of an organization. The formation of a structure that encourages human interaction, idea exchange
and creativity is as needed within the walls of business as it is within
a city.

"I translate the linear centre to business by asking, 'How do you
make a business capable of growing and expanding while maintaining
its integrity and organic wholesomeness?'" he says. "By organic wholesomeness, I mean that the very parts that make the business healthy and
effective are able to maintain a positive relationship to each other, and
are able to expand and change as they maintain mutually supportive
relationships with each other. It means more people can be absorbed
into a business, and communications systems continue to work in a

way that does not regress into a business that requires an enormous bureaucracy that is counterproductive."

Although Safdie also uses artistic design principles in architecture, he takes the concept a step further by applying those principles to communities. Anyone designing an organization of any kind should do the same. In fact, Safdie encourages the application of artistic thinking to organizational or business design because he feels it may help right many of the wrongs he believes exist in the business world today. The main problem he sees through his architect's eye is the breakdown of integrity—a word most think means only moral values, but artists usually take to also mean soundness or, as the dictionary defines it, "a condition that is unimpaired."

"In a sense, the unmitigated marketplace economy means maximization of profit, which is also associated with maximization of growth because so much of profit today has to do with growth," he explains. "[But] a fundamental issue that faces business communities today is the capacity to maintain integrity deep in their minds and hearts, and not succumb to moves which might appear to be profitable short term, but which fundamentally compromise the integrity of what they're doing."

It is Safdie's view that organizations are often badly designed because those responsible think only in terms of function at the outset. This is likely because organizational design principles are often based on the interrelationship of elements that work together to support efficient operations. The basic organizational model involves a combination of:

- systems—methods for allocating and controlling resources;
- climate—the emotional state of the organization's members;
- culture—the mix of behaviours, thoughts, beliefs, symbols and artifacts of an organization;
- strategy—a plan for success in the marketplace;
- policies and procedures—formal rules that define how a company does business;
- structure—a hierarchy of authority.[5]

---

5   Steven Silbiger, *The Ten-Day MBA*, Quill William Morrow, 1999.

A PLACE WHERE EVERYBODY KNOWS YOUR NAME

All structures, including businesses, need a centre, or core. In organizational design, this core comprises the people who are its genetic makeup. To create a sense of community, people need to feel at home and require places to interact.

People—individuals with thoughts, feelings and behaviours—are at the centre of this ring of elements. So both Safdie with his artistic orientation and the basic organizational model with its functional outlook share a common purpose—each shapes the design around its core: people. With Safdie, it is the requirement that people interact within their community; with the organizational model, it is the needs of the individuals who form the base unit of the model. Unfortunately, organizations, particularly businesses with their concentration on intangibles such as profit and growth, often forget that the people who exist in their communities are the essential and basic building block.

Says Safdie: "A community is enriching. It is a group of people that has the potential for enriching each person's experience within the group, through interaction and sharing. I think businesses range from being families to extended families and at a certain stage become communities. When a business has 200 to 300 people it is on the scale of a community. Of course the question then becomes, what constitutes a sense of community? When do people see they are part of a community instead of part of an affiliation, an organization or other parts of our society?"

To Safdie, this sense of community grows out of a sense of place, of belonging. And when companies grow, they often lose this connection. If the communal spirit of an organization withers, it is likely to lose its purpose for being. It becomes overly bureaucratic, and the people that helped it grow are no longer the creative engine that drives it forward. He has seen similar transitions occur with buildings, or collections of buildings, that were meant to house communities.

As an example, Safdie describes his visit to two very different laboratory complexes when he was researching a project that would provide similar facilities to a large group of scientists. One was the Fermi Lab, a 35-storey tower outside Chicago, while the other was Cern, a village-like campus near Geneva. The campus had a sense of community because all services were located in a central square. Everyone working in the lab cluster had to pass through the square to eat, pick up mail and perform other workday functions: this area became the "village" centre where people met and interacted. The tower, on the other hand, did not have a sense of community because there were no gathering places for people. The only space common to everyone in the building was the elevator.

Says Safdie: "An elevator is not exactly a place, and people in tall buildings don't have much chance to interact as they are going in and out by elevator to specific destinations. They don't get to meet gradually; they don't tend to cluster, even if there is a restaurant; each component of community services is detached. So a community needs 'place' [where interaction can occur]. Without place, a community has a hard time surviving."

Organizational designers say it is a rudimentary, but undeveloped, understanding of this concept that compels many companies to refuse to allow staff to telecommute. Although they may not quite understand the theory, these companies implicitly recognize that working alone at home prevents interaction with fellow workers and can create a sense of isolation. If the individual, whose behaviour (and productivity) is a result of his or her feelings or thoughts, is severed from the group, those behaviours can sometimes be counterproductive. This can also be the case with virtual businesses created by the Internet, and many advisors to small, single-person and Internet-based businesses recommend that these people get out and meet other people more often in order to refresh their thinking.

These advisors recognize that we are, in essence, social animals. And Safdie, while recognizing the efficiencies and geographic diversity that can be provided by modern communications such as the Internet and email, also believes it is a basic human requirement to interact with other humans.

Says Safdie: "I am sceptical and old-fashioned, and perhaps very traditional in my assessment of the capacity of the virtual place of communications to replace face to face. I think in my own firm (which has offices in Boston, Toronto and Jerusalem) and in other larger ones with far more sophisticated communications networks, I don't see them replacing the cross-fertilization and excitement and exchange of ideas that occur in face-to-face settings. With the advent of (advanced) communications, the number of professional conferences, of people travelling long distances to meetings, of companies investing in get-aways, is all on the rise. This shows there is a hunger for that which we associate with community."

That hunger, however, while palpable, is often ignored in orga-nizations when they grow out of their infancy and into adolescence. It is not uncommon in business for an entrepreneurial organization in which every worker has creative input and operates across several functions to grow to a size where it becomes industrialized, and work-ers are put on a kind of production line where their work is narrowed to a single task-based function. They are no longer part of the whole, they are simply one its parts.

This mass production model, first designed by Henry Ford when he created car production plants in Detroit, still works relatively well for the manufacturing industries. But it can be dangerous for a com-pany that produces services, especially "knowledge services" that rely on the brainpower and creativity of their workers to perform. Increas-ingly, the Western world's economies are moving to knowledge-based services instead of production of hard goods; the imposition of indus-trial organizational structures on a non-industrial business will create problems.

LESS IS MORE

When designing an organization, one must be conscious of scale. Increased size can create rigidity and result in the slow death of a company's dynamism. That is why many organizational designs now include some way to maintain a sense of intimacy within those structures. Small, comfortable meeting spaces—"gathering places" where people can generate the free flow of ideas—con-tribute to the entrepreneurial quality of the enterprise.

One solution is keeping the concept of "small" in the business. Not only are many micro-entrepreneurial businesses continuing to appear on the scene, but also many small to medium-sized businesses are refusing to grow beyond a certain point in order to retain the nimbleness at the centre of their value proposition. If they do grow, many are now taking great pains to remain entrepreneurial in spirit by creating centres of excellence, cross-functional teams, and by placing more responsibility on individual workers. Small is now considered beautiful—and productive; the concept of top-down, command-and-control management is taking a back seat in the minds of many executives today.

Safdie still sees the industrialized concept of "mega" as a problem, not only in business, but also in society as a whole. This may be a left-over from the twentieth-century concept of industrialization, or it may be an entirely new concept: he's not sure. He is, however, confident from an artistic and architectural point of view that this "mega-zation" is creating tension and is harming the concept of community. He also believes that in the long run it is inefficient, because although it appears to create efficiencies, it eventually destroys the creativity that is at the heart of all organizations.

Says Safdie: "Our culture and our economy tend toward bigness and the massive in everything we do. I feel my mission is the opposite. Mega-scale is dehumanizing; it disconnects our sense of self-identity from the sense of community because it's on such a scale that the community can't really exist. It's not broken down to any hierarchy of places that we can relate to. My whole mission as a designer is to discover the interventions that can modify and mitigate the effect of mega-scale.

"It will be interesting to see how this plays out. There are many, many smaller businesses and there is an interrelationship that functions with smaller businesses. That's really exciting in terms of the capacity of individuals to affect decisions, leadership, and team efforts within these groups. That's really what architecture practice is all about, and we also see it in some medical groups and in the professions. But I can't not be overwhelmed at the same time with what is happening in big business, which is getting bigger and bigger."

KNIT A VARIED QUILT

Once you provide the forum for people to assemble, establish working groups made up of diverse sets of employees. Homogeneity and groupthink do not contribute to the generation of incremental thought; differing opinions are more likely the prescription.

Smaller scale also allows another essential requirement of a community to thrive, Safdie believes. This is simply diversity—of ages, cultures, beliefs, viewpoints and opinions. Diversity begets creativity, which cannot exist in a culture where everyone thinks in unison. That is why a creative culture is an essential building block for every organization. "Diversity is critical for community," he says. "If everybody is exactly the same, that might be an interesting group of people, but I feel that excessive homogeneity is not enriching enough, it is too predictable. It is too familiar. You need the sense of enrichment that comes from surprise."

Throughout history, human social systems have evolved because different viewpoints were introduced to homogeneous groups—it is the essence of creativity, problem solving and innovation to see from a different perspective. New ideas provoke creativity, which in turn encourages innovation, which is imperative in an increasingly competitive business climate.

Therefore, many companies today are encouraging diverse parts of their workforce and operations—their communities—to talk to each other, just as Safdie's citizens interact in the public places he deems so important when constructing buildings. Diversity of views is a concept that almost every business coach and manager is encouraging in organizations, especially in the knowledge economy where information, learning, wisdom, and thereby progress are essential.

"Managers in different [organizational] functions see the world differently, which is good because different challenges confront businesses and different perspectives are required to respond to them," says psychology professor Benjamin Schneider of the University of Maryland. "Simultaneously, however, people in different functions must learn to share some common perspectives, for example, with regard to service quality. Project teams that are comprised of people from different functions are a good way to get people talking."[6]

CREATE A SAFE HARBOUR

People won't share their ideas in a group if they feel those ideas aren't valued, or worse, will be ridiculed or belittled. All employees of every organization must be able to trust that they will be heard, respected and embraced. Effective companies live by the guidelines that there are no stupid questions and no bad ideas. Managers must simply master the art of time and place.

---

6   Benjamin Schneider, *Welcome to the World of Services Management*, University of Maryland, Academy of Management Executive, 2004.

For people within any organization—or public place—to exchange ideas, however, there must be a sense of trust, a feeling that they are respected and can therefore freely speak their minds. Everyone knows of a company where employees are told to just do their jobs and keep quiet. Such companies invariably have high turnover rates because, say organizational designers, the employees are not engaged with the company, do not feel part of it and generally flee such an oppressive situation as soon as possible.

Although these storied companies often believe they function more efficiently by isolating employees, they are in fact dysfunctional. Dr. Peter Eberl of the Institute for Management at Freie Universitat in Berlin, who used game-playing theory to explore the function of trust in organizations, argues that strong trust relationships among workers help make organizations efficient. This trust, he says, should be encouraged through an increase in the frequency of interaction between people, dependencies among people, multiplicity of relationships, co-operative behaviour and support from management.

"In recent years trust has advanced from a border phenomenon to a subject of major relevance in business administration," he writes. "Organization scholars position trust as a central success requirement for new inter- or intra-organizational arrangements. Without a notable dimension of trust, concepts like networks, self-organization or loose coupling seem to promise only a little efficiency. Consequently, trust is even being considered as a strategic competition factor."[7]

To Safdie, trust is an essential aspect of community. If people have a place to meet and exchange ideas, whether in an urban setting or within an organization, they must also feel that their environment allows them to voice those ideas. Without trust, there is no free exchange of ideas and therefore no creative dynamic. And without those, a business is a mere machine instead of a collective of thinking individuals. It is not a community.

"If there is no trust," Safdie explains, "there is a disinclination to make yourself vulnerable, to expose your thoughts and ideas, or to be exposed even physically. Trust is a state of mind needed to partake in the exchange. Sometimes it's simply competition or confrontation, but I think trust is a big ingredient."

Many of Safdie's prescriptions for organizational design, including the need for trust, a continuing exchange of ideas, and a sense of

---

7   Peter Eberl PhD, The Development of Trust and the Implications for Organizational Design: A Game and Attribution Theoretical Framework, *Schmalenbach Business Review*, July 2004.

belonging that is part of community, echo traditional thinking. This is not unusual. For thousands of years, civilizations have used design to reinforce particular belief systems, and every designer, while perhaps searching for a new way of looking at situations, brings to that search a strong sense of history. Indeed, designers and artists often feel their role is to make sense of the past and to integrate it with the future—to sort out the best of the past and marry it with new viewpoints. All design, whether artistic or organizational, involves building upon tradition.

In Safdie's case, tradition involves ethics. And as he views a world in which rampant pursuit of riches at the expense of other human beings is often rewarded, he believes ethics are paramount. "You read about successful businesses that reach quite far by employing oppressive measures," he explains. "But that's a short-term thing. I find myself unable to go beyond the very traditional value systems that have held societies together for thousands of years, which is values that have to do with ethics. It's not a fear of punishment, but it's got to be something. It has to do with some compassion for your fellow human beings, some conviction that this is a better world for pursuing it that way."

SHINE FROM THE INSIDE OUT

We have always heard that a "business is all about the people." For this to be the way a company is legitimately seen by its customers, the structure and organization must, on the inside, provide a fulfilling environment for employees. Discontented team members will not create a face that the company wants exposed to the public.

Safdie also believes strongly that the role of an organization is to create a setting in which people can feel fulfilled—just as it is the role of an urban centre or a building to do the same. The human being's need to be fulfilled has existed since people first began thinking beyond elemental needs such as shelter, warmth and sustenance. In the modern setting, this is often expressed as a desire to do something beyond merely making money. Safdie believes this desire for fulfillment can be fed by a sense of belonging to a community.

"I learned over time in my own business that when anyone ceases to feel fulfilled, they are less productive and less creative," he says.

"You need to be conscious of people's fulfillment as you create a business, because a business is by definition a community of people."

Moshe Safdie is an artist and he brings this viewpoint to his creations, whether single buildings or entire communities. Usually, harmony—a person's sense of belonging to a larger and cohesive whole, a community—is the overarching design element of this paradigm. This principle may be one of an ancient set of design elements, but it has withstood the test of time. It should be the foundation of all modern organizational architecture. Harmony can only exist if every facet of a work of art fits together. Each component must support the others.

5 THINGS YOU NEED TO KNOW

Moshe Safdie suggests that all managers consider these principles of community when designing their own organizations:

1. A Place Where Everybody Knows Your Name

All structures, including businesses, need a centre, or core. In organizational design, this core comprises the people who are its genetic makeup. To create a sense of community, people need to feel at home and require places to interact.

2. Less Is More

When designing an organization, one must be conscious of scale. Increased size can create rigidity and result in the slow death of a company's dynamism. That is why many organizational designs now include some way to maintain a sense of intimacy within those structures. Small, comfortable meeting spaces—"gathering places" where people can generate the free flow of ideas—contribute to the entrepreneurial quality of the enterprise.

3. Knit a Varied Quilt

Once you provide the forum for people to assemble in, establish working groups made up of diverse sets of employees. Homogeneity and groupthink do not contribute to the generation of incremental thought; differing opinions are more likely the prescription.

4. Create a Safe Harbour

People won't share their ideas in a group if they feel those ideas aren't valued, or worse, will be ridiculed or belittled. All employees of every organization must be able to trust that they will be heard, respected and embraced. Effective companies live by the guidelines that there are no stupid questions and no bad ideas. Managers must simply master the art of time and place.

5. Shine from the Inside Out

We have always heard that a "business is all about the people." For this to be the way a company is legitimately seen by its customers, the structure and organization must, on the inside, provide a fulfilling environment for employees. Discontented team members will not create a face that the company wants exposed to the public.

CHAPTER TWO

Strength and Endurance
Family Business and the Napoleonic Art of Victory

FEATURING THE WISDOM OF BEN WEIDER

Family enterprise has been taking it on the chin recently, as the macro-corporate landscape has become more competitive and volatile. Critics say such closely held firms are stodgy, hidebound and too concerned with family stability to be effective in the market that is evolving around them.

Despite this view, the centuries-old family business structure has remained the primary guise of corporate organization in the world. These types of firms still account for more than 80 percent of business activity in North America, driving the majority of the continent's economic output and employment.

Today, the family fiefdom is being forced to keep up with the times. Successors in these kinds of operations are now more often chosen for their managerial skills than for their relationships with the founders. Family firms are becoming more dynamic and innovative in order to cope with the new business climate.

Weider Health & Fitness is an example of a family business that has weathered these challenges, including matters of both succession and evolution. It all started in Montreal more than 60 years ago after brothers Joe and Ben Weider started lifting homemade weights to increase their strength. The enterprise eventually grew into a $500 million publishing, sports equipment and nutritional empire.

Ben's son Eric, an MBA, now heads the company—founder Joe Weider is retired, and Ben is semi-retired—and is leading it into a new era. Another son, Mark, currently heads a division that is developing new products and licensing opportunities.

Over six decades, Joe and Ben solved their issues by maintaining constant communication, understanding each other's strengths, and making decisions jointly. Further, they inculcated the same principles in Ben's two sons so when the time came to pass the baton to the next generation, it was a smooth hand-off.

The Weider organization is now among North America's best-run family firms, largely because all the Weiders, elder and younger, understood that the company must be fit and healthy to see in its next generation.

—⚊—

Update: *Weider retired as President of the International Federation of Body Builders in 2006 and donated his gym to the Knesset, the Israeli legislature. He was promoted to the rank of Officer in the Order of Canada in 2006, after first being appointed as a member in 1975. Until his recent passing, Weider had continued to pursue his love of Napoleonic history and recently published a book on the topic,* Wars Against Napoleon: Debunking the Myth of the Napoleonic Wars. *He was presented with a lifetime achievement award at the Arnold Classic in 2008.*

The family firm has always been the bedrock of the business world, and, indeed, most ventures begin their existence in the domestic domain. When an entrepreneur launches a company to provide a living for his or her family, household members often pitch in. Even though the founder may never bring in a spouse or sons or daughters as actual employees, the business remains rooted in the family paradigm until a wider ownership structure occurs. The family business is the most common form of corporate organization in the world.

Throughout North America, the family-owned business (FOB) encompasses more than 80 percent of all enterprise. It can take the form of private or public ownership (with a family retaining majority control); such firms contribute 64 percent of GDP in the United States and approximately 50 percent of GDP in Canada.[1]

Despite its popularity, however, the family firm has been under increasing attack from many pundits. What was once seen as the natural genesis of a business startup has taken a back seat in the frantic entrepreneurial order of the new millennium. In a competitive environment, the heroic entrepreneur model, usually viewed as a

---

1   Tammi S. Feltham, Glenn Feltham, James J. Barnett, *Facts and Perspectives on Family Business Around the World*, Family Firm Institute, 2005; Are Canadian Family Businesses Ready for Succession?, *Canadian Journal of Policy Research*, Winter 2001.

one-man or one-woman show, began to be viewed as more nimble, responsive and innovative than the tradition-bound and often stagnant family enterprise.

Modern forms of business structure usually separate ownership from operational control, which allows professional managers, rather than shareholders, to navigate the day-to-day affairs. Theoretically, this enables the organization to respond more quickly to changing business conditions than would be the case with family members in charge.

"Many studies have highlighted the complexity of running a family business," explains Dr. Jim Lee, a researcher for the Family Owned Business Institute. Lee adds that family firms must worry about creating a balance between equity and efficiency; deciding on a succession plan; and avoiding putting the family's interests ahead of company performance. Another major consideration: the family is likely to limit top management positions to family members rather than hire more qualified or competent outsiders. As well, Lee says, family members can sometimes distribute excessive compensation or special dividends to themselves, and this may adversely affect employee morale and productivity.[2]

Similarly, many modern analysts believe that the family firm, focused as it often is on stability, sometimes plays it too safe and emphasizes reduction of downside risk instead of taking advantage of opportunities for aggressive growth. These firms, which are typically started by a single founder, often morph into family operations and therefore have difficulty operating effectively in a dynamic environment.

"The rules of the global business game have changed and everybody knows it," explains a trio of researchers from the Wharton School of Business. "Nowhere is the ambiguity surrounding the business game more perplexing than in the family business arena. Families wrestle with the legacy of their assets versus their competitiveness capabilities. They live in an arena where selling (even at a premium) or utilizing traditional growth strategies—going public, forming a strategic alliance, leveraging the company—can be viewed as a failure, rather than successful wealth creation."[3]

---

2 Jim Lee, The effects of family ownership and management on firm performance, *SAM Advanced Management Journal*, 9/22/2004.

3 Timothy G. Habbershon, Joseph Pistrui, Michael N. McGrann, *Enterprising Families: Mindset and Methods for Wealth Acceleration in a Dynamic Marketplace*, www. Wharton. Upenn.edu.

Family enterprise, seen so often as stagnant, rife with nepotism, and content to merely provide a living for its kin instead of expansion in the best interests of the company, is staging a comeback of sorts and recapturing some of its previous lustre. In the post–technology bubble environment, rampant entrepreneurship has been shown to have many downsides—an investor-driven overemphasis on hypergrowth at all costs, for example. The family firm is increasingly being viewed as an oasis of prudent sustainability. Also, a renewed preference for family control has emerged after several high-profile U.S. public companies—scandals involving Enron, Tyco and WorldCom, for example—indicated that some professional managers put their own interests above those of the shareholders.

Today, family firms are changing to take into account the new dynamics of their surroundings. Over the past decade, many have evolved to adopt best practices that can position a business to operate better within these new market realities. Some of these changes are:

- *A focus on generational transitions rather than business succession.* This includes more than just finding a family member to take over the business. It also encompasses an entire strategic direction that will be taken by new management.

- *Management and ownership is becoming a team effort.* The days of the autocratic patriarch are passing and owners from a younger generation are more likely to operate as part of a team than as a single authority.

- *Increasing financial sophistication.* Unlike old family firms whose primary purpose was to generate cash for the family, these enterprises now often feature complex share and valuation structures. In this, they mirror the financial world around them.

- *Increasing managerial professionalism.* Traditional idiosyncratic and entrepreneurial managers are giving way to family members who meet or exceed the highest levels of executive professionalism and training.

- *Refining retirement.* The traditional struggle for control between elder leaders and their successors is disappearing. Many elders now give way to successors but remain with the company as consultant, advisor or governor.[4]

A family business that has witnessed many of the traditional challenges yet has emerged a leader in this new marketplace is Weider Health & Fitness of Woodlands, California. It is the parent company of Weider Publications LLC, until recently a publisher of fitness magazines, and Weider Nutrition International, which produces more than 2,000 vitamin and food supplements, controlling more than one-quarter of the sports nutritional business worldwide.

The Weider organization was launched in Montreal in the 1940s by Joe Weider, now 84 and retired, and Ben Weider, now 81. Ben recently retired as head of the International Federation of Body Builders (IFBB), an organization the Weiders established in the early days and which grew to encompass 173 member countries today. An Order of Canada recipient and 1984 Nobel Prize nominee for his efforts to promote the sport of bodybuilding—recently deemed an Olympic trial sport—Ben also founded and still oversees the International Napoleonic Society. The Weider organization is currently headed by Ben's son Eric, 42, an MBA graduate of University of Toronto's Rotman School of Management. A younger son, Mark, 40, whom Ben Weider describes as "street smart," recently joined the firm as head of a division that is developing new food and clothing licensing products utilizing the strength of the Weider brand.

The firm's roots go back to the 1930s when Joe and Ben, a couple of scrawny kids from the poor side of Montreal looking for a way to deal with the bullies who routinely challenged them on their way home from school, began exercising with weights assembled from old railroad parts found in a junkyard. In 1942, Joe started *Your Physique*, a 12-page magazine that offered instruction on weightlifting and nutrition. By 1943, the magazine had attracted readers across Canada, and Joe added an equipment mail order business to serve them. Ben, who had recently returned home from Army duty, joined the enterprise, and the brothers began organizing bodybuilding contests for other weightlifters. By 1947, Ben was in Europe organizing the IFBB, which from then on became intricately tied to the Weider empire.

---

4 Craig E. Aronoff, *Megatrends in Family Business*, Family Firm Institute, 2004.

The business grew exponentially as *Your Physique* circulation rose and orders for equipment multiplied, so Joe moved to the U.S.—eventually to California—to manage publishing and production demands. The company began selling nutritional food supplements—protein, vitamin and mineral formulas that were specially designed for athletes—and *Your Physique* eventually became the monthly magazine *Muscle and Fitness*, which now has more than seven million readers in 16 countries. Eventually Weider Publications also offered such award-winning fitness and health magazine titles as *Shape*, *Men's Fitness*, *Flex*, *Jump*, and *Natural Health*. In 2003, Weider Publications was sold for $350 million to American Media Inc. As the Weider business grew, Ben was also growing the IFBB, which Weider magazines sponsored and heavily cross-promoted.

The brothers' division of duties was an innate skill they developed along with their muscles and their company. Although neither finished high school, they were avid readers and students of the world around them. Joe was considered the dynamic one, an organizing genius with an odd high voice and a Montreal French/Jewish accent who could swing a business deal as easily as he could hoist a barbell. Ben was the diplomat and salesman, a student of other cultures who possessed an ability to empathize with anyone, regardless of their language or station in life. He had a remarkable talent for convincing people of the benefits of fitness. From a small home office in Montreal to a half-billion-dollar manufacturer and marketer of home fitness equipment and nutritional supplements, the Weiders together defined a personal fitness culture now practised by millions.

But the history of the Weider organization is also one of constant change and obstacles in trying to create awareness of health and fitness, educate a marketplace on its rewards and methodology, and establish bodybuilding as a legitimate sport. It was a campaign that received a considerable boost in the 1970s when a canny Joe Weider brought a young bodybuilder from Austria who had won his Mr. Olympia contest to America to promote the sport and fitness lifestyle. Arnold Schwarzenegger, who went on to become an American film icon and eventually Governor of California, proved to the world that you could be fit, muscular and smart at the same time. The quest for fitness grew into a worldwide phenomenon.

Throughout the life of the Weider organization, Joe and Ben experienced many of the problems all family businesses encounter along the way. They met them as resolutely as they had the bullies who bothered them in their school days. When a problem occurred, they faced it side by side, and have continued to do so for over 60 years. Today, Ben's sons are continuing down the path that was laid out before them.

GOOD SPOTTERS COMMUNICATE ON THE BENCH

A family that is managing a company, not merely earning a living from it, must take a modern team approach—and that means constant, honest communication with each other. All family members must set aside personal feelings to work together to build the business. Failure to do so can lead to chaos.

The most significant challenge the brothers faced was quite typical in family-run firms: how to ensure family issues do not unduly influence sound business decisions. Too many companies seize up when family issues such as jealousy, rank, old memories and rivalries inject themselves into the veins of the operation. But business concerns and family dynamics are different and must be kept segregated at all costs.

To avoid this problem, many experts suggest that the family firm build a pyramid of relationship approaches similar to team building methodology used by many project management groups today. At the foundation of this pyramid is continuing open and honest communication, something that is often easier in an arm's-length company.

Above this foundation lies agreement on common values and expectations, followed up the pyramid by shared visions, identification and understanding of team members' roles, and an accountability process for all actions. Near the top, the family management team should have a system of decision-making, as well as procedures for conflict resolution and compromise. At the top of the pyramid, the point where a family management team needs to be functioning extremely well, sits mutual respect and trust.

Many members of modern family firms have learned to create this team-based approach through trial and error. For those who cannot, advisors suggest they begin with regularly scheduled family council meetings to discuss the business. If family issues still cloud the discussions, they recommend that an outside advisor or manager chair the meetings.

"Regularly scheduled family meetings are fair, open and honest conversations that address the tensions faced by every business family," says consultant Henry Landes. "These meetings provide a safe place for all members to share aspirations, concerns or fears about the family business, and to nip simmering conflicts in the bud.

"Another tool is a board of directors that includes outside directors. Such a board not only brings invaluable business perspectives, it helps to mediate the inevitable conflicts that bubble up in the family. Usually the ratio is four 'outside,' three 'inside.' The deck needs to be stacked in favour of objective, trusted outsiders. Such a board enhances accountability by individuals in the family business [and maintains] big picture perspective."[5]

A TEAM FORGED OF IRON

All businesses have crises, but they may be exacerbated in family firms if unpleasant personal issues are bared under pressure. Managers of such firms must resist these emotional storms and stand even more solidly together when the business faces a difficult challenge.

Ben and Joe Weider, who had a very strong relationship throughout their lives, didn't use formal council meetings; however, they had formed a very close bond when young. When issues came up, they would hold frank face-to-face discussions in order to overcome them. Family members involved in a business, says Ben, must first decide if these concerns are indeed business issues, and if so, get them out in the open where they can be analyzed and solved. And they must definitely try to separate their own family problems, if any, from those of the company.

"You can't allow family or [spouses]—because that happens sometimes—to interfere with the operation of the business," he explains. "My brother and I each had characteristics that the other didn't have—he was very good at organizing, and I was good at talking to all kinds of people. By respecting these abilities and talking through whatever had to be talked about, we got results. We had differences of opinion on the way things should be done from time to time, but we'd say 'Okay, let's talk it out and whatever decision we make, we're together and let's make it happen. Once a decision is made, we won't go our own way, we'll go forward.' "

---

5   Henry Landes, Though Conflict Comes with the Territory in Business Families, There is Hope for Resolving It, *Conciliation Quarterly*, 2002.

This open dialogue is especially important during times of crisis. All businesses experience periodic turmoil, usually at "inflection points," when changes in the marketplace, financial challenges, growth or operational matters necessitate the formation of new strategies. Companies must stop, analyze, and craft solutions that could change the very essence of the company.

This can be a wrenching process for any business, but it is doubly so for a family firm, because times of crisis can often unearth long-buried family disagreements. Managers in family firms may have established working relationships when the business was functioning well, but the pressures created at these inflection, or crisis, points can cause that harmony to deteriorate rapidly.

"Most businesses can survive the threats of competition, economic cycles, changes in technology, or other factors, but the deterioration of interpersonal relationships will devastate the business and tear apart the family," observes Wayne Rivers, co-founder of the privately held Family Business Institute Inc. "Both the direct and opportunity costs can be monumental."[6]

In the modern business landscape, the foundation of open communication that helps a family business function in the good times becomes even more important in the bad ones. These are the moments, advisors say, when the relationship pyramid must be examined and fortified. If the family management team reaches a level of trust and mutual respect, and has its conflict resolution and other procedures in place, then exercising open and honest conversation will allow the team to get the company back on track without finger pointing. Since business today sees continual change and requires nimble response to market conditions, the family will gain priceless experience for the next set of hurdles.

"The implementation of these skills will improve existing relationships and help build new relationships that are lasting and fulfilling," says Rivers. "We must constantly work to build goodwill and improved relationships. Families that work together… are mutually dependent on both the business and the family. Good relationships will cement the successes of both."

Working with his brother for more than six decades ensured that Ben Weider would be familiar with this process and the solutions it

6   Wayne Rivers, Relationships key to family business success, *Family Business Review*, 2002.

required. Throughout most of its life, the Weider organization was forced to carve out new business territory and therefore faced much unfamiliar terrain. The one he remembers best, and which set the tone for years to come, occurred when the company had become a powerful magazine publisher, and its newsstand distributor went bankrupt.

This bankruptcy arrived at a critical time for the Weiders, who had expanded their magazine array to 10 titles over the previous decade and were stretched very thin financially. Under the distribution system of the time, the distributor would hold back payment for newsstand sales of four issues per title, and that amounted to a lot of money. When the distributor folded, the Weiders were owed payment for sales on 40 magazines; in turn, they also owed many suppliers. As a result, they were now essentially insolvent.

Ben wanted to declare bankruptcy because he felt it was the only way out. Joe disagreed and insisted that all suppliers should be paid every cent owed. It was the classic fork in the road that all companies face at some time. As usual, they made their decision together. They agreed to avoid bankruptcy by cutting back to one magazine title and embarking on a long journey to repay more than $2 million to suppliers.

"I said we should go bankrupt because it wasn't our fault and paying them back would slow our expansion," Ben recalls. "But my brother said, 'No, we should pay what we owe,' because that's what our father had taught us, and that was how we had been running the business. He was right, but practically speaking, he was wrong.

"Whenever there was any business issue, I would look at it and think: 'Is it worthwhile to break with Joe and have my way; is it going to hurt the company badly; and is having my way worth the feelings that would create in Joe?' So, in this case, I had a similar choice, and because of what we always had between us, I went along with Joe. It took us about five years to get out from under, and it delayed us from building up our business again for some time. But I'm glad we did it, because it was the honest thing to do."

CHOOSE MUSCLE-BOUND SUCCESSORS

Only 30 percent of family firms survive into the second generation, largely because successors are typically chosen more for their familial relationship than their ability. Ensure that the next generation are not only qualified for the job, but also appropriately trained for, and have earned it.

The brothers also applied this type of upright communication and clear analysis when thinking about succession issues in their company. When pondering the question of who will take the helm in operating a family firm, most founders intuitively look to their children first. But sometimes they can let family feelings cloud their judgment. The market is littered with failed companies that saw family feuds break out over who would rise to the top post. Perhaps that is why only 30 percent of family firms survive in the second generation, and only about 10 percent in the third.[7]

These sobering statistics are especially true in small family businesses in which the second generation often prefers to follow outside interests instead of joining the firm. Since the technological revolution has changed the nature of business considerably over the past thirty years, the prospect of taking the helm of existing "old-economy" companies is torment to sons or daughters who would rather engage in more exciting, modern careers.

Some studies have shown, however, that in contrast to the small family firm, larger ones often surpass widely held companies in economic performance and ability to adopt modern business methodology. This is largely because the company—usually operated by a focused family shareholder group—can change with the times and therefore present a more interesting option for the second generation. Wal-Mart is a good example. The world's biggest retailer is famous not only for its operational innovation, but also for including members of the Walton family in the operation itself from very early on.

"The family business of the twentieth century was generally led by a strong entrepreneur who exercised autocratic management and operational control over virtually every aspect of his company," observed Rivers of the Family Business Institute. "[The] controlling owner type of company will be a thing of the past. There is a definite trend toward sibling partnerships and cousin consortiums as ownership models. This means the next generation of family business owners will not only need to be strong business leaders, but will also need to be tactful diplomats. The trend also implies a strong need for more structure and coaching in managing family communications and conflict." [8]

---

7 *Succession planning*, Business Development Bank of Canada, www.bdc.ca, 2003.
8 Wayne Rivers, The future of family business, *Family Business Review*, 2002.

In the Weider case, Joe had a daughter who wasn't interested in the business, but Ben had three sons who might have moved into the firm. So the Weiders began watching Ben's children while they were young to see if they were interested and if they had the right stuff to lead the company. "At the beginning, both Joe and I decided to watch and see what were their strengths and weaknesses," Ben explains. "We took into consideration all the things we had learned through trial and error. We asked ourselves if they had the right characteristics. Were they diplomatic, respectful of people, able to show sensitivity, able to handle money, and did they do what they promised?

"We never, ever tried to control the children—to make them report to us on everything they did, every decision they made, or every dollar they spent. We gave them a free hand, within reason, to make decisions, to make errors. Then we picked who we thought would be most capable of leading the company and gave him his head."

Quite early, it seemed that Eric fit the bill. At a young age he showed an ability to understand his mistakes and learn from them—a required trait in an up and coming leader. This was confirmed years later when Eric was studying in Paris and ran out of money. Rather than ask for help from his father, the younger Weider busked in a Paris Metro station to earn enough to live on.

Eric was first brought into the business as a lowly shipper in a small town in New York. After attending business school, he joined the firm and apprenticed at the side of a professional CEO/manager who had been brought in to guide the company. Eventually, after he had proved himself to other workers and managers, he took the reins as CEO.

"My work at U of T gave me a solid grounding in many of the financial analytical skills that I still use every day in running the business," Eric has observed. "In a general way, the sense of balance and work ethic that I had to develop in order to succeed in the MBA program were the perfect preparation for work in the business world. But more specifically, having majored in marketing, I took several courses in which I acquired many of the formulae that we use on a daily basis in evaluating the profitability of our magazine and many of our other products."[9] Ben's youngest son, Mark, followed his brother into the firm after graduating from Concordia University in Montreal. He now

---

9 *Voices of Alumni*, University of Toronto Alumni Association, 2004.

heads a recently created division of Weider Health & Fitness that is developing new markets. For example, he is cultivating a "smoothie" business that can be sold in health clubs and at retail. He is also pursuing licensing opportunities for clothing and other sports gear to carry the Weider name.

All three of Ben Weider's sons had something their father and uncle were looking for—minds of their own. (Ben's eldest son, Louis, now an antique dealer, wasn't interested in joining the firm, but Eric and Mark were.) They weren't reckless, but were independent enough to ask for advice, measure it, and then make their own decisions. The founders knew that this independence was a requirement for a business landscape that was changing: a new kind of managerial talent was required to navigate this horizon.

FITNESS REGIMES DIFFER

Successors often have business skills learned in a different environment from the parent company. For a transference to proceed smoothly, founders must avoid trying to force their own viewpoints on those chosen to take over. Hand them the equipment, and let them use it in their own way.

A failure to recognize this need for independent thinking can often result in the downfall of a family firm. Too often, founders try to retain control by micro-managing children who have taken over; as a result, they snuff out any innovations their successors may initiate. Whether they don't trust their children or just cannot relinquish control is debatable—it can sometimes be a bit of both. Either way, it is destructive behaviour that removes the individualism from management.

What's important is not why they do it but the effect it has on the company. While these differences in approach do not always result in a struggle for control, they are a common feature when a company passes from the controlling founder to the next generation. Researchers say understanding these differences is often a necessary part of this transition.

"At this time, the family enterprise formally declares itself ready to operate differently," says the Family Firm Institute, an organization of family businesses. "It involves actually implementing the changes in the structure and helping (or requiring) the environment to deal with the new system. The tasks often include the withdrawal of the prior leaders from critical roles in operations, important changes in support systems and individuals, and the implementation of new policies and routines."[10]

Eric learned how to manage change because he was involved in new initiatives undertaken by the Weider organization throughout the 1980s and 1990s. Weider bought a Los Angeles maker of high-energy nutrition bars to add to its food division; it phased out the longstanding mail order business and began selling Weider products in retail stores instead. It began using new marketing methods, such as placing magazine subscription ads inside video and equipment items to spur wider interest in the subject of fitness.

Perhaps the biggest example of the second generation's differing view of the business, however, involved the sale of the company's flagship publication division to American Media Inc. (AMI) in 2003. Weider Health & Fitness was built on the back of publishing and still continued to generate substantial revenue from its seven magazines with a combined circulation of 22 million. But in a changing business scene, it became clear to Eric Weider that the organization's core business had evolved from publishing to producing nutritional supplements, equipment and products for licensing. The six-decade-old company had changed with the times and to grow further had to jettison what didn't fit its new direction. At Eric's suggestion, the Weiders put the muscle and fitness magazines, which were the advertising vehicles for many of the Weider organization's other pursuits (such as the IFBB), up for sale in order to determine the company's worth, and eventually received $350 million from AMI. Eric and Joe sealed the deal with AMI owner David Pecker over dinner.

Ben Weider says the recommendation to sell the magazines came from Eric, but the young CEO ran it by him and Joe first—in keeping with the communication system they had established long before. "It wouldn't have happened if we hadn't agreed, because, after Eric took over, the three of us discussed things just like Joe and I had done before," he pointed out.

To Ben, the sale made good business sense because the AMI organization could grow the magazines for a wider mass audience, while the Weider group could continue to have strong input into the magazines' content.

---

10 Kelin E. Gersick, Ivan Lansberg, "Stages and Transitions: Managing Change in the Family Business," *Family Business Review*, December 1999.

ONLY SPOT FOR THE FIRST COUPLE OF SETS

Too many founders who stay on after retiring refuse to turn over full control to successors. If you stick around, use the strengths you have gained—wisdom, experience and perspective—to help the new in-charge. Be a mentor and guide, but let go of being the boss.

However, while Ben discussed the move with his son, it was clear he was doing so as an advisor, not as a "boss." The Weiders had ceded managerial control to Ben's son and continued to act as advisors and consultants. This form of succession has often caused conflict in some businesses in that "retired" founders keep interfering in their successors' management of the operation. The founder's inability to let go, for emotional reasons or otherwise, is especially problematic in the family business in which the successor is the child of the founder rather than an outsider.

For that reason, a founder's retirement was often an either/or proposition: either the founder remained in control until death or disability precipitated a succession, or he or she passed the baton to a successor and disappeared from the scene altogether. Increasingly, however, a new role has emerged for founders—that of mentor or counsel to successors. According to the Family Firm Institute, some one-third of family business leaders now stay on in some capacity after officially retiring.

"A person who has devoted a lifetime to a business, deriving fulfillment and identity from it, must transition to something also filled with meaning and identity," it says. "And if the elder stays with the business, he or she is more likely to have a clear role and to clarify who the new leaders are by deferring to them. Family business leaders who will hang around increasingly pass the baton but stay on to watch, help and cheer."[11]

Ben Weider describes his current role with the Weider organization as more of a sounding board for his son than an overseer. He has faith in his son's abilities and generally defers to his decisions. "Eric works with us and treats us the same as I acted with Joe," he says. "When something comes up, before making a decision he'll come to us and tell us why he's doing it, give us his reasons and take us right through the whole thing. Ninety-nine percent of the time he's right."

---

11 Craig E. Aronoff, "Megatrends in Family Business," *Family Business Review*, September 1998.

For his part, Eric Weider has nothing but respect for his father and his accomplishments and likes to tap into his experience and wisdom for business purposes. "He's never achieved his objectives at somebody else's expense," he says. "So many successful people feel that they're playing a zero-sum game in which their success must by definition come at the expense of somebody else's. And while there's some truth to that in my opinion, my father has never approached what he tries to do in that way. There's always competition in business, but he never preached the gospel of destroying your competition. He just focused on what he was doing."

Ben Weider also remains active with his other love—the life of the famous French emperor and general, Napoleon Bonaparte. Throughout his life, Ben Weider has had an obsessive fascination with Napoleon. He founded the International Napoleonic Society and co-authored a book that proved the exiled emperor died of poisoning instead of cancer, as had been believed for more than 150 years. The book sold more than a million copies and earned Weider the French medal, the Légion d'Honneur, which was created by Napoleon himself.

Weider has the world's largest private collection of Napoleonic memorabilia, and for most of his life he has been learning from the master general and conqueror. One lesson he has taken from his historical subject: an organization must be coordinated in that an enlightened leader consults with colleagues, makes decisions, and then acts on them. "My business is to succeed and I'm good at it," the great general once said. "I create my Iliad by my actions, create it day by day."

But Napoleon also said something else that Ben Weider took to heart, applied to his own organization, and which should provide a lesson to all family firms operating 200 years later.

"The secret of war lies in the communications."

5 THINGS YOU NEED TO KNOW

The Weider family has been able to continue to operate its business successfully for more than 60 years because it rigidly adhered to the following principles:

1. Good Spotters Communicate on the Bench

A family that is managing a company, not merely earning a living from it, must take a modern team approach—and that means constant, honest communication with each other. All family members must set aside personal feelings to work together to build the business. Failure to do so can lead to chaos.

2. A Team Forged of Iron

All businesses have crises, but they may be exacerbated in family firms if unpleasant personal issues are bared under pressure. Managers of such firms must resist these emotional storms and stand even more solidly together when the business faces a difficult challenge.

3. Choose Muscle-Bound Successors

Only 30 percent of family firms survive into the second generation, largely because successors are typically chosen more for their familial relationship than their ability. Ensure that the next generation are not only qualified for the job, but also appropriately trained for, and have earned it.

4. Fitness Regimes Differ

Successors often have business skills learned in a different environment from the parent company. For a transference to proceed smoothly, founders must avoid trying to force their own viewpoints on those chosen to take over. Hand them the equipment, and let them use it in their own way.

5. Only Spot for the First Couple of Sets

Too many founders who stay on after retiring refuse to turn over full control to successors. If you stick around, use the strengths you have gained—wisdom, experience and perspective—to help the new in-charge. Be a mentor and guide, but let go of being the boss.

CHAPTER THREE

Bliss Girl

Bootstrapping Rhinestones into Diamonds

FEATURING THE WISDOM OF MARCIA KILGORE

Thousands of people make the entrepreneurial leap every year, hoping to turn an idea or a dream into a fiscal reality. Most don't make it, but many do, creating viable businesses that in some cases grow into sizeable, industry-leading enterprises.

Although the media, particularly during the heyday of the late '90s, was riddled with stories of companies receiving millions from venture capitalists, new entrepreneurs most often begin by bootstrapping—starting a business with little or no money and growing it through sweat equity. Bootstrapped ventures usually start very small and rely on the entrepreneur's personal energies and talents—as well as a good dose of luck—to succeed.

One of the great bootstrapping stories involves Marcia Kilgore, a charismatic young woman from Outlook, Saskatchewan (pop. 2,600), who became the toast of Manhattan by growing a tiny aesthetician practice into Bliss, one of the world's top spa and beauty chains. Beginning in her kitchen, Kilgore used an eye for detail, a canny marketing sense and, not least, a self-deprecating sense of humour to grow a luxury spa and beauty product business that quickly had celebrities and the crème de la crème of New York fighting for appointments.

Within a few years, Bliss was an industry leader that generated $18 million a year in revenues and drew the envy of some of the pre-eminent beauty manufacturers in the world. By 1999, Kilgore had sold a 70 percent interest in Bliss to France-based LVMH for a reported US$30 million and become *a multimillionaire. In 2004, the interest was sold again to the giant Starwood Hotels & Resorts, which plans to rapidly expand the Bliss brand in North America through its signature W hotel chain. Kilgore is still a minority owner in Bliss, and she remains the company's creative director and its chief product designer.*

Kilgore's journey from small-town Saskatchewan to New York doyen of the world's beauty scene is a lesson—and an inspiration—for every person who has ever dreamed of building something, but wasn't quite sure how to get to the starting line.

—⁓—

Update: *Marcia followed up her success with Bliss by launching Soap & Glory, a mass-market brand of inexpensive beauty and bath products. The line retains much of the same humour and funky packaging—one of their most popular items is a lip plumper called Sexy Mother Pucker. She has also moved outside the cosmetics industry to launch FitFlop, flip flops designed to tone legs and reduce cellulite. Wearers quickly discovered that the shoe also corrected posture and alleviated back pain, and the shoe is now sold in 28 countries. In May of 2008, FitFlops were featured on Oprah Winfrey's Top Ten list for summer picks.*

Every company starts somewhere, and it's often humble—a desk in a corner of a bedroom, a garage, or a rented room above a store with a couple of card tables for desks. This is bootstrapping at its finest; a budding entrepreneur begins with little more than an idea and a mission to succeed. Through hard work and sheer determination—often peppered with a little luck—a business is born.

Throughout North America, hundreds of thousands of people venture out on their own every year, typically under extremely modest circumstances. Of course, not all these fledgling businesses grow into confident and full-bodied enterprises; some never make it beyond their first phone bill. Those that do, however, often survive because their founder has one driving passion—to answer to no one other than the customer.

This freedom is the very essence of entrepreneurship and millions of North Americans have elected to walk through its doors. Census figures in the U.S. show that some 17 million self-owned businesses operate beside more than four million firms that employ fewer than 20 people—the high water mark for a typical small or micro-business. In Canada, some 2.5 million people are self-employed, while smaller businesses employ 42.5 percent of the labour force.[1]

This desire to run the show is a common attribute of habitual entrepreneurs, according to most researchers. In fact, they say, those who possess an entrepreneurial mindset usually:

- Passionately seek new opportunities. Entrepreneurs stay alert and look for places to profit from change.

- Pursue opportunities with enormous discipline. Not only do entrepreneurs spot opportunities, they also act on them. Most entrepreneurs maintain a basket of ideas and revisit them often.

- Pursue only the best opportunities and avoid exhausting themselves by pursuing every option.

- Focus on execution—especially adaptive execution. People with an entrepreneurial mindset get things done, even if it means they have to do it themselves.

- Engage the energies of everyone in their domain. Rather than going it alone, entrepreneurs engage everyone they meet to help them reach their goals.[2]

But it usually takes more than simply the mindset to actually build a new company. Most new entrepreneurs are unlikely to have had much training and will get thrown into a very steep learning curve. While the traditional educational channels, as well as new ones offered online, have made this collective knowledge and advice easier to secure, most learning still comes from the trial-and-error of doing. This is especially true in the case of bootstrapping—the kind of quick, opportunistic learning by fire that is the most common classroom for new recruits. Bootstrappers are master information gatherers and, because of this, many go on to become excellent managers. Most, however, enjoy the process so much they go on to repeat it again and earn the badge of being "serial."

---

1 Canada Labour Force Survey, Statistics Canada, 2004.
2 Rita Gunther McGrath, Ian MacMillan, *The Entrepreneurial Mindset*, Harvard Business School Press, 2000.

In his e-book, *The Bootstrapper's Bible*, entrepreneur and business advisor Seth Godin sums up how most new entrepreneurs (should) think in his "bootstrapper's manifesto":

"I have initiative and insight and guts, but not much money. I will succeed because my efforts and my focus will defeat bigger and better-funded competitors. I will leverage my skills to become the key to every department of my company, yet realize that hiring experts can be the secret to my success. My secret weapon is knowing how to cut through bureaucracy. My size makes me faster and more nimble than any company could ever be. I'm in it for the long haul. Building a business that will last separates me from the opportunist, and is an investment in my brand and my future."[3]

Unfortunately, many entrepreneurs don't follow Godin's advice and end up stumbling on execution. While their ideas may be sound, they are unable to move from "interesting on a napkin" to profitability. Going solo can be daunting—it's a grind to build a business from nothing—and the statistics around success rates are not encouraging.

According to business speaker and author Frances McGuckin, the first few years of a business can be difficult because the person who operates it may have as many as 60 different jobs to juggle. "By learning how to circumvent operational stumbling blocks, your business has a better chance of success," McGuckin writes. "The secret is to take the time to learn how. Most proprietors are 'too busy' working *in* their business to work *on* their business."[4] Any small business owner will acknowledge that it is common to be CEO one minute, and janitor the next. And then marketing person, salesperson, accountant, and manager—the list goes on.

The early years, during which the founder is the backstop for everything, provide priceless training and perspective until employees are more affordable. Many businesses fail, however, because founders never grow out of this martyr role. Multitasking can teach the entrepreneur to understand the details of a business, but this knowledge is useless if it exists in a vacuum and is not applied to strategic issues as the business expands. The concept of working *in* a business instead of *on* it is a constant refrain among advisors to small businesses and it is the most common reason companies hit a growth ceiling.

3   Seth Godin, *The Bootstrapper's Bible*, www.changethis.com, 2004.
4   Frances McGuckin, *Big Ideas For Growing Your Small Business*, McGraw-Hill Ryerson, 2001.

For all businesses, bootstrapped or otherwise, there comes a time when the entrepreneurial attitudes that sustained them through start-up and early stage growth need to give way to the hands of a professional. The enterprise is now mature and has grown beyond the seat of its own pants. With arm's-length management in place, the company is less reactive and more structured in identifying and pursuing opportunities. It also becomes more organized, with a set of clear goals and processes everyone in the company understands and follows. It may still be an entrepreneurial business in its heritage and spirit, but it is no longer a startup.

In 1993, Marcia Kilgore, a young woman from Outlook, Saskatchewan, population 2,600, began a process that took her through all the stages of entrepreneurial growth, including eventual sale of the business, which turned her into a multimillionaire. Kilgore started a small business in New York that provided facials for friends and which eventually morphed into the spa chain Bliss, a pinnacle of the Manhattan beauty scene. More remarkably, she positioned Bliss as the "best of breed" in a sector in which every participant is trying to do the same. In the spa world, there is little consolidation or the equivalent of the big box store or fast food outlet.

Through canny management and insight, Kilgore's bootstrapped venture grew at lightning speed—within a few years, she had emerged from the chaos of startup mode to managing a full-blown enterprise that was approaching US$20 million in sales. The company was quickly purchased by a beauty and fashion consortium for a reported US$30 million. In the process, Kilgore helped launch the spa revolution that was a dominant feature of the hospitality industry of the late 1990s and the early part of the twenty-first century.

Kilgore grew up in humble surroundings—her father Monty, a real estate salesman, died when she was 11, and her mother Lorene was a clerical worker. At age 18, determined to do something with her life, Kilgore left Canada and moved to New York to join her older sister Jodi, a model, and to try and make it in the Big Apple. An earlier visit had whetted her appetite for the vivacity and life the city promised.

"I had $300 plus pocket change and no return ticket," she says of her move to Manhattan. Kilgore had planned to attend Columbia University, but her funding fell through. It certainly didn't take her long to bounce back. Back in high school, she had taken up bodybuilding and by the time she graduated she had developed muscles "like a ballet dancer." So she put her hobby to work in New York and began working as a personal trainer for models, celebrities and others connected to the fashion world.

YOU ARE THE CHIEF COOK AND BOTTLE WASHER

When you start a business, especially if it is bootstrapped, keep your ego in check (particularly if you came from a large corporate environment); you will inevitably be doing everything yourself. To build a best-of-breed company and maintain the highest possible quality control, you must remain very close to all aspects of the business. Even after you can financially afford to forgo the bottle washing to focus on being the chief cook, you should still scrub the occasional bottle to keep close to customers and stay on top of your game.

In 1990, frustrated with the bouts of acne she occasionally suffered, Kilgore decided to take a skin-care course. Before long, in addition to her training clients, she was giving facials to friends and models in her sister's apartment. Encouraged by their response, she enrolled in a crash course in cosmetic chemistry at California's UCLA. Soon after, in 1993, when she was just 23 years old, she used all her savings to open Let's Face It, a small skin care centre in Manhattan's trendy SoHo district. "It was [basically] a one-woman show," she recalls. "I did the laundry, the leg waxes, answered phones, vacuumed the floor between facials, unpacked the products, welded leaky pipes. The three-room facial and nail place in SoHo had a small but fab staff, a groovy trompe l'oeil paint job and a $4,000 antique French sofa. You know, even back then, without a nickel to spare, I'd rather have been broke than expect our customers to sit on featureless furniture."

In 1996, when Let's Face It outgrew its tiny borders, Kilgore opened the 5,600-square-foot Bliss. It was the beginning of BlissWorld, an $18-million-a-year spa empire that by its third year—because of strong marketing, and Kilgore's own unlimited energy—included two New York branches, a popular mail-order catalogue called *Bliss Out*, and an online store (*blissworld.com*). Almost instantly, Bliss, with its easy-going attitude, cheeky and cheery view of its own business, and superb service, was a hit.

Bliss drew celebrities and the elite of New York's young singles set—it could take up to six months to get an appointment, prompting actress Julia Roberts to complain to *People* magazine that even she couldn't get in—and that eventually drew the attention of the French luxury products group LVMH (Louis Vuitton Moet Hennessy). In 1999, it paid a reported US$30 million for a 70 percent interest in Bliss.

At the tender age of 30, the optimistic kid from Saskatchewan had become a multimillionaire and was now managing an empire that soon grew to include three additional day spas—two in New York, one in London—plus a catalogue business, two product lines (Laboratoire Remede skin care and Bliss Labs), as well as a department store outpost in Paris. Bliss products are currently sold in about 279 stores globally, including Bloomingdale's, Harrods, Holt Renfrew, Neiman Marcus, Nordstrom, Saks Fifth Avenue and Sephora.

Soon BlissWorld would grow even larger. In 2004, LVMH, in a divestiture, sold its interest in Bliss to Starwood Hotels & Resorts Worldwide Inc., operator of the W, Westin and Sheraton Hotel chains. Starwood plans to install Bliss Spas in some of its new, more cutting-edge properties.

Kilgore, who is routinely described as "feisty," "cheery" and "incredibly bright," helped launch the 1990s spa phenomenon by taking the matronly stuffiness out of the experience and turning a visit into a good time. Using a quirky sense of humour that translated into names like the "quadruple thighpass"—an anti-cellulite treatment—for her products, Kilgore turned an hour or two at the spa into a form of social time with good friends—an experience.

THE ANGEL IS IN THE DETAILS

To build a "five-diamond" service business, pay religious attention to detail and ensure that the highest standards of quality are maintained. Occasional missteps are okay, but own up to your customers quickly and without excuses. Every great restaurant and hotel knows that attention to the fine print, great service, consistent quality and a rapid, apologetic response to any failure to meet such standards is the key to long-term staying power.

Kilgore has primarily succeeded because, even as her business grew, she maintained a fanatical attention to detail. Although she is no longer majority owner, she still gives facials from time to time just to keep in touch with customers. She also writes most of the copy—particularly the popular Bliss Girl column on trends—for her catalogue, which has over 10 million subscribers annually. She keeps a strong hand on the development (especially the naming) of her product lines.

Kathy Phillips, a former English beauty writer who is converting to a beauty mogul herself, described Kilgore, her "heroine," as an obsessive observer of business details. "Marcia was once discovered lying on the floor analyzing why a treatment-room door wasn't closing quietly enough," she marvels.[5]

Kilgore likes to regard such obsession as just knowing her business thoroughly, a habit she acquired in the early years when she did everything, and she believes it is the primary driver behind her success. "Any brand can be mediocre, average, or as expected," she points out. "What sets it apart is when a company does the unexpected, goes the extra mile, takes care of those extra details." Kilgore cites the example of former New York Mayor Rudy Giuliani stopping squeegee-wielding beggars from soliciting drivers using the Holland tunnel to enter New York. He didn't want these panhandlers to be visitors' first view of the city.

Says Kilgore: "[Giuliani] said large things matter, but they usually take care of themselves because they're obvious. But it's the really small things, the details that no one thinks about, that really set you apart from the competition. I try to follow that. I'll look at all the details—like why are the housekeepers carrying garbage down the hall during working hours when they should be taking it out the back door. The housekeepers may not understand that it's a luxury spa, and that's not done."

Kilgore's attention to her customers is almost legendary in the beauty business. One oft-told story concerned the discovery of a mouse in her spa. Immediately she sent letters to 10,000 customers notifying them of the uninvited guest and explaining what would be done about it. This staved off that hard-to-counter bad publicity that can rocket through a customer base by word of mouth and destroy a service business almost overnight. The letter, written in her usual humorous style, drew rave reviews both inside and outside her business. More important, it put an

---

5   Josephine Fairley, Kathy Strikes Oil, *The Mail on Sunday*, 5/2/2004.

honest face on a business that is all about personal bonding. Too many companies will do everything but apologize for a mistake they make, or where their service is not up to snuff. It doesn't matter whose fault it was, or the nature of the problem: how it is handled is what a customer remembers.

Kilgore still follows the same principles, even though the spa chain is now corporately managed and she is no longer solely in control. In her capacity as Bliss's creative director, she visits spas regularly, spending several hours at a time watching how work is done, observing details she considers so critical to customer service—the reason for Bliss's success. Having worked on almost every aspect of the business, she has a good picture of the operation from a managerial point of view and understands its needs right down to the miniscule.

Without management training, Kilgore learned how to run an entrepreneurial operation by just doing it. She innately understood that every entrepreneurial manager must earn an MBWA—"management by walking around."

Says Kilgore: "Very often you'll see people who have gone to business school, and they see everything from a macro level. I think it can be more difficult for someone who comes from a stuffed-shirt, high-education background to come up with a creative concept or understand how much the details can affect revenue. Once you get to a larger size, this helps. You know that you don't have to pay $450 to get that light bulb changed because you have climbed up on that ladder and done it yourself. Many companies bought by larger companies are often started by people who don't necessarily have business training. These people think everything matters."

This knowledge of the nooks and crannies of a company is a route that many prestigious business schools are now attempting to map for the growing number of students who desire to become entrepreneurs instead of divisional managers in large corporations. Almost every MBA program today has added coursework that focuses on the functional management of the entrepreneurial operation—the kind of thing that Kilgore learned the hard way. "Entrepreneurial management is not simply inspiration: There's a lot of perspiration," notes Howard H. Stevenson, the Sarofim-Rock Professor of Business Administration at the Harvard Graduate School of Business. [6]

---

6 Entrepreneurship: It Can Be Taught, Harvard Business School *New Business*, Winter 2002.

LAUGH AND THE WHOLE WORLD LAUGHS WITH YOU

In many service businesses, especially in the leisure and entertainment sectors, customers are paying for an experience. They want it to be warm, wonderful and magical, and nothing makes people feel better than a good laugh. So, while it is critical to demonstrate how seriously you take your operation and the products and services you provide, mixing in a little humour pays dividends by building bonds with your customers.

While Kilgore is very serious about the managerial aspects of her operation, she does not let it brand her business as stiff or unfriendly. From the beginning, she recognized that what made her spa stand out from the field was her personal and quirky sense of humour. Her rise from the first facial she did in her sister's apartment to eventual market domination was not only due to know-how, it was that she had a good time along the way. A small-town bundle of effervescence, straight shooting and understanding, she also had a constant desire for a good laugh. This combination made her clients feel as if they were at a friend's place for a get-together, not at some we-take-ourselves-seriously beauty factory where every flaw is treated as a life tragedy.

Kilgore's spas are oases of calm and luxury, where women—and men—can indulge themselves. Not only do Bliss staff treat everyone with good humour—it is not unusual for a customer to be offered a glass of champagne and a chocolate at the door—but the *bonhomie* also translates into the services and the products used. Bestsellers include the zingy Lemon Peel body smoother, Hot Salt Scrub, Glamour Gloves, Softening Socks and the Carrot and Sesame Body Buff.

"Prior to us, most spas were rather snobby and they would try to intimidate you into buying products or make you feel you should come in through intimidation," Kilgore says. "We were the exact opposite. Bliss was about coming in and saying, 'I need to lie down,' and a woman would be there that you could tell all your problems to. And she would say, 'Poor you, and here's a crème by the way.'

"It was a girlfriend kind of atmosphere: we were there to give them a fantastic treatment and we weren't taking ourselves very seriously, although we were serious about making sure that people had a great time. It was about whatever made the customer feel best—inclusional, not exclusional. It's a special Bliss branding, being funny, to make you laugh a little, which is really the best way to relax."

Bliss Spas featured such treatments as "Arm-istice," which promised women who spent "waking hours connected to a keyboard and feeling wrist-ricted" a "part physio, part pampering" that would "kick your carpals back into their tunnels, making typing a lot less terrifying." For men, there was the "the manly-cure," a manicure treatment insisting that "guy grooming just got groovy" and that "manly-cure maketh the man."

The Bliss nonconformity and humorous outlook extended to its catalogue, which reaches 750,000 readers *monthly*. Crazy puns and quirky names drive the Bliss business, especially in the direct mail sphere. For example, "fat girl slim" is a "caffeinated cocktail of choice" that promises to attack stubborn fat deposits and slim down the user. This spirit seeps into the corporate communications as well: press releases are headlined "Publissity."

Then there is the fictional Bliss Girl—"beauty product addict extraordinaire, tester of every lipstick ever and connoisseur of cosmetics"—who offers a regular column with her funny take on the world of beauty. It was no secret that Bliss Girl was Kilgore, who always insisted that Bliss's playful sensibility was what made the spas and the catalogue such a success. It was one reason the first Bliss spa to open outside New York was in London, which Kilgore insists is a city with a strong funny bone. "Not everybody got my sense of humour whereas in Britain everybody seems to get it," Kilgore says. "Bliss and Bliss Girl are very self-deprecating and the Brits understand that.

"[Our catalogue] really started mostly as a reflection of my personality after we first opened Bliss," she adds with her usual laugh. "I wrote most of it because we couldn't afford a copywriter and it just came out that way. I found out through the grapevine later that after we mailed out this catalogue that was kind of stuck together with a glue gun and some shoelaces and had me as copywriter and a friend as a photographer, [that] Calvin Klein called an 'emergency meeting' to discuss our catalogue with his team."

SHE BLINDED ME WITH SCIENCE

Even if your business is not in the technology space, don't ignore its benefits. Few businesses can survive and grow without continually applying the latest technological advances to improve product and service development, as well as cost and pricing structures.

While life may be a laugh at Bliss in the customer's eyes, the company is very, very serious about its products. Kilgore studied skin chemistry extensively and, while she may have dreamed up funny names for them, the method behind the madness was extremely earnest. They usually included the latest in scientific research regarding various chemical reactions in the body. "Fat girl slim," for example, boasted a "new advanced technology adipose antagonist (in layman's terms, that's fat fighter)." To be sure, Kilgore does her (science) homework.

If that sounds like weird science, it isn't. In fact, it's a Kilgore trait to delve deeply into the chemistry of skin products to arrive at the perfect concoctions. Her design of some of her Remede line is typical of this process. Kilgore had been hearing from clients that they had skin problems that seemed to defy the traditional categories of normal, dry and oily skin. "It became obvious that, although most people had pinpointed their skin type, there were always other concerns—about sun damage, wrinkles, hyperpigmentation and the toll of travel," she told *W* magazine. "Let's say you're travelling to the Bahamas, recently started smoking, but usually have sensitive skin—what do you do then?"[7]

Kilgore's solution was to dream up a basic system that would act like a pharmacopoeia of different products, and she converted her team of chemists to the idea with such brain teasers as: "If you were on a desert island, and you could take only one cleanser/moisturizer/etc. with you that you had to use every day for the rest of your life, would this be the one that you would consider taking?" The entreaties worked. Eventually the team arrived at a line of four basic products that could be "amplified" with supplementary products to treat just about any skin problem.

This hard science demonstrates something all bootstrappers require at the root of their businesses: a quality edge that differentiates their products or services from those of larger competitors and that

---

7   Patricia Reynoso, Late-Breaking Bliss, *W*, 9/1/2000.

allows them to make noise in the market that translates into sales. In the modern landscape, smaller and newer companies will be drowned out if they go head-to-head with established players. Most successful small businesses avoid this run-in by emphasizing their X-factor— the something that distinguishes them. This can be better and more personal service, or higher-quality products and services for the same price.

GROW OLD GRACEFULLY

As the business matures, the entrepreneur needs to know when to delegate an appropriate level of control to a team of professional managers. To maintain the highest standards, a company needs to upgrade processes and personnel or the founder will become the bottleneck. Knowing how, when, and to what extent to let go, is the key.

"For too many bootstrappers, sales is an afterthought," says author Seth Godin. "It's the thing you do that allows you to do what you really want to do. Big mistake. In fact, sales is the reason for your business to exist. If you can't sell what you make, you can't help anyone, influence anyone, or make anyone's life easier, better, or more convenient. If you can't sell what you make, you can't pay yourself. You're finished."[8]

Marcia Kilgore lived by this edict from day one, recognizing that Bliss would only succeed if it stood for something that other spas didn't. When she started her business back in the '90s, she saw an opportunity: most of her competitors were boring. They either served the matronly set, or tied the spa experience to some kind of spiritual awakening.

"Something had to be done," she says. "The spa selection at the time was so uninspired. A person who just wanted to get rid of their large pores had to choose between new age music, incense and the endless spiral of worshipping the inner child—I mean, really, who needs a facial at the mental age of five?—or it would be some stuffy old spa with guard towers, run by eastern European Nazi types who would chastise you if you came in with a pimple. That wasn't what Bliss was about." So at Bliss, even standard spa services had a fun aspect: pedicures, for example, took place in a room built to look like a beach.

---

8   Seth Godin, *The Bootstrapper's Bible*.

Celebrities like Uma Thurman, Cindy Crawford, Julia Roberts, Oprah Winfrey and Madonna became fixtures. This attracted editors and writers for beauty magazines, who helped spread the word farther. Soon, it could take months to get an appointment at Bliss, which in the competitive New York atmosphere made it even more desirable.

"Uma Thurman's makeup artist came in and had a great treatment and told [Thurman] she had to go," says Kilgore, explaining her marketing methodology. "So she comes in and tells her brother, who also is an actor, and he tells his friend. It's word of mouth, even with celebrities. [Celebrities] are important for getting your name out there at the beginning, because if people see their favourite celebrities go to an establishment, they want to go there too. But at the same time, if they go to an establishment because a celebrity goes, and they have a rotten experience, they're not coming back. So you have to have quality. I think there are a lot of brands right now that are offering a kind of hollow promise. That's why it's so important for me to have quality at the highest possible level."

This desire for quality began long ago when Marcia Kilgore's father died and life as she knew it changed drastically. Soon her mom began to fret over finances. "I saw my mother always worrying about money," she says. "I remember thinking, 'When I grow up, the last thing I want to worry about is paying the electric bill.'"

She doesn't have to worry any longer. Smart marketing, an eye for detail, and an unfailing sense of direction have made Marcia Kilgore, at the age of 35, a rich and fulfilled woman. Her personal life has been equally rewarding. In 1998, she married Thierry Boue, who had come to work with her in Bliss. Last year she took the next step in her own personal evolution by giving birth to her first child. She now spends much of the time she once devoted to work with her "cute baby boy."

By the straps of her boots, Kilgore built a dream into an empire. She accomplished what many people don't even have the fortitude to imagine, let alone pursue and flourish. When asked for the secret to her success, she quotes not business school texts or management gurus, but Dr. Seuss:

"Be who you are and say what you feel, because those who mind don't matter and those who matter don't mind."

5 THINGS YOU NEED TO KNOW

Marcia Kilgore built her best-of-breed company from the ground up by relying on the following principles:

1. You Are the Chief Cook and Bottle Washer

When you start a business, especially if it is bootstrapped, keep your ego in check (particularly if you came from a large corporate environment); you will inevitably be doing everything yourself. To build a best-of-breed company and maintain the highest possible quality control, you must remain very close to all aspects of the business. Even after you can financially afford to forgo the bottle washing to focus on being the chief cook, you should still scrub the occasional bottle to keep close to customers and stay on top of your game.

2. The Angel Is in the Details

To build a "five-diamond" service business, pay religious attention to detail and ensure that the highest standards of quality are maintained. Occasional missteps are okay, but own up to your customers quickly and without excuses. Every great restaurant and hotel knows that attention to the fine print, great service, consistent quality and a rapid, apologetic response to a failure to meet such standards is the key to long-term staying power.

3. Laugh and the Whole World Laughs with You

In many service businesses, especially in the leisure and entertainment sectors, customers are paying for an experience. They want it to be warm, wonderful and magical, and nothing makes people feel better than a good laugh. So, while it is critical to demonstrate how seriously you take your operation and the products and services you provide, mixing in a little humour pays dividends by building bonds with your customers.

4. She Blinded Me with Science

Even if your business is not in the technology space, don't ignore its benefits. Few businesses can survive and grow without continually applying the latest technological advances to improve product and service development, as well as cost and pricing structures.

5. Grow Old Gracefully

As the business matures, the entrepreneur needs to know when to delegate an appropriate level of control to a team of professional managers. To maintain the highest standards, a company needs to upgrade processes and personnel or the founder will become the bottleneck. Knowing how, when, and to what extent to let go, is the key.

CHAPTER FOUR

Success Toolbox

How Mindset and Outlook Can Impact Performance

FEATURING THE WISDOM OF JOHN ASSARAF

What differentiates successful entrepreneurs from those who fail? Can the way we think affect our reality? Can we harness the power of the mind to accomplish our goals?

Despite the long-standing practice of self-help, positive thinking, affirmations and personal coaching, the induction of those philosophies in a corporate context is a relatively new trend within mainstream business literature. With the popularity of books like The Secret, *these concepts have migrated into the mainstream, and readers have expressed a willingness to explore the impact of mental mindset on real-life success.*

While skeptics dismiss these principles as nothing more than a clever marketing ploy, there are those who swear by them—and have the track record to prove it. One of those people is John Assaraf, a highly successful entrepreneur, author and business consultant.

For years, Assaraf has been trying to understand the true nature of success. As a troublemaker during his youth, he narrowly avoided incarceration before deciding to pursue a better future. Determined to rise above his humble beginnings and guided by mentors, he embarked on an entrepreneurial journey that would result in the creation of four multimillion dollar companies.

These include RE/MAX of Indiana, a real estate company that currently generates sales that exceed $5 billion dollars annually, as well as an Internet company called bamboo.com which had a market value of $2.5 billion.

Unlike many self-help gurus, Assaraf did not build his empire by selling how-to books. He did it by building thriving businesses in several different industries that allowed him to retire in 2000. He has since gotten back to growing another franchising business, OneCoach.

He began coaching others simply because he discovered a genuine satisfaction in helping entrepreneurs overcome challenges and fulfill their highest potential.

His experiences sparked a curiosity about the way the mind accomplishes goals. His research in quantum physics, psychology and brain physiology would be used to establish a framework that he believed helped outline the path to success. He made his first foray into coaching literature with his book Having It All, *which placed on the* New York Times *and* Wall Street Journal *bestseller lists and ranked as a number one seller at Barnes and Noble.*

His latest book, The Answer, *explores the skills and methods needed to turn any business into a thriving and profitable venture. The book, too, was on the* New York Times *and* Wall Street Journal *bestseller lists shortly after its release.*

Assaraf currently runs OneCoach, a company dedicated to providing small business owners and entrepreneurs with the necessary skills, tools and resources to allow them to succeed.

In 1905, a young German patent officer named Albert Einstein proposed a mathematical equation that would one day become so famous it would be instantly recognizable around the world amongst scientists and laymen alike. Unable to explain the behaviour of light within the confines of Newtonian physics, Einstein's equation proposed a radical new viewpoint that bridged the long-standing gap between energy and matter. $E=MC^2$ stated that Energy (E) is equal to Mass (M) multiplied by the speed of light squared (C^2). At its simplest level, Einstein was able to recognize that energy and matter were different forms of the same thing. More important was the realization that both matter and energy could be transformed into the other, meaning that energy could become matter, and matter could become energy.

His theories would pave the way for scientists to seek out the mechanics of the universe at the smallest levels of subatomic particles and waves, a field of study that is now known as quantum physics. At its most minute part, the universe is made of tiny bundles of energy called quanta that underlie the neutrons, protons and electrons that form atoms which eventually form the molecules that make up everything in our world.

Ultimately, the things that surround us in daily life, from plants and animals to furniture and electronic devices, are all fundamentally made of the same material: quanta, or put another way, energy. Interestingly, these energy bundles were capable of influencing each other in a way that defied any logical explanation. Scientists called this property entanglement. Hence, if two particles were entangled, any type of stimuli applied to one particle would impact its twin, regardless of distance or space between them. In his *New Scientist* article "Entanglement: The Weirdest Link," author Michael Brooks explains the implications of entanglement on our everyday lives. "Set things up correctly, and you can instantaneously affect the physical properties of a particle on the other side of the universe simply by prodding its entangled twin," he writes. "This is no longer just a curiosity of the quantum world, visible only in excruciatingly delicate experiments. Physicists now believe that entanglement between particles exists everywhere, all the time, and have recently found shocking evidence that it affects the wider, 'macroscopic' world that we inhabit."

Another interesting characteristic was that the very act of observing the quanta caused them to change their behaviour. Scientists at the Joseph H. and Belle R. Braun Center for Submicron Research in Israel conducted highly controlled experiments monitoring electron behaviour and the impact of observation at various stages. They concluded that "the greater the amount of 'watching,' the greater the observer's influence on what actually takes place." This meant that in every experiment where scientists attempted to study an electron, their very intent of observing it actually affected it. We are only beginning to discover how thought, or intent, is able to affect matter in the physical world.

According to John Assaraf's book *The Answer,* if everything in the universe is fundamentally composed of energy, and energy is interchangeable with matter, our thoughts can have a more tangible impact on our environment then we previously realized. Assaraf considers himself to be an example of how the application of these principles can yield extraordinary results. He has transformed himself from a troublemaking destitute teen into a billionaire and successful entrepreneur.

Assaraf still remembers the day his journey started, all those years ago. It was 1982, and while perusing a newspaper, an ad caught his eye. It was simple and to the point: become a real estate agent with Century21 and make $25,000 a year, guaranteed. For Assaraf, then 19, the idea was enticing. It certainly appeared to be a better option than his current position at Mycom, a Philips subsidiary where his annual salary was between eight and nine thousand dollars. Intrigued, he attended an opportunity meeting. "I met a whole bunch of people there, and they told me that they were learning skills and studying," he recalled. "I heard what they were all earning, and I thought, 'I could do this.'"

While he didn't join Century 21, he did enroll in a month-long real estate seminar. Assaraf suddenly found himself engulfed in information. "The owner of the company, Alan Brown, gave me books to read and he would say, 'Read this book on listing, read this book on closing, read this book on marketing, go to this seminar, go to that seminar,'" Assaraf laughs. "At that point I really started to understand that there was a recipe that most successful people were following."

That recipe seemed to encompass two things: changing his behaviour and changing his thoughts. He quickly realized that he needed to train his thoughts. "That was the first glimpse that I had into the world of learning more about me, more about the universe," he says. "There were some natural laws, like gravity, that were irrefutable. If I lived my life and built my business based on these natural laws, while at the same time retraining my brain, or as I called it upgrading my personal software, then I would be able to achieve success greater than I ever imagined." Assaraf credits his mentors with pointing him in the right direction. After all, he realized that whatever they were doing seemed to be working.

Despite his initial skepticism, he committed to at least giving their advice a chance. After all, they were reaping successes while Assaraf was, he says, "insecure, unhealthy and flat broke." As he began to see positive changes in his life, he became a dedicated student. "I busted my butt working 70-80 hours a week to learn as fast as I could," he says. "There was a formula and a process that answered the question of 'Why should I do that?'" He became knowledgeable in the fields of positive psychology, visualization and affirmations and started applying these principles as a newly licensed real estate agent.

In his first year as a realtor Assaraf made $30,000. In his second he earned $150,000. Soon, he was looking for a new challenge. It would present itself in the form of an offer to own the sub-franchising rights of RE/MAX® in the state of Indiana. Market conditions were daunting; better-known and larger competitors owned over 70 percent of the market, but Assaraf was determined. He turned again to his affirmations and outlined what he hoped to achieve. Sure enough, within five years the company was generating over $1.2 billion in sales. Not being satisfied with this success, he moved his family back to Canada to contemplate his next move. He continued reading everything he could get his hands on about quantum physics, brain physiology and philosophy.

In 1998, a friend's invitation to see a new technology altered the course of his life. The idea was simple: allow online users to conduct virtual tours of cars and hotel properties online without the use of plugins or downloads. Seeing unlimited applications, Assaraf moved to San Francisco to partner on this venture. Bamboo.com was launched in early 1999. Nine months later they took the company public, and after a merger of equals with another company, the venture had a market valuation of $2.5 billion.

In 2001, Assaraf found himself in a position most people would envy. A self-made multi-millionaire, he had complete financial freedom to live out his life in leisure and luxury. However, Assaraf was never one to sit still for long. As he pondered the events that had catapulted him into the business elite, he realized he wanted to help other people achieve their own business and life goals. He started OneCoach, an organization devoted to teaching the skills and strategies that he had learned to those who needed help achieving their goals.

You Are What You Think

Assaraf knew his clients would have to start at the very beginning, just like he did. The first step was recognizing that every thought, be it insecure or confident, happy or sad, had the power of impacting their success. He found that the biggest limitations faced by business people were the ones they set themselves. "Once we are impregnated with an idea, most people will discount it, and think 'I can't do that,' and come up with the all the reasons of why they can't based on their past and on their beliefs," he says. His research into the psychology of success has shown him that the exact opposite action is needed. "If I have the thought, then somehow there must be within me and around me the resources and tools to be able to achieve it," he says. "If you can hold on to an image of what you want, then you can achieve it."

That is the crux of what many refer to as the Law of Attraction. It builds on the notion of like particles attracting each other and extends to include thought. Positive thoughts will attract other positive thoughts, while the same is true for negative ones. "Everything in this universe, everything, is made up of something called energy. If you look at your hand through an electron microscope, it will be vibrating; vibrating packets of energy. It is vibrating and emanating energy," he explains. "And we know from quantum physics that things that resonate will make themselves known to each other. We can start to understand that our thought is the most potent form of energy known to man, it travels faster than the speed of sound, light, faster than the speed of anything we know on a physical and non-physical scale."

This means that the links between the matter and thought are more connected than originally believed. "We are starting to look at some new research that is pointing to the fact that our thoughts really do matter. Not only do they matter, but at the subatomic level everything is a field of possibilities," he said. "So if we have a thought that we focus on, regardless of who is doing the focusing, whether it's a bus driver, a homemaker or the CEO of a company, we are actually causing something to occur, something to go from wave to a particle, from potential to the physical."

The bigger the dream, and the more meaningful it is for the dreamer, the better. "You need to understand that you can achieve a lot more than what you believe you can achieve."

Assaraf is a firm believer in creating vision boards to help drive his focus. He will often cut out images from magazines or newspapers that represent the goal he is trying to achieve. It helps reinforce the strength of the idea to the subconscious mind. He recalled a particularly emotional experience with his vision boards in 2000. Having recently relocated to California, he was in the process of unpacking boxes shipped from a storage facility in Indiana, where they had been languishing for several years. Upon opening the box he discovered vision boards he had created years earlier. One in particular caught his attention. Much to his surprise and delight, the vision board contained a picture cut out from a magazine of the exact house that he had moved into a few months prior. Years earlier, he had come across an image of that house, and to him it had represented the type of financial freedom he one day hoped to achieve. Living in Indiana's winter climate, he had envisioned his dream house, nestled on the coast, facing the ocean. He had forgotten all about it, until that moment. Assaraf remembers that experience clearly because he realized at that moment that he wanted more then anything, to show others the techniques that had served him so well. His latest book, *The Vision Board Kit*, shows people exactly how to create their own vision board and specifically what to do with one once they have it.

YOU ARE WHAT YOU THINK

Matter and thought are more connected than originally believed. Therefore, if your idea contains positive or negative energy, then it will attract a similar energy. Every thought causes something to occur, a reaction is happening that moves from potential into the realm of the physical. Focus thoughts on the types of things you want to attract into your life and corresponding ideas that resonate at the same frequencies will be presented to you.

Rethink the Way You Learn

When visualizing a goal, it is best to be as specific as possible. One of the major tenets of positive psychology is the ability to define the meaning of success down to the smallest details. Whether your version of success involves a Ferrari or a summer house in the Hamptons, the more intricate your vision the easier it will be to achieve it.

"When you start to help somebody understand why thought is so powerful, they begin to understand why having a clear, precise vision of is so critical," Assaraf says. "As soon as we have that thought, and we hold onto that thought on both a conscious and unconscious level, we are now taking the most sophisticated piece of equipment known to man, the brain, and we're tuning it to the frequency of that vision, of that thought," he explains. "The more specific the thought, the more the mind becomes attuned to its frequency, which in turn will attract related ideas, helpful solutions or tools in the conscious level that taps us into anything or anyone with that same frequency."

For organizations, this translates into having a shared vision that percolates to every level of the organization. Employees not only understand the vision, but also possess thoughts and perceptions that are aligned with it. An entire organization can become one synchronous being, moving collectively towards achieving a single goal. "When everybody is vibrating and beaming at the same frequency, it becomes contagious," he says. Unfortunately, the same is true of the reverse. "When you have a fractured vision and an incoherent message things will start to break down."

Fine-tuning this visioning process requires reprogramming how humans learn. Assaraf's research outlines four different levels of human learning:

1. *Unconscious Incompetence*—when an individual is unaware of what they don't know. Assaraf describes this stage as someone who is "in a prison and they don't even know they're in a prison."

2. *Conscious Incompetence*—when an individual becomes aware of what they don't know, and faces a choice between continuing on to the next level of learning and remaining with the status quo. This is often a critical stage, as it involves taking accountability for previous mistakes and missteps and actively seeking better solutions. Too often, many will choose continuing to embrace feelings of victimization and helplessness, locking them into the same cycle of defeat.

3. *Conscious Competence*—when an individual is making an effort to become competent and seeks new knowledge. Skill is acquired through practice and repetition over time.

4. *Unconscious Competence*—the highest level of learning and performance, which occurs when a person unconsciously is acting in a way or thinking in a way that brings success either due to a genetic disposition or through practice and training.

Assaraf states that the majority of businesses and individuals never make it past the third level due to a lack of know-how. He credits the success of *The Answer* to comprehensively outlining the necessary methods needed to ascend to the final level. The book provided in-depth research coupled with actionable tips geared towards business owners and entrepreneurs who were interested in strengthening this particular skill set.

RETHINK THE WAY YOU LEARN

A clear vision of end goals is critical in creating the right mindset for success. Entrepreneurs can train their brains to learn at a subconscious level to attract the right types of thoughts needed to achieve their goals. The more specific your vision is, the easier it will be for your subconscious mind to help you achieve it.

Your Gut Is There for a Reason

One of the best ways to train your mind to operate on the unconscious competent level is to develop an intense awareness of your intuition. Successful entrepreneurs seem to instinctively do this. We all know the business owner who, faced with all the research outlining the infeasibility of an idea, decides to follow his hunch and do it anyway. Or maybe it's the entrepreneur who always seems in the right place and at the right time when opportunity presents itself.

Assaraf believes the more you allow yourself to listen to this voice, the stronger it will become, and the more helpful it will be in guiding decisions. "Intuition is a mental faculty of the mind that picks up the vibrations that's all around us. It's like the thermostat that picks up a deviation in the temperature of the room," he explains. "It picks up everything we read, everything somebody says to us. Intuition is what you know before you think; the way the brain works is that we're actually gathering information up to half a second before we're consciously aware of it."

That information is then processed through deductive reasoning faculties, internal cognitive maps based on a combination of genetics and past experiences. According to Assaraf, some of the most successful entrepreneurs have been those who have been able to hone this instinct. "If you poll CEOs, most of them say that they use their intuition most of the time to make decisions after they've got all of the facts and figures," he said.

In his book *Blink: The Power of Thinking Without Thinking*, author Malcom Gladwell tells the story of a Greek statue purchased by the Getty Museum for under ten million dollars. Prior to the sale, the museum followed normal authentication protocols, including extensive geological testing that had confirmed the authenticity of the piece.

However, when art historian Federico Zeri saw the statue, he instantly decried it as a fake. Another expert experienced a wave of "intuitive repulsion" upon seeing it. The controversy led to more in-depth investigations and it was discovered the statue had in fact been forged in Rome. Despite over a year of analysis by museum staff, it was the historians' hunches that alerted them to the deceit.

A study on the relationship between intuition and business success at the New Jersey Institute of Technology examined the executives of companies whose profits had doubled in the last five years. Over 80 percent of them possessed above-average precognitive powers.

YOUR GUT IS THERE FOR A REASON

You intuition is an instinctive form of deductive reasoning that allows you to process information before it reaches your conscious brain. It works in alignment with the subconscious mind to filter information relevant to goals. Training the mind to recognize signs from the intuition will greatly increase chances of success.

Feed What Fuels You

Once the idea is conceived, the vision has been fine-tuned and the intuition consulted, there is another element that must come into play: passion. Passion will play a dominant role in determining entrepreneurial success.

Passion stems from not only doing something you love, but also doing something that also adds meaning and value to your life. "Never ask yourself if you are worthy of the goal," explains Assaraf. "Always ask whether the goal is worthy of your life." He encourages entrepreneurs to spend time reflecting on what they are doing and whether they will look back on their accomplishments later in life with pride or regret.

Questions each entrepreneur should ask themselves regularly:

- Am I trading my life for what I love?
- Am I trading my life for what I want to contribute?

And it's never too late to start. "The one thing we do know for certain is that you can teach an old dog new tricks," says Assaraf. "You have to give clients hope that their life is not over, that they can make more difference in the next three to five years than they have in the last sixty." That hope leads to an open-mindedness that is willing to explore new possibilities. For Assaraf, being 47 is a time for reflecting on his success not in terms of finances but in terms of contributions made to the world. OneCoach has provided a deep sense of meaning and value to his life. He also recognizes the skepticism he faces. "There's an old saying that when the student is ready, the teacher appears," he says. "Our job is not to change anybody. I want to help the people that have their hands raised like I did as a kid and who want someone to show them the path." These are the people who want to try something new, and were willing to ask for help. "I don't know where in history we got caught up in the idea that we have to do it on our own," Assaraf says. "My belief is that we have to do it by ourselves, but we can't do it on our own."

FEED WHAT FUELS YOU

True success is the level of meaningful value contributed to society, as opposed to financial success. Following passion will always yield better results then the pursuit of material things. The excitement and happiness of doing work you truly love will help broadcast energy out into the world, resulting in a multiplicative effect of opportunity.

Get Off Your Ass

Entrepreneurs have the ability to envision and manifest great things with the power of their mind. However, Assaraf is quick to stress the differences between his philosophies and other "fluffy, frou-frou, esoteric, sage-y, mystical stuff," that promise millions of dollars and big screen TVs just by sitting on the couch and thinking in a certain way. To him, those types of philosophies overlook one very essential law that often results in failure for frustrated readers who think and think and think of what they want without seeming to get anywhere. "It's called the law of G.O.Y.A." he deadpans. "That's the law of 'Get Off Your Ass' and do something."

Many entrepreneurs are adept at researching and evaluating information but are unable to take that decisive action. Assaraf compares it with the high rate of people who break a diet regime. "Ninety-nine percent of people who go on a diet stop the diet within 72 hours," he says. "Why is that? Their intent is there, they consciously want to look better and they want to feel better." It is the subconscious mind that needs to be involved in this process; it regulates nearly all thought patterns, perceptions and behaviours.

"The reason we started OneCoach wasn't so that we could give people the right information, it was to put in a team around them that would create an environment of change," he explains.

Actions reflect an underlying set of beliefs that create what Assaraf calls "the world of causes." OneCoach specializes in dealing with uncovering the cause of the belief pattern that creates undesirable behaviour. "We teach at the level of causality," he said. "If you want longer-term results, then you have to change the software, you have to change what's causing you to act in a certain way."

Confucius famously said, "A journey of a thousand miles begins with a single step." Instead of feeling overwhelmed, taking small steps in the general direction will go a long way to helping you achieve goals.

Tama Kieves, a motivational speaker and author of *This Time I Dance*, often tells her clients to envision driving on the highway on a cross-country road trip. Instead of feeling overwhelmed at the sheer distance that needs to be travelled, she suggests concentrating on the upcoming 200 feet. Bit by bit, step by step, one will gradually make significant headway towards the final destination. All that matters is that some form of positive action was taken.

At the end of the day, all the planning and preparing and visualizing in the world will be meaningless if not reinforced with action.

Assaraf recalls working at the RE/MAX office in Indiana, where he would invite the best motivational speakers to come speak to his team. "People would take copious notes for a day, two days, for three days and say this has changed my life, it's unbelievable; and then within a week they weren't doing anything with what they learned," he says wryly. "You know what I should have done in retrospect? I should have hired a clown to entertain them. They would have had the same amount of fun and it would have cost me a hundred thousand dollars less each time."

GET OFF YOUR ASS

It is important to understand the underlying beliefs and mental schemas that influence your perceptions and actions. Understanding the causes of a particular behaviour is essential in overcoming it and replacing it with more positive actions. Regardless of the amount of time spent thinking or "manifesting," nothing will happen if you don't actually do anything. So, in other words, get off your ass and do something.

Conclusion

Assaraf has devoted his life to helping entrepreneurs and business people achieve their life and business goals. He feels as though he has finally found his calling, the true contribution he was meant to share with the world. He is consumed with a powerful curiosity to unravel some of the mysteries of the universe, and remains awed at what he learns. He looks forward to the journey ahead, anticipating the discoveries that will shed light on the workings of the human mind, and allow humans unprecedented opportunity to harness their full potential.

Scientists have only scratched the surface in decoding the true link between thought and matter. One of the most powerful tenets of Assaraf's teachings is the concept of gratitude, of truly appreciating the small things in your life. He considers himself blessed, and it is this grounded outlook that has allowed him to generously share his teachings with entrepreneurs all over the world without losing his authenticity. From a struggling teen in Montreal, hungry to make something of himself, to a successful entrepreneur who has realized all of his dreams, his journey so far has been an exciting one.

Asked whether he had any regrets on his life so far, his first answer is a simple no. "Actually," he says a few seconds later, "I would have risked a lot more, a lot earlier."

5 THINGS YOU NEED TO KNOW

1. You Are What You Think

Matter and thought are more connected than originally believed. Therefore, if your idea contains positive or negative energy, then it will attract a similar energy. Every thought causes something to occur, a reaction is happening that moves from potential into the realm of the physical. Focus thoughts on the types of things you want to attract into your life and corresponding ideas that resonate at the same frequencies will be presented to you.

2. Rethink the Way You Learn

A clear vision of end goals is critical to creating the right mindset for success. Entrepreneurs can train their brains to learn at a subconscious level to attract the right types of thoughts needed to achieve their goals. The more specific your vision is, the easier it will be for your subconscious mind to help you achieve it.

3. Your Gut Is There for a Reason

You intuition is an instinctive form of deductive reasoning that allows you to process information before it reaches your conscious brain. It works in alignment with the subconscious mind to filter information relevant to goals. Training the mind to recognize signs from the intuition will greatly increase chances of success.

4. Feed What Fuels You

True success is the level of meaningful value contributed to society, as opposed to financial success. Following passion will always yield better results then the pursuit of material things. The excitement and happiness of doing work you truly love will help broadcast energy out into the world, resulting in a multiplicative effect of opportunity.

5. Get Off Your Ass

It is important to understand the underlying beliefs and mental schemas that influence your perceptions and actions. Understanding the causes of a particular behaviour is essential to overcoming it and replacing it with more positive actions. Regardless of the amount of time spent thinking or "manifesting," nothing will happen if you don't actually do anything. So, in other words, get off your ass and do something.

CHAPTER FIVE

What's Next:
Business Basics

FEATURING THE WISDOM OF DEBBIE LANDA,
FOUNDER OF DEALMAKER MEDIA

NEXT GEN COMPANY BUILDING

In Mountain View, California, a speed-dating event is taking place. Nestled in the heart of Silicon Valley, a group of men and women are meeting each other through a series of three-minute "dates." It's a popular event; last year alone, 19 successful matches were made, and long waiting lists are commonplace. However, the people here are not singles looking for love, but startup companies and investors searching for the perfect match.

Dealmaker Media is a San Francisco company that specializes in producing conferences, roundtables and seminars specifically designed to connect entrepreneurs with executives, investors and analysts. Created by CEO Debbie Landa in 2000, the company has an impressive list of success stories. Through Dealmaker events, key industry players (including Yahoo, Google, Oracle, Cisco and Fox) have acquired numerous technology start-ups.

Landa grew up in Saskatoon, Saskatchewan, far from the harried pace of Silicon Valley. After a successful career in fashion, Landa soon realized that her skill as a connector and her keen eye for talent were being misplaced. It wasn't the divas that needed her the most, it was the entreprenerds.

Dealmaker's success owes a lot to Landa's instincts and keen sense of timing. A large part of her daily responsibilities will typically involve listening to the pitches of eager young entrepreneurs who are convinced their idea is the next big thing. In the past two years, she has witnessed a significant shift in the attitudes and strategies of entrepreneurs. Landa herself is a part of the change she is seeing: a new wave of young, networked and tech-savvy entrepreneurs who are entering the market and changing the way companies are being built and managed.

YOUR NETWORK IS YOUR NET WORTH

The rise of social networking, led by Facebook and MySpace, means people are connected to a vast network of friends, colleagues and business associates. These relationships are fostering the birth of new companies and facilitating communication between businesses and consumers. "Being networked is the most important part of being an entrepreneur. People don't just buy products, they buy from people who they are friendly with, and who they have a relationship with," says Landa. Doing business through your personal networks is not new. But technology has changed the game; the Internet and the web are like steroids for networkers. It has never been this easy to communicate with so many people so quickly. And that is changing the way we do business.

IT'S CHEAP; YOU'RE YOUNG AND HAVE NOTHING TO LOSE

The Internet has also dramatically reduced the barriers to starting a new business. For web businesses in particular, the costs for offices, equipment and infrastructure are negligible. Facebook, Digg and StumbleUpon are a few of the sites started in dormitory rooms and parents' basements. It's not unusual to see three or four entrepreneurs living together and working out of the same house. "These guys are working all night and day to build this technology. They don't look at it and think, I need some nice office chairs or a CEO; they don't care," says Landa. "They'll meet in coffee shops, sit there all day and then go home and work all night. They hang out with their roommates and talk about technology."

And this has changed the world of venture capital. In the pre-bubble days, every young tech entrepreneur was trying to raise tens of millions of dollars from VCs while pitching them on how their companies were going to be worth billions. And while those stories still exist, there are lots of entrepreneurs today who are seeking funding from their networks instead of immediately approaching outside investors. "They're not as hungry to go to the venture capitalists," Landa says. "They'd rather go to family and friends and are willing to sacrifice more. They'll network them-selves to death to find the angel investor that really gets what they're doing and who is willing to fund them."

It is easier than ever to experiment through trial and error, and it is costing less and less to build new businesses because of the power of technology. With such low opportunity costs, some of the most successful entrepreneurs have left the classroom early and ventured out into the real world. This is a shift from the perception that a formal post-secondary education is essential for success. A degree, even an MBA, is not as appealing to these young entrepreneurs as it once was.

"When you're young, you just want to get out there. You might not create the hugest company ever, but you can hire someone to do things for you, like bookkeeping and human resources, to figure out what you don't know," says Landa. Her father had given her that same advice a few years earlier. "He told me I didn't need to know accounting," she recalls. "Just hire a good accountant. That advice has stuck with me."

Even if the company is not successful, failing is a setback that pro-vides valuable experience for next time. "Business school is great," adds Landa, "but if you've got a burning desire to go out and make something happen, just do it. It's cheap; you're young, and you've got nothing to lose." The street has replaced the business school as the learning vehicle of choice.

ADAPT OR DIE

This experimental mindset is present all the way through to market launch. Even if the product is one hundred percent ready, the feedback from consumers, investors and analysts is invaluable in refining the busi-ness concept. For Landa, launching your product is essential: "You have to put your stuff out there for people to want it and discover it."

Once in the market, adapting quickly to consumer response is a key differentiator of success. Today, technology allows consumers to share opinions instantly, and companies who want to succeed should sit up and take notice. According to Landa, successful companies "are built by those who are willing to listen to feedback."

Dealmaker Media recently launched operations in Los Angeles and plans to expand to New York. As for what's next for her, Landa is unsure but optimistic. The marketplace is rife with possibility. "Global is wide open, everything is wide open, there's so much opportunity that nothing has been figured out yet."

PART TWO

---------------------------- 🍁 ----------------------------

Second Period

The Brand

CHAPTER SIX

Brand Era
Creating and Delivering "The Big Idea"

FEATURING THE WISDOM OF BRIAN FETHERSTONHAUGH

After graduating from McGill University in 1979, young Montrealer Brian Fetherstonhaugh joined Procter & Gamble's marketing department. Four years later, he moved to Ogilvy & Mather Canada, beginning a career that now has him as CEO of OgilvyOne Worldwide, the Ogilvy Group's global consulting, direct marketing and interactive arm. Fetherstonhaugh, 47, has become an acknowledged world expert on the subject of global branding.

Fetherstonhaugh began with Ogilvy Canada working on international accounts such as American Express and Kraft. His tenure there was marked by roles of increasing management responsibility that culminated in his appointment as President of Ogilvy & Mather Canada in 1994. During his three years as President, Ogilvy's Canadian business grew by 50 percent and the team's creative work received more than 100 awards for excellence.

Fetherstonhaugh moved to the global stage in 1997 when he relocated to New York to become Ogilvy's Chief Operating Officer, with responsibility for its largest global account—IBM. In 2000, he was named to the Ogilvy & Mather Worldwide board of directors and in 2002 he was named Chairman of Ogilvy Global Brands. In late 2004, he was elevated to his current position.

Fetherstonhaugh describes his time on IBM as an intensive learning experience. In the beginning, the IBM brand was drifting and unfocused, reeling from the effects of new technology and competition. Five years later, IBM's fortunes had revived to a point where it was considered one of the best-marketed companies in the world, with a "brand value" of $50 billion.

What did Fetherstonhaugh learn by being a part of this historic turn-around? The first lesson was to rally behind one simple idea. Eliminate the multiple messages IBM was sending out and establish one "Big Idea": that IBM was the leader in e-business. The second was to then drive that idea through every aspect of communications—through advertising, direct mar-keting, the Internet, communications to investors, employee programs—in fact, to every point where the brand touched a customer or opinion leader. According to Fetherstonhaugh, this strategy of pairing a big idea with an in-telligent multimedia approach is the best way for marketers to cope with the increasing complexity of the twenty-first century consumer landscape.

Update: Fetherstonhaugh continues to lead OgilvyOne as CEO. In 2007, the agency experienced significant business growth, added clients to their already impressive portfolio, and launched creative groundbreaking campaigns. New clients included Aflac, DoubleClick, The Economist, Marsh and Pitney Bowes. Fetherstonhaugh speaks at events all over the globe, sharing his tremendous expertise on branding in a new technological era with companies who are eager to take part in the digital revolution.

Who are you? What do you do? What makes you different? We know from our daily lives how hard these "simple questions" are to answer. A person asked "who are you" will often customize an answer to fit the situation based on relation to something or someone: manager of a particular company; a husband or wife; a father or mother; a dog owner. They may further define themselves by their buying habits—they spend thousands every year on the latest communications tech-nology, or they buy a new car every four years, for example. But they also know that the real answer is much more complex and that they are only answering with the blinds partially open—delivering just small bits of their own reality. The true answer is that each individual has many different personal aspects that together form a very complicated and intricate whole.

But that's a little difficult to get across at the water cooler or a cocktail party. When a relative stranger asks a simple question such as "Who are you?" he or she is not expecting a treatise on your per-sonal likes and dislikes. Such a long-winded explanation would like-ly bore your listener to death unless you have already thought long and hard and have come up with a short, simple, all-encompassing statement about yourself. A personal elevator pitch—so to speak. Very few people, even if asked, could do so.

Now you have an insight into the problems a marketer faces. They boil down to one simple question for most people: who are you? (And, for their corporate cousins: what are you?) That is why marketers talk incessantly about brand, a much-misunderstood word that has become so misused in business it's almost been rendered meaningless. Brand simply represents a business's most basic proposition—what are you? Without a good cohesive answer, customers don't have the basic foundation from which to know how to interact with a company. It is the marketing equivalent of speaking different languages.

Like the succinct answer to the personal question, a brand tells the world—customers, employees, critics, competitors, colleagues, suppliers—what your company is all about. It could mean your organization is sincere and trustworthy, clever and exciting, innovative and adventurous, slightly boring but solid and reliable. Or it could mean something else entirely. The same range of characteristics could be ascribed to you personally, creating your own unique brand. Brand is shorthand for how hundreds, thousands, perhaps millions of individuals perceive you. A brand is also about reputation and how the world values it. You and your company may have a positive or a negative brand, but one thing is certain—you have one.

The word is originally taken from the Old West, when cattlemen would burn their ranch's mark on the haunches of their cattle so they could figure out who owned which cow on the open range. In the early years of advertising, many people subscribed to the theory that a brand was merely a logo and the advertising of that logo. A concept could be drummed into people through repetition. It would eventually lodge in their minds and influence their buying patterns.

David Ogilvy was one of the early pioneers who saw a broader concept of what a brand can be. He defined a brand as "the intangible sum of the product's attributes: its name, packaging and price, its history, and its reputation. It is also the impression that you have of the people who use the product, as well as your own experience with the brand."

Another definition stresses the uniqueness of each brand: "a brand is the distinctive . . . character that sets a product, service, person or place apart from other products, services, people or places." [1]

---

1   Debbie MacInnis and C.W. Park, *Branding and Brand Equity: Clarifications on a Confusing Topic*, MarketingProfs.com, February 17, 2004.

There are examples everywhere and each means something different. Tide is a brand with a distinctive name, package and set of product ingredients; Fidelity is a brand with a unique set of service deliverables; Martha Stewart is an example of a personal brand that sets standards for decorating; Paris Hilton is a personal brand with a reputation for establishing what's hot; Disneyland and Las Vegas are brands about fun, the former innocent and the latter risqué. But in each case, the brand is a simple, understandable concept that characterizes the product or the company that produces it.

By extension, branding is a verb that describes a set of strategies and tactics that influence perceptions about what the brand stands for. If a brand is a concept, then branding is the art of its delivery. This used to be a synonym for advertising. Certainly, you might find new methods of messaging—putting ads in washrooms, posting a banner or search ad on a particular website, or painting an entire section of a town pink, as Mattel did in England for a Barbie launch—but, in essence, communication was still being transmitted from the top down to consumers.

In a modern globalized world, however, product parity, increasing commoditization and incessant advertising—3,000 or so advertising messages are beamed to the average person daily—have resulted in consumer wariness and brand backlash. Therefore, branding has had to take on a new meaning. No longer considered just advertising, branding now must communicate a company's core reason for existence—its *raison d'etre*, so to speak—in many different ways.

Someone who intimately understands this turn of trends is Brian Fetherstonhaugh, a Canadian born in Montreal. In 2004 Fetherstonhaugh became CEO of OgilvyOne Worldwide, a division of Ogilvy & Mather, the New York-based advertising giant. Prior to his current position, Fetherstonhaugh served as Chairman of Ogilvy's Global Brand Community, representing 20 of its largest global clients, such as IBM, American Express, Kodak, DHL, Cisco and Nestle's.

One of Fetherstonhaugh's earliest lessons in the power of branding came when he was the new brand manager for Mr. Clean at Procter & Gamble. In his first days on the job, Fetherstonhaugh was reviewing consumer research in the household cleaner category. He discovered that when consumers did a performance comparison between unmarked bottles of Mr. Clean and a generic yellow cleaner, the Mr. Clean would win by a narrow margin. But in research where the brand names were revealed, the Mr. Clean would always win by an over-whelming percentage. The power of the brand extended far beyond any technical cleaning advantage. The brand carried an extra level of trust. Since Mr. Clean was also by far the best-selling cleaner in Canada despite a premium price, it was also clear that this brand trust advantage translated into real sales.

Fetherstonhaugh is an acknowledged expert and frequent speaker on the demands of the rapidly changing marketing landscape. He un-derstands implicitly that individuals are made up of an intricate system of various beliefs, tastes and interests and that marketing must be a made-to-order process for each. For example, Fetherstonhaugh is not only immersed daily in worldwide marketing campaigns, he is also a family man with two daughters, a regular hockey player, and a guitar-playing musician with a local rock band called Plan B. Each of his dif-ferent roles—marketer, family man, hockey player and musician—is an aspect of a personality that makes up the whole of Brian Fetherston-haugh. Each of these idiosyncrasies results in a consumer of relevant services and products. Similarly, every person in the world represents a unique basket of different tastes and requirements. The messages sent to those consumers must be small enough to reach their individual targets, but large enough to break through the clutter of messages they are inundated with. The task is to create mindshare and lodge the mes-sage in their psyche forever.

It was this understanding of the growing complexity of market-ing that Fetherstonhaugh brought to the IBM account. The IBM and Ogilvy teams devised a strategy to rebuild the perception of the com-pany, not from the top down, but from the consumer up. They started, not with the traditional reams of technical data, but with a global brand audit—an insightful qualitative study among IBM employees, custom-ers, prospects and industry opinion leaders. The results were strikingly consistent around the world. IBM was seen as a trustworthy company with lots of great, patented technology, but needed to be more nimble, flexible and human. This led to the "solutions for a small planet" cam-paign that sparked the IBM brand transformation.

By the mid-1990s, the technology landscape was changing rapidly. Powerful new competitors like Dell and Microsoft were emerging, and consumer interest in the Internet was exploding. IBM needed to respond to a rapidly changing world or risk being left behind. The company developed a powerful vision for the future: offer businesses a combination of traditional information technology plus the power of networks. Originally dubbed network centric computing, the idea never really took hold. Only when the idea was brought to life as e-business and branded with a red E, and defined in a compelling eight-page manifesto, did it reach its full potential.

Next came a narrowing down of IBM's dozens of messages to those that reinforced the "e-business" concept. Fetherstonhaugh calls this "360-degree branding," in which all communications reflect the same big idea. Ogilvy used advertising to define the IBM brand around e-business, build broad awareness and define the company as a thought leader. Then it used direct response marketing to create tailored communications, develop one-to-one relationships and ensure that key constituents understood the IBM e-business message. After that, Ogilvy put the concept online to establish interactivity with it, to demonstrate e-business capabilities to a broader market and to provide deeper content. In essence, to show it practised what it preached.

Collectively, these techniques were successful in helping turn IBM's brand around, but in the few years since the campaign started, marketing, as a discipline, has changed even further. Fetherstonhaugh notes that the brand manager's job is growing more difficult because change is accelerating as target markets fragment and multiply. Marketers now have to tailor messages to many more markets and therefore have an even greater need for a unifying Big Idea that can overcome this fragmentation.

Currently, market researchers analyze this segmenting marketplace by grouping people into models based on their distinct needs to determine what types of consumers will be most receptive to a particular product or marketing message. To develop these models, they classify consumers according to a set of demographics and geographic variables (age, race, education, location). More sophisticated models also include psychographic and behavioural variables such as attitudes, lifestyle, values, ideology, risk aversion and decision-making patterns.

Other classification systems can add greater clarity by predicting consumers' purchasing power, motivation and self-orientation. Perhaps the best known of these is the VALS system of segmentation, which postulates that consumers buy products and services by seeking experiences that fulfil their characteristic preferences and give shape, substance and satisfaction to their lives. The VALS system, which is owned by SRI Consulting Business Intelligence, clusters consumers into eight types, based on motivation:

- *Innovators*, formerly called actualizers, who are successful, sophisticated, take-charge people with high self-esteem. They are motivated by ideals, achievement and self-expression.
- *Thinkers*, formerly called fulfilleds, who are mature, satisfied, comfortable and reflective people. They are motivated by ideals.
- *Achievers*, who have goal-oriented lifestyles and a deep commitment to career and family. They are motivated by the desire for achievement.
- *Experiencers*, who are young and often impulsive and seek variety, excitement and the new. They are motivated by self-expression.
- *Believers*, who are conservative, conventional and have concrete beliefs based on traditional established codes such as family or religion. Believers are motivated by ideals.
- *Strivers*, who are trendy, fun-loving and concerned about the opinions and approval of others. They are motivated by achievement.
- *Makers*, who are practical people with constructive skills and often "work on things," such as building a house, raising children or fixing a car. They are motivated by self-expression.
- *Survivors*, formerly called strugglers, who have few resources, are comfortable with the familiar and are primarily concerned with safety and security. They have no primary buying motivation.[2]

Fetherstonhaugh believes buying decisions are decentralizing at a more rapid pace than most people suppose. Marketers must also understand how buying decisions are evolving and what factors will go into these decisions in the future. Primarily, he says, several people share buying decisions at the same time, and each brings a particular view or emotion to the equation.

2   http://www.sric-bi.com/VALS/.

For example, in the business-to-business space, at one time only one person—perhaps the Chief Information Officer in the case of an IBM product—may have made a decision about a purchase. These days a committee of stakeholders, which includes the heads of finance, marketing and operations as well as a consultant, may collectively make that decision. Similarly, in the consumer space, democratization of the family means all family members—especially children—have increasing input into decisions regarding not only major, but also minor, household purchases.

BUYERS GO FORTH AND MULTIPLY

Buyer decision-making has been decentralized. At one time purchasing was simply advertisement-induced. Now buyers reach conclusions based on multiple influences and emotions. Feed these different inputs with a Big Idea that is clear and understandable, and, most important, delivers a clear window into how it will affect an individual's life. There should be a persistent hunt for the answer to the question "Why should I care?" Recognize the multiplicity of buyer touchpoints and hit them all.

Given the diversification of buyers, how does a company effectively deliver messages to each decision maker? Fetherstonhaugh points to the IBM scenario, which involved thousands of products and as many as 15 to 20 different market segments in 100 countries. Each segment required a different message and the complexity of managing all these messages was overwhelming. So he used two interrelated strategies. The first was the "really big brand idea"; the other was tailoring messages that grew out of this idea to specific buyers.

The big idea was IBM as the facilitator of e-business, which created a framework for adapting messages downstream. An individual consumer was told that IBM's portable computer, the ThinkPad, was a tool that would open up the world of e-commerce, while a chief financial officer was told it was a tool that would lower costs by replacing paper-based functions with the Internet. This paradigm can be applied to most businesses, Fetherstonhaugh adds. "The skills that a brand manager needs to develop for the future include a big unifying brand idea, then lots of really smart, tailored, individual communications programs," he explains.

Says Fetherstonhaugh: "Take BP, the oil company. They chose a big brand positioning, which was beyond petroleum—a play on their name—that brought to life a business strategy that said, 'We're not just about oil, not about traditional ways of selling gas, we're going to make our best effort to be a more responsible oil company.' It's a big brand idea that employees, people in retail stores, the gas buyer and the big industrial buyer can wrap their minds around."

To understand this new, targeted buyer and to create more customized messaging for him or her, Fetherstonhaugh's company sometimes uses a form of "cultural anthropology." For example, instead of using focus groups to determine buyer attitudes, it performs deeper research, sending a videographer and a skilled researcher to spend a weekend with a family in order to see what their tastes really are.

Says Fetherstonhaugh: "If you talk to people about, say, asthma in a focus group scenario, they say, 'Oh yeah, my asthma is okay and I've got it under control.' But if you live with them for a weekend, you discover how profoundly asthma affects them, how they actually become hyper achievers to prove to the rest of the world, 'I'm okay, nothing wrong with me.' They wouldn't admit that in a focus group. This is observing and interpreting behaviour as opposed to just reporting back what they said. If you actually see them, you have a much deeper appreciation of how their tastes and decisions are informed."

ONE MESSAGE, MANY PATHS

Information channels have also been decentralized. Just as there is more information that goes into buying decisions, there are increasing numbers of channels to deliver that information to buyers. This means that the Big Idea has to be disseminated across multiple messaging channels, each message carefully crafted with the idiosyncrasies of the specific medium in mind.

While buying decisions have been decentralized, messaging channels have also exploded in recent years. The proverbial 500-channel universe exists, but in the messaging realm, it's not 500, it numbers in the millions. In the traditional domain, there are television and radio stations, magazines, newspapers, billboards and posters, as well as newer carriers of message boards, such as public transit and business vehicles.

Alternative communications channels have also sprung up. The Internet has altered the way we communicate. Direct mail has not died; it has morphed into a newer, more universal format—e-mail—as just about everyone who uses this ubiquitous communication tool can attest. Wireless telephones now carry ad messages, and, of course, there is the World Wide Web with its millions of sites that are increasingly becoming preferred platforms for marketing messages. This is particularly true post-dotcom bubble, as profit models for online marketing are starting to prove credible.

Each of these channels has a different character, as do the people who use them, so marketers now have to tailor each message, not only to the actual buyer, but to the medium that carries it as well. A print ad will not necessarily work on the Internet; a television ad will not necessarily work on radio; an Internet ad will not necessarily work on TV. "The proliferation of channel choices, the number of different ways you can reach the buyer now is mind-boggling, and today's brand managers could easily be overwhelmed," Fetherstonhaugh says.

At the same time, the nature of messaging itself has changed. Despite its proliferation, or perhaps because of it, advertising has lost its former power as the sole voice for brand. Instead, to impart more specific thoughts or information, some believe advertising has been joined on the podium by public relations. One role of PR, for example, is to encourage media outlets to run stories that feature information the company wants delivered. In the book *The Fall of Advertising and the Rise of PR*, authors Al Ries and Laura Ries assert: "Advertising has no credibility with consumers, who are increasingly skeptical of its claims and whenever possible are inclined to reject its messages. To get something going from nothing, you need the validity that only third-party endorsements can bring."[3]

While the claim that advertising is dead is likely over-reaching, there is something to the Rieses' assertions that advertising is only one of several methods marketers now must use to reach consumers in an age of multiplicity of information channels. Certainly Brian Fetherstonhaugh is of this belief. He often uses a process called "open channel planning" when deciding on a marketing campaign. Simply, this technique identifies a specific target buyer and then follows him or her through the buying process, looking for touch points where that buyer finds information that goes into a purchasing decision.

---

3   Al Ries and Laura Ries, *The Fall of Advertising and the Rise of PR*, HarperCollins Publishers, 2002.

Says Fetherstonhaugh: "We start with a blank piece of paper and a clear understanding of who our target audience is, and then map out the customer shopping and buying journey. We look for where they get the information that leads them to making a purchasing decision and then we look for the touchpoints that really make a difference. But you don't then try to hit all the touchpoints. For example, if they're looking for a digital camera and you discover that their price range is at the high end, there are really only three decisive points. One is at the point of retail, one is at the third-party level when people search on the web, and one is in high-end photography magazines because really keen people buy them."

Fetherstonhaugh also pays attention not only to people's actions but to their words as well—because the two can often differ, especially in buying categories involving taste or preference. "This allows us to really understand some common beliefs about people's tastes, which they may have said, but don't do," he argues. "For example, people say they don't buy sweet wines. Well, yes they do. Or Canadians used to say they were offended by American beer and would never drink it. Well, that's not true either. In many of these categories, people say sometimes what they believe to be true, but it doesn't stack up with their actual behaviour."

This complex buying behaviour, combined with the proliferation of message channels, means that today's managers have a much more difficult time directly influencing consumers' buying decisions than was the case under the old advertising model. Therefore, marketers are increasingly turning to the points of influence among consumers. These "influencers" are people with the power to sway or affect attitude or behaviour within their communities of reach.

REACH OUT AND TOUCH A TASTEMAKER

Those who influence buying decisions are growing more accessible and transparent every day. New, independent opinion leaders are emerging by the minute, with better and faster ways to pontificate. If you manage a brand, you must identify these individuals and have the means to reach them. Only five years ago this was very difficult to do as most were hidden behind relationships that guarded their access. Today, it is only a matter of identifying them and being tenacious.

Traditionally, influencers were people with prestige, ability or position, perhaps all three. The traditional model called for targeting the vehicles to access these opinion leaders—the news media—using public relations as the primary way to influence consumers' perceptions of a brand. This is still the case to some extent—most traditional media is now segmented into sectors such as music, technology, fashion, business—but the news media has lost its hegemony over access to tastemakers. Increasingly these new influencers have formed cluster points that consumers turn to in order to form their own opinions. Moreover, these influencers have new channels such as the Internet through which to deliver their views. The middleman is slowly getting cut out. It has never been easier to make your opinion public—just ask the many bloggers who are starting to be seen as one of the rising media through which to spread thought, and thereby brand leadership.

Tastemakers have become far more transparent and accessible than they once were. Oprah Winfrey has a huge influence on women's issues, and book sales. Paris Hilton, like her or not, impacts young women in terms of trends and uses a multiplicity of channels—television, magazines, tabloids and the Internet—to spread her influence. On the Internet, potential buyers can access the opinions of their peers at hundreds of opinion junction points.

If you want to buy a particular car, you can research it on the web, gathering reviews and finding out what other buyers of that car think; if you want a digital camera, there's an opinion site where other buyers express their thoughts on specific models; if you want to see a movie, you can find out everything about it on websites where thousands of people voice their opinions. So most consumers now gather several opinions in order to put together an accurate picture.

"You can't buy anything now without getting 10 opinions; it's very, very accessible," says Fetherstonhaugh. "Anytime you go shopping, you can get more opinions than you'd like. The Internet is particularly powerful—Yahoo! can make or break a movie in 24 hours. And eBay is another enterprise that has done a fantastic job managing purchase relationships. One of the keys to eBay's success is peer influence—the rating of buyers and sellers—is built right into it. It's incredibly powerful, but it needs to retain its independence or people will turn it off. Concepts like eBay and movie reviews are built around trust. You can make or break a market, a seller or a buyer in 24 hours. It's peer government in a way, total transparency."

START A CRUSADE

Opinions, or tastes, have been democratized; buyers now often trust their peers or respected opinion leaders more than they do traditional marketing. Influence these opinions by inspiring people to be "evangelists" for your product or service.

The rise of these opinion clusters, often involving peer influencers, means that brand management is increasingly about nurturing people's opinions, and not just managing buying behaviour, Fetherstonhaugh adds. And since opinions are often influenced by those who gain respect through integrity, the world is seeing a corresponding rise of the "opinion brand"—tastemakers who are independent of marketers schooled in the old top-down, command-and-control advertising model. These opinion brands—Oprah Winfrey is one of the best-known examples—retain their position through trust. Buyers listen to them because they have formed trusting relationships with them. In Oprah's case, just think of the "Oprah's Choice" stamped on the front of books at the bookstore and you'll understand the personal brand she has garnered and the leverage it has.

Brand managers who aim to establish all-important relationships with customers would be well advised to study these opinion brands, and to learn from them. Generally, brand managers attempt to establish relationships with customers by having a brand promise with distinct messages, by growing a unique identity in the marketplace, by nurturing the relationship over time, and by reinforcing the message all the time.

Similarly, opinion brands, or opinion leaders, either by design or simply by displaying integrity and consistency, present a distinct promise through a unique identity. They form long-term relationships with those who seek their opinion and continually reinforce their trusted stature, or brand. A technology reviewer, for example, gains respect because followers believe that his or her opinion will not be coloured by an attempt to curry favour; it is presumed the reviewer will offer the straight goods, and will do it independent of the brand owners.

"I think the game now is going to the quality and integrity of opinions," says Fetherstonhaugh. "It's a looser leadership style. But what it means for brand managers of the future is that they can rapidly lose control of their own brands. Now, you don't have anywhere near the control you used to; you have people churning opinions—good, bad and ugly—about your product. So, you have to try to nurture your brand and inspire people to become evangelists for it. It's more about influencing and trying to find evangelists who decide on their own to back it."

PEOPLE ARE BRANDS

Many people have learned that strong corporate brands are built through a clear mission, and trust that is earned over time. Fetherstonhaugh believes the same is true of individuals and their career brands. A career is a surprisingly long journey. And once again, clarity of purpose and trust are vital ingredients to success.

In his comments, Fetherstonhaugh is touching on an issue that is becoming more common as the increasing numbers of communications channels allow more people to voice their opinions. If a brand is about opinions or perceptions, now, and even more so in future, the brand and its necessary Big Idea are being perceived as one and the same. Your opinions define you, so increasingly your brand is you. (In business, this was always the case to some extent, but it is only now being seen as an important branding exercise instead of a downgraded personal issue.)

A well-known example of personal branding is Richard Branson, head of the Virgin empire. Branson delivers a consistent message about all his diverse businesses, a message that is intricately entwined with his own personality. Branson's personal brand implies fun, creativity and service, as does the brand of all his companies, despite their diverse industries. Other examples abound in the entertainment and sports fields, but personal branding is increasingly rearing its head in the field of marketing. In investing, for example, Warren Buffett has a personal brand that says "sage investment thinking," which infuses his holding company, Berkshire Hathaway, and has made its shares among the most valued in the world.

Brian Fetherstonhaugh believes that many of the principles that apply to corporate brands also apply to personal brands as people pursue their careers. Like marketing brands, personal brands are built on human relationships, established at particular "moments of truth" over time. As with a marketing brand, customers, or other people who form relationships with you, if only briefly, will be gauging whether you delivered what you said you would and met expectations, or you over-promised and underdelivered.

Personal branding takes on even more importance in light of the multiplication of communication channels. There is a reason, says Fetherstonhaugh, that personal meetings and other face-to-face interaction are increasing at the same time that electronic methods of communication such as e-mail, and web- and tele-conferencing are increasingly removing the need of physical presence. People prefer relationships that mean being in regular contact with others. Face-to-face contact is still the best way to gauge what another person is really all about—hence the increase in conferences, executive education, networking events, and personal networks in general.

Personal branding plays a very large part in another field that Fetherstonhaugh has recently turned his attention to—career planning. He believes implicitly that people embarking on a career have to recognize that it is really a very long exercise in developing a brand around yourself. In a speech to MIT's Sloan School of Management in December 2004, Fetherstonhaugh pointed out that people today have more years of career after they're 40 than before. And that the average person accumulates over 90 percent of their personal wealth after the age of 40. Therefore, the early part of a career should be spent building "rocket fuel" for the latter part.

"The big idea is to have two or three rewarding career options in your forties," he says. "Look at all the successful 'career brands'; they have a relatively small handful of truly successful human relationships that they built up over time that enabled them to succeed. So it's a long journey. And it's about how much brand equity you build over time, the quality of the relationships you build up."

Fetherstonhaugh has observed that people with really successful long-term careers have proven themselves trustworthy and valuable day in and day out. The same people always seem to be in demand when a tough or interesting challenge comes up. This is branding at work.

Fetherstonhaugh's Big Idea is about more than career options, however. In the personal realm, it includes how you want to be viewed by your peers, and by others. In the business field, the details may differ, but the principle is the same: businesses need to pay close attention to how they are perceived—by their customers and their competitors. The best way to manage a positive perception of an organization is to form a Big Idea about its products and services and then continually and consistently deliver that view at every important contact point. Deliver one easy-to-understand message and serve it when and where it will make a difference. Do the same thing for yourself.

"I often ask people in our company to think about what they have done to earn the trust of those around them," Fetherstonhaugh says. "What kind of client questions are you a superb answer to?"

More pointedly, "If you were put up on eBay—who would bid for you?"

5 THINGS YOU NEED TO KNOW

To survive in a changing marketing landscape, Brian Fetherstonhaugh believes brand managers must recognize that:

1. Buyers Go Forth and Multiply

Buyer decision-making has been decentralized. At one time purchasing was simply advertisement-induced. Now buyers reach conclusions based on multiple influences and emotions. Feed these different inputs with a Big Idea that is clear and understandable, and, most important, delivers a clear window into how it will affect an individual's life. There should be a persistent hunt for the answer to the question "Why should I care?" Recognize the multiplicity of buyer touchpoints and hit the right ones.

2. One Message, Many Paths

Information channels have also been decentralized. Just as there is more information that goes into buying decisions, there are increasing numbers of channels to deliver that information to buyers. This means that the Big Idea has to be disseminated across multiple messaging channels, each being carefully crafted with the idiosyncrasies of the specific medium in mind.

3. Reach Out and Touch a Tastemaker

Those who influence buying decisions are growing more accessible and transparent every day. New, independent opinion leaders are emerging by the minute, with better and faster ways to pontificate. If you manage a brand, you must identify these individuals and have the means to reach them. Only five years ago this was very difficult to do, as most were hidden behind relationships that guarded their access. Today, it is only a matter of identifying them and being tenacious.

4. Start a Crusade

Opinions, or tastes, have been democratized; buyers now often trust their peers or respected opinion leaders more than they do tradition-al marketing. Influence these opinions by inspiring people to become "evangelists" for your product or service.

5. People Are Brands

Many people have learned that strong corporate brands are built through a clear mission, and trust that is earned over time. Fetherstonhaugh be-lieves the same is true of individuals and their career brands. A career is a surprisingly long journey. And once again, clarity of purpose and trust are vital ingredients to success.

CHAPTER SEVEN

Pitching Up the Wazoo

Managing Communications
in the New Media Millennium

FEATURING THE WISDOM OF BONNIE FULLER

TV, magazines, newspapers, books, radio, newsletters, the web, email, blogs—people are now bombarded by media on all fronts. While there are more channels than ever to disseminate information, it has never been more difficult for a business to cut through the noise to reach a customer. Every company must clearly understand how to work within this media-saturated world; it must know not only what its own story is, but also how to tell it so that it falls upon the right ears.

One person who excels at this skill is Bonnie Fuller. In 1982, at the age of 26, she became editor of Flare, *a Toronto-based fashion magazine that spoke to young Canadian women. Fuller dramatically increased* Flare's *circulation and by 1989, she had moved to New York to become editor of the struggling teen magazine* YM. *She turned it around and then moved on to do the same with* Marie Claire, Cosmopolitan *and* Glamour.

Fuller significantly built circulations at every magazine she touched, and by 2003 reached an apex in her career by turning around the moribund Us Weekly, *a feat that earned her the title of Media Person of the Year in an online poll conducted by* I Want Media *and* The Week *magazine. That same year, she jumped to American Media Inc. as Editorial Director. There she oversaw a diverse group of media properties, from supermarket staples (*Star Magazine, The Globe *and the* National Enquirer*) to a host of fitness magazines, including* Shape, Men's Fitness *and* Natural Health.

Fuller specializes in pumping up periodicals for owners who feel their progeny aren't living up to their potential. Her golden knack for successfully growing magazines is tied to her intuition about what her target readers are looking for. She knows what her customers want, and she makes sure they get it.

Fuller's intimate knowledge of the media landscape provides a lesson for every company trying to navigate its way through this dense forest.

—m—

Update: *In May of 2008, Bonnie stepped down as Executive Vice President and Chief Editorial Director at AMI Inc., a position she had held since 2003. She will remain as Editor at Large at* Star *magazine and will serve as a consultant to AMI Inc. Chairman and CEO David Pecker. In recent interviews, Bonnie has revealed that she is working on a new online venture, but details are not available at the time of this writing.*

One hundred years ago, businesses discovered that new modes of transport, such as trains and trucks, allowed them to greatly extend the reach of their product. Similarly, modern communication channels now help companies not only touch many more buyers, but at the same time speak to each of them much more directly and personally. Companies can deliver a product easily to a distant customer, and they can communicate and close the sale without ever meeting him/her in person. Communication strategy is to the companies of the twenty-first century what transportation changes were to the twentieth.

But just as the transportation revolution created a spiderweb of routes that travellers had to learn to navigate, the communications revolution is also creating a labyrinth of channels that communicators must master. The increase in channels has revolutionized business by dramatically expanding the potential market for every producer of a product or service, large or small. Moreover, the quality of outlets on those channels has allowed companies to have a greater influence on buying decisions. It is a truism that businesses have always needed to learn to communicate more effectively with their customers. Now, however, it is even more important: if you can't articulate your value proposition in a convincing manner, you can be sure at least one of your competitors will.

Communication strategy is the most important tool in the corporate arsenal. Those who aren't proficient at it will die on their own sword. U.K. consultant and professor David Clutterbuck examined the communications strategies of ten businesses and discovered that four factors were present in all successful companies: clarity of purpose; effective interfaces; information sharing; and consistent leadership behaviour. He noted, "We found that it was the communication competence, not just of the communication function, but of the business as a whole, that determined its success."[1]

This communication competence, however, becomes difficult because of the sheer number of vehicles to manage. Not only is there a dizzying multiplicity of outlets, each has its own distinct characteristics and personality. When engaging with customers, a communicator still has traditional media—television, newspapers, newsletters, magazines, radio stations and billboards. But the advent of the networked world means that a universe that was once stable and predictable has exploded.

"Today, media is a collective term for the producers of content for mass consumption," explains U.S. consultant and author B.L. Ochman. "Newspapers, radio and TV each are powerful mediums, but they are no longer the only—or necessarily even the best—outlets for news about your company or product. Websites, e-zines, newsletters, mail lists, online forums, newsgroups, blogs (weblogs, or online diaries, some of which are becoming full-fledged publications in themselves), reputation management sites and email also are powerful mediums created by the Internet. They can have as much or more influence than the (traditional) press. In fact, journalists troll these mediums for stories."[2]

This exponential increase in conduits has come at a price. Most media outlets, whether electronic or traditional, are businesses as well. So they act like any other company: each targets a particular market and therefore further segments the audience for information delivery. This increased capacity to communicate has placed a correspondingly greater burden on companies to get their messaging right and ensure that it reaches the correct audience.

In the content-saturated world of the twenty-first century, choosing the right channel and putting the right message into it is an art

---

1   *Linking Communications Competence to Business Success: A Challenge for Communicators,* International Association of Business Communicators, IABC Research Foundation, 2001.
2   B.L. Ochman, *The Principles of Reality PR,* MarketingProfs.com, 2002.

form. Too many companies, however, are incorrectly pursuing it solely as a science.

Communication skills—conveying, through an assortment of channels, outlets and styles, the right information that encourages the right listener to make a buying decision—are paramount. All enterprises must now invest more time and money to understand how to communicate with their markets. Similarly, today's managers must be as schooled in the logistics of communication as they are in the logistics of running the day-to-day of the business itself.

The modern communications toolkit includes three major areas of focus: which *market*, which *outlet*, and which *message* should be used? Each is important in its own way, but gains more importance in its relation to the others.

The first consideration should be the choice of market. A manager must investigate a wide array of options. The days when a company developed products for a vague mass market are over. Markets today are extremely segmented, so managers must examine each stratum.

For example, a company selling music (in whatever form) would obviously want to target its typical buyers. If the choice is Big Band, or "swing," which was most popular in the 1940s and 1950s, the primary market would most likely be the elderly, since those who grew up with one type of music tend to favour it later in life. This does not mean the elderly form the only market, however. Certainly members of other generations—particularly young adults who have discovered swing music as a retro movement—would form a parallel secondary market. (Of course, this is a simplified example, as you would likely do a far deeper dive into the demographics.)

After identifying the customers, the company must next sift through the collection of messaging channels to determine how it will reach them and understand their buying patterns. The best messaging channel for seniors who like swing music would probably be television and radio, followed by ads in traditional, but targeted, print media, such as magazines for seniors. But for the secondary "retro" market, composed of young people who are most comfortable with the Internet, it might be more appropriate to message through online music sites and forums devoted to swing music.

Probably the most important communications choice, however, involves the actual message itself. A company must speak to its customers in their native tongue. So, to continue with the music example, it would be silly to communicate with seniors in a discourse that would appeal to teenagers. Seniors are experienced, and therefore have memories, so messages to them often begin with "Remember when…" to evoke nostalgia. But the opposite would be needed for the retro market of young people who like swing music. In their case, it's as much about experiencing the milieu as the music, so messages would likely need to be shorter, punchier, perhaps with slang that was around at the time of the music and which is now part of the whole retro scene. The first message is about remembrance, the second about education.

This understanding of messaging is apparently not obvious to many executives. Companies often choose wildly inappropriate messages and channels when attempting to speak to their customers. Members of the marketing communications profession—once known as Public Relations, or PR, but now frequently referred to as "Marcom"—routinely trade stories of clients who were determined to talk to potential customers in the language *they* wanted, instead of the language the customers spoke, usually with disastrous results. Similarly, there is no shortage of examples of well-polished marketing messages being sent down channels that were completely misfired.

Whether this is done out of arrogance by the product provider, or out of naiveté, the results are the same—a failure to connect. Marketing communications involves building a rapport with an audience, and that means constant dialogue between a company and its customers in a language both understand. If a business is to use marcom effectively, it had better clearly understand who it's dealing with. Unfortunately, a lot of organizations do not.

A guru and oasis in this complicated new media stage is Bonnie Fuller, currently the editorial director of American Media Inc. (AMI), publisher of magazines and newspapers such as *Star*, *The Globe*, *Mira!*, *Thalia*, *National Enquirer*, *National Examiner* and *Weekly World News*, as well as *Shape*, *Men's Fitness*, *Fit Pregnancy*, *Flex*, *Natural Health and Muscle & Fitness*. The AMI publishing array exemplifies the new face of the media industry—extremely targeted and subject-specific.

Fuller is a master at catering to this new targeted landscape of readers; she has been pursuing them throughout a 23-year career. In 1982, she began a career trajectory as the editor of *Flare* magazine in Canada and has since sat at the editor's desks of some of the world's top magazines. She has had stints captaining *YM* magazine—which prompted her move to the U.S. in 1989—*Marie Claire*, *Cosmopolitan*, *Glamour*, and most recently, the extremely successful *Us Weekly*. Fuller has posted large circulation gains at every magazine she's touched and in turn almost minted money for publishers such as Gruner + Jahr, Hearst and Condé Nast—among the largest in the world. Fuller has done this, and continues to do so at AMI, by aligning the magazines with an unerring sense of who her readers are and what they crave.

This golden touch has made Fuller, who is married and has four children, possibly one of the highest-paid and most successful editors in North America. The contract she received with AMI when she went over from *Us Weekly* in July 2003 called for a salary of US$1.5 million a year for three years plus hefty bonuses for circulation increases.

The Fuller advantage is her legendary insistence that her staff "get it right"—deliver information her readers want and in language they use, not the diction the writers favoured. She is well known for churning through employees because she works them blisteringly hard at writing, rewriting and rewriting again so that the messages her magazines deliver to her readers are clear, to the point, and exactly what they want.

DON'T BUILD CUSTOMERS IN YOUR OWN IMAGE

Make sure you know the difference between who your customers are and who you want them to be. Most companies fail to understand this basic distinction and end up chasing the wrong audience, selling disjointed products and pitching incorrect messages.

"It's all about knowing the reader," she told one interviewer. "And it is important to be able to communicate to readers both visually and textually. The physical package has to attract them. You can know what readers want, but if you can't communicate to them and sell it on every page, you're going to be in trouble."[3]

This doesn't mean Fuller gains an understanding of her readers by analyzing mountains of data about them. Rather, her knowledge is all about instinct and intuition honed through years of working with

---

3   Patrick Phillips, Bonnie Fuller: It's All About Knowing the Reader, *I Want Media*, 03/25/04.

them. According to an article in *New York* magazine, Fuller is a well-known idea machine when it comes to talking to her readers.

Says the author: "Many of the ideas that come into her head are uncannily in sync with a broad base of women's magazines readers—especially those who buy at supermarkets. 'Bonnie is a fan' says an editor. 'She is her reader—that's why she understands her reader. These are questions that she genuinely has.' When focus-grouping potential covers with a gaggle of staff—mostly women in the *Us* demographic, 25–39—she would repeatedly bark: 'No thinking! No thinking! It's got to be visceral! *Visceral!*'"[4]

This is marketing at its most laser-focused, with a clear understanding of the mind of the user—the reader—and it is a signature Fuller technique that has worked at every magazine she has edited. And it continues to work every time. Fuller was involved in the planning of a new AMI homes magazine and brought this understanding of a market segment to bear: "It's aimed at couples in their twenties and thirties. It's for the guys as well as the women. A lot of couples do their homes together. I think there is a real need there."[5]

It is also a marketing technique that other businesses would be well advised to study and emulate, since a clear and unrelenting eye for her readers' needs and desires has propelled Fuller for more than 20 years. If a company can do the same with its product, it is bound to succeed. Yet, she says, many advertisers and businesses that try to use media to communicate their own messages often do not employ this technique. Instead, she adds, they would rather follow their own ideals about who their customers are.

"One of the biggest mistakes I see with companies trying to reach the public is that they have this fantasy of who their customer is," she explains. "They don't want to know the reality of who their customer is. Sometimes, it's that they may not even like their customer."

Fuller is referring to an everyday phenomenon in the business world—companies delude themselves into believing their customers have certain characteristics that may or may not exist. And they often form that belief more from their own corporate identities and personalities than from those of their actual customers. Worse, they

4 Carl Swanson, What Makes Bonnie Run? *New York* Magazine, July 14, 2003.
5 Patrick Phillips, Bonnie Fuller: It's All About Knowing the Reader, *I Want Media*, 03/25/04.

don't bother canvassing their audience to see what their feelings are about a product or service, perhaps because they are consciously or subconsciously afraid to do so. Moreover, they may stubbornly refuse to hear what their customers are telling them. They become guilty of "drinking their own bathwater," of building a demographic in their own image.

MCLUHAN WAS RIGHT

The medium truly is the message. In a media-dense world, with consumers displaying ever-decreasing attention spans, companies must spend more time exploring how best to reach their target market. Choosing the right channel is now just as much an art form as the message itself.

Occasionally, companies misalign their focus because they would prefer to operate in a market that is different from the one that actually aligns with their product. For example, a company might target the premium market because that is where higher profits exist. However, the company's product may be completely unsuited to that segment, and no amount of wishing is going to change that. Wal-Mart figured this out and became one of the largest retailers in the world, and so did Yahoo!, which is now the dominant Internet portal on the planet. Google delivers to its users exactly what they need—specific information—and now captures 80 percent of Internet searches because it understood who it was serving. That, in essence, is the key—companies need to remember they are serving a customer base and not the other way around.

The only way to determine which customers should form the target market is to drill down through data to gain a psychological picture of them—not the ideal candidates, or the ones a company would like to have, but the ones it really does have and can speak to. Moreover, once the data has been secured, the company must accept and come to terms with it.

Marcom practitioners group people by their distinct needs to determine what types of consumers will be most receptive to a particular product and message. First, they classify consumers according to a set of demographics and geographic variables such as age, race, education and location. Then they may include more sophisticated data like attitudes, lifestyle, values, ideology, risk aversion and decision-making patterns. Other classification systems are used to predict consumers' purchasing power, motivation and self-orientation. At the end of this data accumulation and correlation lies a very strong picture of the demographic for a product.

As an editor, Bonnie Fuller is very familiar with this approach. All publications, especially larger ones, continually survey their audiences, hold focus groups on their likes and dislikes, and invite comment so they can better measure their audiences' minds. But Fuller, like many in the media, also relies heavily on instincts for insight. She talks to her readers, essentially becomes one of them, and this helps her form an understanding of what that reader might like. She is astonished when companies promoting products in her magazines don't do the same thing. It is, however, a more regular occurrence than you would think.

Says Fuller: "Companies make a lot of assumptions about who the customer is, age-wise, economically, how they look, their education and what their opinions are," she explains. "They gear their messages and products towards that customer when in fact that may not be their customer at all. They want to have a certain customer instead of the customer they have, or they may not appreciate the value of the customer they have.

"To know your customer, you have to be open-minded. If you're a retailer, you have to pay attention to everybody who comes in your store, not just the ones you want to see. You have to also be a customer for your own product or service. If you have a product, you have to use it, see how it feels, how you feel about it, how it works, what it does for you."

Marcom professionals say they regularly encounter situations in which a company wants to convey a message of some sort, but doesn't understand what it should say or to whom it should be sent. This is invariably because organizations don't understand their own story, that little piece of drama or critical hook. These messages need to break through the first line of defence of media outlets and then through to the actual end users.

All messages answer a basic question everyone in the media will ask because they know their audiences will ask the same: what's your story—who are you? What do you do? Although the questions sound simple, they can be challenging. Perhaps the company hasn't thought it out clearly. How will others embrace a story if an organization doesn't even put the time and energy into crafting it?

To understand this concept better, think of the potential media outlet—and hence the customer the company is trying to reach through the media—as a potential investor, and form an "elevator pitch" for that investor. An elevator pitch—the 30-second-tell-and-sell as it has also been called—is an example of what marcom is really all about—breaking down doors by whetting someone's appetite to look further and ask more questions. Too many companies work backwards and develop complex media plans before they think about the elevator pitch. By then, the message is likely too late and already convoluted. You must start with the pitch first, get it simple and easy the first time, and then draft the plan from that.

According to consultant Chris O'Leary, a good elevator pitch contains six basic elements:

1. It's short.

2. It positions your idea and company.

3. It talks about pain (and corollary pain relief).

4. It's memorable.

5. It uses one of the three power phrases (first, most widely used, or top-rated)

6. It's used over and over again.[6]

The clear, simple story also has to be tailored to a particular media channel. Since all the elements of drama are in the pitch already, this is not an arduous task. For example, a panel of journalists from four of the top news outlets in the U.S., speaking at a conference in San Francisco, listed these essential elements of a media pitch: conflicts, obstacles, drama, trends. "Realize that we make decisions based on what our readers want to see, or what we like to write about," the panel explained.[7] While they were talking about the more traditional news media, similar principles apply to all media, whether traditional or new media, such as websites or blogs.

6   Chris O'Leary, Pain and the Pitch, MarketingProfs.com, 2001.
7   Allen Weiss, *Public Relations and the Press*, MarketingProfs.com, 2000.

Bonnie Fuller echoes these sentiments, but like most journalists shapes them for her own particular needs. Fuller's largest magazines mostly target women readers and emphasize celebrity, beauty and fashion coverage. Pitches aimed at her fitness magazines would have to concentrate on lifestyle. Generally, however, she requires that pitches be "easy to read, packed with information, involve a personal story, be interesting and well written."

While Fuller is referring to pitches for print media, the principles apply across the board. "We have to learn to write with a voice that is true to our clients, true to their customers and true to the culture of communicating online," says web copywriting guru Nick Usborne. "Even today, companies online still don't get it. They still write their online text in the slick corporate style of offline writing. The text of e-commerce has no character, no humanity, no recognizable voice."[8]

Journalists and marcom professionals agree on one point: anyone pitching a story should have a clear knowledge of the nature of that media outlet in question—and its audience. You need to grasp both facets. But most journalists can recount anecdotes about terrible pitches that were totally misaligned with the interests of that particular medium: long, lumbering releases sent to tabloids, television stations or electronic outlets that require short, punchy statements; press releases that take three or more pages to describe technology in numbing detail, but without describing any of its benefits; ego statements that are all about the company and its operations, but not about why the customer (or the media outlet) should be remotely interested.

"Amateurs and flacks look upon PR as a sales job—you whip up a news release, send it out to a large pool of media and then 'sell' that media on your story," explains veteran journalist and news strategy coach Rusty Cawley. "Forget whether the story is something the media outlet can actually use. But you must know your customer (the media outlet) and you must design your product (the story) to meet that outlet's needs. Often, your story will appeal to a specific audience: an industry, a community, a profession, a customer base and the like. As a result, you must choose which media reach these audiences."[9]

---

8   Nick Usborne, *You'll be Judged by Your Voice*, MarketingProfs.com, 2001.
9   W.O. Cawley Jr., *PR Rainmaker: Three Simple Rules for Using the News Media to Attract New Customers and Clients*, www.prrainmaker.com, 2003.

THE MEDIA IS A STRATEGIC ALLIANCE

Just as many organizations fail to properly understand their customers, too many do not spend enough time understanding the
media and the differences between media outlets. Media channels are businesses too, and the failure to understand their needs
will inevitably lead to failure in the relationship. The media should
be managed like any other strategic alliance. You wouldn't walk
into the boardroom of a potential partner without understanding
their makeup and what value you can add.

Most journalists suggest that anyone attempting to place a story
about their company with a media outlet online first become intimately familiar with it—its styles, requirements and followers. Just as Fuller
appeals to her readers by thinking like them, to appeal to a media outlet, you must think as if you worked there.

As an editorial director of magazines with very large circulations,
Fuller rarely takes direct pitches from companies, although they do
flow non-stop to her individual publications. However, although she
may not see all the incoming pitches, she is aware of them. She recognizes the troubles companies can have in messaging. Sometimes, she
says, it's their own fault because they haven't researched the particular
magazine or taken the time to understand its readers.

Says Fuller: "Advertisers often don't read a media vehicle, or if they
do, don't understand it. When I was at *Cosmopolitan*, there were certain advertisers who didn't want to talk to 'Cosmo girls' because they
had their own ideas about who they were. But I knew my readers—
they were smart, active women who were engaged in careers and life,
were well educated and very self-actualized. They would have liked
those products and they weren't what these people thought Cosmo
girls were."

Fuller alludes to something all companies hoping to influence
opinion about their product or service should remember: the media
will rarely help you in your quest. Editors and journalists are far too
busy and too deluged by competitors to bother guiding you through
the process. If you want to speak to customers through the media,
you're going to have to hand over that message on a platter, prepared
and ready to consume. Make it easy for them or you won't be in the
game.

You may have an attention-grabbing message, you may have established a relationship with a journalist, and you may have thoroughly researched a particular channel. However, if you make that outlet work too hard to tell your story, it simply won't bother.

In some cases, it might even result in negative, not positive, coverage. This is especially true in the blogosphere—the large network of weblogs that has passed into the millions of pages and is growing exponentially by the minute—where opinions matter more than information. Blogs have quickly become one of the most important media for marketing today. Bloggers often take a subversive slant, and a company that sends some pompous, badly prepared message to them will only be providing fodder to be used against it. In such a case, bloggers are more likely to use this communiqué as the basis of a joke or tirade. To make matters worse, given the viral nature of blogs, other bloggers will pick it up and link to it. The turned around, savaged and ridiculed message will spread quickly throughout the Internet and, possibly, to the traditional media, which mines such sites for stories.

To avoid bad messaging, there are standard methods involving distribution and follow-up to make the information exchange easier. But the crux of the issue is writing style. All communication involves writing and it must be appropriate to the eyes and ears that receive it. If a website or e-publication favours a satirical or sardonic tone, tell your story that way. If the writing is lofty and academic—the *Harvard Business Review*, for example—focus your style in that direction. "Good webtext has a lot in common with good print text—it's plain, concise, concrete and transparent," says writing instructor Crawford Killian. "Like good print text, webtext carries a nonverbal message or subtext. The message may be, 'I'm comfortable with this medium and I understand you, my reader,' or it may be, 'I'm completely wrapped up in my own ego and my love of cool stuff'."[10]

THE MAYOR OF SIMPLETON

No one runs at a faster pace than the media, especially now with the just-in-time demands of the Internet. Companies working with the media need to make it as easy as possible for their media partners. Like a child with a short attention span, the minute things get confusing or difficult, they will move on to something else.

---

10 Crawford Killian, *Writing for the Web*, Geeks' Edition, Self-Counsel Press, 2000.

"You have to assume that whoever you are dealing with [in the media] is extremely pressed for time, so you have to make it totally easy to work with you," Fuller adds. "You can't assume [they] will come to you; you have to go to them. If you send out information about yourself and your company, you've got to make sure that it's full of information, has everything they need, like contact numbers and email addresses. You have to follow up, because you can't expect them to call you back. These people are busy and they're bombarded. So you have to go the extra mile, make the extra effort. And not feel bad about it, because that's just the way it is." Savvy politicians who have learned how to feed up "sound bites" that are nothing more than easily digestible content for media outlets have mastered this technique.

If there is likely to be a traffic jam at a particular media outlet's door, pick another, but similar, outlet that is less popular. Too many companies want to use the same media vehicles as their competitors, a kind of pack mentality that often results in ferocious bottlenecks for media mindshare. Companies are always looking for underserved niche markets, so why not apply the same thinking to communications strategy?

ZIG WHEN THEY ZAG

Too many companies try to use the same media vehicles as their competitors when going after their target audience. With media channel and outlet diversity, however, comes choice. Just as a company might elect an underserved market for its product to minimize threat from the field, a company might choose an underutilized media channel to allow its message to rise above the competitive noise.

Find an alternative medium that targets your customers directly and exploit it. Try ignoring the most popular mass newspaper, magazine or website in favour of a more specific trade magazine, newspaper, website or blog. A company may receive a far more sympathetic hearing from a media outlet that doesn't have armies of messengers knocking at its door. And the resulting exposure will be far more effective since it will be directed at a more specific customer who is more likely to be interested in that company's product.

This is an especially effective strategy for smaller companies without the means to pay professional fees for help to gain exposure in the larger media outlets. A small company must operate its entire business guerrilla-style, and certainly should approach communications from a guerrilla viewpoint. Such a company will need quick, targeted and creative messaging campaigns aimed at newer or less popular (to other companies) areas.

"You have to get out of your silo," explains Fuller. "Look for media that might be underutilized. For example, everybody in the fashion world spends a lot of time pitching to *Vogue* or *Harper's Bazaar* because they are the traditional places that you go to when pitching fashion or beauty products. But not everybody that is interested in fashion reads *Vogue* and *Harper's Bazaar*. They may read *Star*, even though we're not thought of as a traditional fashion or beauty publication. So while the editors at *Vogue* and *Harper's* are overwhelmed with pitches and it's hard to get into their pages, over here there's *Star Magazine* with more fashion and beauty pages than most monthly magazines."

Fuller isn't just talking about her own magazines. As a representative of a media outlet that receives many pitches, she's also a manager of a business and has to make her own pitches to other media to get the word out about her own product. To do so, she follows her own advice to the letter: "I have been in situations where I need media to work for me too. But all my competitors and established magazines pitch the traditional ones up the wazoo. So we have to think, 'Okay, where else can we go that also reaches our readers that isn't getting pitched up the wazoo?'"

Being fluid and accommodating is now even more important because the media scene has changed so much, and there are so many alternatives to work with. It's a different world than it was before the Internet, and any company wanting to work successfully with media has to be more creative, has to think broader, look harder and be more non-traditional. It has to go up, around, over, or under in order to navigate the logistics requirements of twenty-first-century communications.

Think about this—the Internet telephone company Skype (based out of Luxembourg) has exclusively relied on the media to spread the word about the company. It started with a groundswell through blogs and Internet reviews which led to the mainstream media picking up on the phenomenon. Today, the company has over 90 million downloads of its soft phone, making it one of largest telecoms in the world—all without a penny spent on traditional marketing.

So, if you are having trouble getting your message out, consider Bonnie Fuller's advice. "Take the blinders off," Fuller advises. "Find another way."

5 THINGS YOU NEED TO KNOW

Bonnie Fuller's insights in working with the media in the new millennium include:

1. Don't Build Customers in Your Own Image

Make sure you know the difference between who your customers are and who you want them to be. Most companies fail to understand this basic distinction and end up chasing the wrong audience, selling disjointed products and pitching incorrect messages.

2. McLuhan Was Right

The medium truly is the message. In a media-dense world, with consumers displaying ever-decreasing attention spans, companies must spend more time exploring how best to reach their target market. Choosing the right channel is now just as much an art form as the message itself.

3. The Media Is a Strategic Alliance

Just as many organizations fail to properly understand their customers, too many do not spend enough time understanding the media and the differences between its outlets. Media channels are businesses too, and the failure to understand their needs will inevitably lead to failure in the relationship. The media should be managed like any other strategic alliance. You wouldn't walk into the boardroom of a potential partner without understanding their makeup and your value add.

4. The Mayor of Simpleton

No one runs at a faster pace than the media, especially now with the just-in-time demands of the Internet. Companies working with the media need to make it as easy as possible for them. Like a child with a short attention span, the minute things get confusing or difficult, they will move on to something else.

5. Zig When They Zag

Too many companies try to use the same media vehicles as their competitors when going after their target audience. With media channel and outlet diversity, however, comes choice. Just as a company might elect an underserved market for its product to minimize threat from the field, a company might choose an underutilized media channel to allow its message to rise above the competitive noise.

CHAPTER EIGHT

On Underwear and Seduction
The End of Selling
in a World that has Everything

FEATURING THE WISDOM OF NICK GRAHAM

In North America today, the underwear of choice for the hip young man about town is probably a pair of Joe Boxers. Until the Joe Boxer brand hit the scene, men's underwear was just a commodity—generally dull, boring, uninspired and relatively inexpensive. Now millions of guys are willingly paying a premium for their undies.

Joe Boxer is only one example of a business that has successfully carved out higher ground in a market that used to be quite pedestrian. Luis Vuitton did it with handbags, Manolo Blahnik with stiletto-heeled shoes, Starbucks with coffee, Virgin with just about everything. While the traditional suppliers in each sector griped, "No one will pay that much for that product," consumers proved them wrong. Shoppers quite happily chose, and in some cases rushed to purchase, the premium products sold at much more lucrative margins.

Nick Graham, an itinerant musician from Calgary, Alberta, with an eclectic background—among other things, he's related to the famous Canadian newspaper magnate Lord Beaverbrook—discovered this oddity about consumers in the 1980s when he started to make novelty underwear in his San Francisco apartment. Through a series of wacky attention-getting stunts, Graham's modest home-based business eventually grew into a US$100-million-a-year fashion aristocrat—Joe Boxer—which he ultimately sold in 2001 and which went on to become a house brand for Kmart.

So what was the secret to getting men to shell out 25 bucks for a pair of skivvies? As Joe Boxer founder and CUO—Chief Underwear Officer—Nick Graham discovered, it is all about learning how to lead horses to water, and getting them to arrive there thirsty.

—∿—

Update: *Since launching 100 Minute Company, Nick's firm has become home to several brands, including NickIt, American Iconic, U.S.U.K and National Underwear. In 2007, he teamed up with Goodwill to launch William Good, a line of one-of-a-kind clothing and accessories made from Goodwill donations that were destined to be tossed out. Nick also expanded into the food and beverage industry, where he joined renowned San Francisco restaurateur Stephen Weber in opening the area's first Best-O-Burger, a gourmet mini burger franchise, in 2008. Currently, in addition to managing all of his ventures, Nick travels the world and speaks to leading organizations about the importance of branding.*

Manolo Blahnik stilettos may have had the women of *Sex and the City* agog, but are they really that much better than similar shoes on sale at the nearest discount shoe store? Are they worth a price that can be more than 10 times higher than shoes from Wal-Mart? Similarly, is that $1.60 cup of coffee at the nearest Starbucks truly that much better than the old 50-cent cuppa Joe you could get at the corner diner? Likely, the answer is no. The higher price point obviously includes something else—an intangible value that the producer and consumers have agreed is present and worth every cent. That x-factor is what makes Manolos, Starbucks and many other brands considered to be premium products in a sea of commodity-priced competitors.

Premium pricing is a technique used by some manufacturers who want their products to be considered a cut above. They believe consumers will pay more than the going rate in a given category. After covering costs (which are often not more than those of low-cost competitors), the premium product producer adds on a tremendous mark-up or margin. He or she does that not only to ensure a hefty profit, but also as a marketing technique. In other words, the premium product manufacturer can say *my product is better simply because I am charging you more for it* (Not *I am charging you more for it because it is inherently better.)* This takes advantage of consumers' blind tendency to believe you get what you pay for.

While pricing techniques are not necessarily the most interesting part of marketing, premium pricing is a hot topic and has been a growing trend in the marketing world over the last decade. Since the 1950s, product pricing has been one of the key building blocks of the marketing mix strategy routinely taught in business schools. The basic strategy asserts that when selling a product, marketers must focus on Price, Product, Promotion and Placement (referred to as the "4Ps"). Historically, the price equation has been simple: sell for as much as you can without scaring off the buyer. But this simple formula inevitably crumbles as competitors leap into a market and start lowering prices to grab market share. Soon all prices must climb downward to match and the commodity-pricing cycle begins.

In a world of product parity where almost every item is comparable to others in its category, premium pricing has become a way to achieve market differentiation. Companies use premium pricing to give a product cachet. The technique is a natural outgrowth of the segmentation of mass consumerism where some individuals have indicated they are willing to pay for the allure of exclusivity, or quality, or some other intrinsic "value." It is this value that producers emphasize when they put a premium price on their goods.

But what is value? Simply making a product more expensive than others in its category is unlikely to say "value" to the buyer. Traditionally, value was a top-down message from the manufacturer to the customer—"value is what we say it is." Today, however, consumers are saying that value is what *they* perceive it to be. When the two definitions are in sync, the product becomes a success; when they are misaligned, failure is inevitable. When you get it right, you have created an inimitable brand.

During the 1990s, some pioneering companies recognized this segmenting consumer base and designed their products to appeal to it. For example, some automakers that had spent the previous decade improving quality realized that every other automaker had done the same thing. There was no longer any competitive advantage in boasting about quality—consumers had simply grown to expect it. They also recognized that car buyers were injecting something else into their buying habits—their personal identities. In short, buyers would pay a premium for a car that reflected back their perceptions of themselves.

Young hipster on the make? A high-performance, fuel-inefficient-but-stylish muscle car. Who else would buy a car that can only get you as far as the next gas station before you have to fill up again? Family man concerned with safety and control? Buy a Volvo. Volvo's marketing message is a very interesting example—they don't sell cars, they sell safety. Similarly, Mercedes and BMW are selling a message to the successful businessman—we will give you the luxury you deserve. And the Japanese carmakers, Nissan, Honda and Toyota—we will get you where you want to go, reliably.

Carmakers were also changing the way their sales forces communicated with customers. We have seen the advent of the no-dicker, friendly buying and servicing system that doesn't assume the consumer is uneducated and naive. This appealed particularly to the upwardly mobile female buyer who was tired of condescending car salesmen. This new alignment of values was not top-down delivery of a desired trait; it was bottom-up. It matched the product to buyers' feelings about themselves. Because of that emotional connection, it was all the more powerful.

Then there was Starbucks, the now ubiquitous chain of coffee shops that managed to convince people they should pay considerably more than the usual price for a cup of coffee. Starbucks, while at its core a coffee purveyor, offered something far more than a cup of coffee. It updated the coffee shop, a gathering place where people could meet, talk, and even work. The company created a third space where people could assemble between their homes and offices. It was a very European concept, but carefully and intelligently translated to North America—the cup of coffee as the basis of an experience. It's often said that with Howard Schultz and Starbucks, experience marketing was born.

At the same time, there was someone else around who took another ordinary item—men's underwear—and turned it into a premium experience. Nick Graham, a punk rock musician from Calgary, Alberta, landed in San Francisco after kicking around Europe for a while. Broke and needing to eat, he decided to earn a few bucks by using some self-taught design skills to make and sell novelty ties to hip local businessmen. While the ties were moderate sellers, Graham needed something bigger.

What turned his attention to underwear was nothing more than a moment of his own need—for underwear! "Actually, I really needed some, because I think the last pairs I had I probably bought at Canadian Tire," he jokes. A buyer for Macy's whom he had befriended pointed out that underwear was a really, really boring clothing line that might benefit from Graham's odd sense of humour. What eventually transpired from this conversation was a company that managed to turn men's underwear—which is about as common an item as you can get—into a consumer phenomenon. Graham started Joe Boxer in 1985 and used his off-base sense of humour and some shrewd marketing skills to create a business with revenues of US$100 million a year before it was sold, in 2001, to the apparel licensing giant Windsong Allegiance Group, LLC, of Westport, Connecticut. The next year, Joe Boxer allied with Kmart to supply its stores with Joe Boxer apparel and home decor.

One of the keys to the Joe Boxer success story is Graham's weird sense of humour, which he describes as Monty Pythonesque. "All the great comedians in the U.S. come from Canada because, like the British, we have a great sense of irony," he says. "America suffers from irony-poor blood." Mike Myers, Jim Carrey, Dan Aykroyd, Martin Short, and a long line of other Canadian comedians would no doubt agree.

After deciding to combine humour and underwear, Graham made a few mockups and came up with his first product—a pair of tartan boxer shorts with a detachable raccoon tail. He called it the Imperial Hoser, Canadian slang for a dozy backwoods beer-drinker, and it was an instant hit. The Imperial Hoser and other boxers with happy faces and bold, humorous designs took the staid anti-fashion world of men's underwear by storm. Until then, men's underwear offered an amazing array of two options: simple briefs, now known as tighty-whities, and boxers, supplied by traditional underwear manufacturers.

Men didn't like to shop, so the theory went, and they especially didn't like to shop for such a utilitarian item as underwear. Traditionally, a man would hit a store, grab a few pairs, usually at less than $5 apiece, and get it over with as quickly as possible. The only requirement was comfort. Suppliers might have offered the occasional item that showed some flair for the more daring fashion leaders among the emerging gay and singles markets. But the mass market got plain and simple underwear, similar to the 50-cent cup of flat, stale diner coffee.

> **THE "MORE" FACTOR**
>
> Understand your buyer and recognize when he or she is tired of the same old thing. Today's sophisticated consumers want more, and you have to keep up with their desires—even when they may not be able to clearly articulate what those are. People gravitate toward things that spice up the mundane.

Until Joe Boxer. This product was just plain fun. Each morning anyone could go to the office looking like his normal buttoned-down self on the outside—but wearing underwear covered with happy faces or that said "No, no, no" in the light and glowed "yes, yes, yes" in the dark. Or wearing boxers that quacked or inflated. All day long he could pretend to be a normal uptight lemming, but underneath he knew he was really a rebel. Or at least, that is what Joe Boxer wanted him to believe.

Men lined up to indulge their sense of humour at up to $25 a pop, and soon Joe Boxer was being featured in such upscale American stores as Saks Fifth Avenue and Bergdorf Goodman. Casual and lounging apparel quickly followed and was available in more than 4,000 department stores, specialty shops and catalogues. Then Graham branched out and licensed the brand for everything from furniture to other types of clothing, and from fashion accessories such as sunglasses and watches to basics like napkins and toilet seats. Eventually, Joe Boxer was producing 1,000 eye-catching designs a year, earning Graham several fashion industry awards.

Nick Graham saw his unique marketing ideas spread like wildfire throughout the clothing industry. Those ideas grew out of his ironic view of life combined with an understanding of trends he gained while travelling around Europe, where he had noticed that underwear was changing into a fashion item. He had tucked that thought into his backpack and revived it when he left his band, the Scream of Dreams, to start his home-based tie-making business in San Francisco. Nick Graham had tapped into something that is now much talked about among marketers. It goes by various names—branding, buzz-building or experience marketing—but Graham just sees it as a way of appealing to previously ignored emotions in the buying public.

Says Graham: "We didn't have a plan, and looking back on it, naiveté can be a good thing in business sometimes. Now I call it "emotional market share" but I had no idea at the time that I was doing that. There's a whole realm of other people who have a sense of humour and that's the emotion I appealed to. Somebody with an incredible sense of humour is going to wear [the product], and only those who know them really well are going to see it. It's still like that, but now there are 10 pairs of underwear on the floor and each one represents a different emotion, and customers have hundreds of emotions. So you have Fruit of the Loom, for instance, and it's basic underwear that says 'I'm a boring guy.' And you have Calvin's, which says 'I have an incredible body, or I don't, but I'm going to wear this underwear and maybe that will happen to me.' And you have Joe Boxer, which says, 'I'm fun.'"

His hypothesis had proved to be very astute. Nick Graham may not have been able to articulate it at the time, but he was ahead of the curve. Ten years after Graham launched and carved out a sizeable piece of a market that had grown to an estimated US$2–$3 billion, designer underwear had become a staple on advertising billboards around the country. Underwear was no longer just a useful garment: it represented a worldview. Or at the very least, a worldview of what was in a man's pants.

Although hindsight allowed him to get a better understanding of it, at the time Graham was really following his own instinctive marketing muse. Unable to view it any other way, he designed the zany underwear because he was the kind of character who loved a good laugh. "Look, it's a garment, but it's one of the few garments you can put a real sense of humour into and sell a lot of," he says. "Underwear is a very intimate thing. It can be naughty, nice, or whatever. By putting some fun into it, making it irony-rich, it's having a laugh. And that's very sexy. One thing a woman finds most attractive in a man is a sense of humour. I think that's an interesting combination, that being funny is also very attractive."

That "funny" could be attractive was the secret to attaching higher price tags to a pair of Joe Boxers. "Lowest price" didn't enter into the equation.

What did factor in was the relationship Joe Boxer established with its customers. Early on and without any marketing training, Graham realized that to sell something in a world that was flooded with products, you had to seduce buyers, to establish a relationship or emotional connection with them. Consumers were moving away from judging on quality or price alone and toward investing some emotion into the buying process. There had to be a reason this ordinary individual should buy from you and not from your competitors.

Modern marketers call this "brand equity" or "the confidence gap," which represents the consumer's inability to distinguish whether a product or service is any better than, or different from, any other product or service. Most businesses can't even satisfactorily address this question for consumers, often because they haven't figured it out themselves. Business coach Tom Peters has referred to this difference as "the Wow factor"; others have given it different names. But it all means the same thing—a clear understanding of what a business is delivering to its audience and why it is important. This is the "value proposition" of the product, or the emotional benefit it will provide to a purchaser.

SOME ENCHANTED EVENING

Sale of premium products is a seduction process. It's all about establishing a relationship between your brand and the customer. Consumers want a connection to what they buy, and that's what your marketing strategy must achieve. They no longer want to be sold to—they insist on ownership of the buying process.

Nick Graham doesn't talk about confidence gaps, or value propositions, or any of the other typically tossed around marketing terms. He simply calls it "seduction," and his Wow factor, or method of seduction, was humour—and entertainment. "I look at business as a kind of flirting," he says. "If you're looking to create a relationship with the consumer, you have to go through this process of courtship. It's no different than being picked up in a bar. How do you flirt? How do you create a relationship and how do you keep that relationship going?"

A customer browsing through shelves of underwear who has no previous knowledge of Joe Boxer may not get the emotional connection. So the Wow factor has to be communicated. Graham's seduction had to be reinforced through the larger creation of a brand identity. To create this identity—in this case, a sense of fun and craziness on top of a quality product—Nick Graham used a form of marketing that fit his identity perfectly. Unlike most garment makers, who relied on expensive, and distant, advertising campaigns to establish themselves in the minds of consumers, Graham turned to a new form of selling which was just emerging—guerrilla marketing.

THE MEDIUM IS THE MESSAGE—GO GUERRILLA

Even if your product is as ordinary as underwear, find a way to make it stand out and be used as a vehicle for people to express their individualism. Once you have found this x-factor, use extraordinary methods to tell people about it. Unique products deserve creative ways of spreading the word about them.

First coined in 1983 in a book of the same name by Jay Conrad Levinson, the term guerrilla marketing refers to chasing the conventional business goals of sales, profits and growth using unconventional means. Instead of spending money on advertising, for example, guerrilla marketing suggests companies invest time, energy, imagination and knowledge. Tactics include free publicity, special events, product giveaways and simply handing out flyers on the street. Forget focus groups or demographic analysis or any of the other traditional tools used by advertisers. Focus instead on your gut feelings about your target market, on delivering the right message through unconventional means, and especially on imagination.

Guerrilla marketing has another feature—it allows the little guy or newcomer to compete with the established companies, because it is less budget-driven. Today, guerrilla marketing is a respected discipline often used by smaller businesses and startups that don't have the war chests available for large advertising campaigns. But in the 1980s and 1990s, it was a revolutionary concept.

Nick Graham was the very definition of a guerrilla marketer because it fit his own personal view that imagination and fun trump advertising any day, especially when you're turning the plain into the amazing. When Joe Boxer underwear hit store shelves, Graham was ready to tell the world about it, unconventionally and at low cost. He used a series of outrageous stunts to ensure that Joe Boxer was on everybody's minds. It worked, and students of marketing should pay close attention.

Some of his wackier marketing tricks included sending 100 pairs of underwear to then-U.S. President Bill Clinton to coincide with his first 100 days in office. He included a note that read, "If you're going to change the country, you've got to change your underwear." Then there was the record for the "highest unmanned underwear rocket launch" in Black Rock, Nevada. Graham sent a Joe Boxer rocket, which contained a pair of underwear from Joe Boxer and a pair from a Russian manufacturer, 66,000 feet into space. You could also get underwear to go from the Joe Boxer underwear vending machines, known as the Undo-Vendo, which were installed at universities, fitness centres, airports, comedy clubs and bookstores. Complete with a motion sensor that spoke to passersby when triggered, the machine offered up a greeting, a joke and underwear when customers inserted their credit cards.

How about the first-ever in-flight underwear fashion show on Virgin Airways' inaugural flight from London to San Francisco? Passengers heard the following announcement after the show: "U.S. Customs requires that all passengers change their underwear."

The stunts kept coming. In 1998, Graham, revelling in his newly acquired position in life, felt he needed to acquire a title to go along with the success. So he purchased one—"The Lordship of the Manor of Balls Bedfordshire"—through the Manorial Society of Great Britain. "I had been looking for a couple of years for the right title, and the Lord of Balls fell into my lap," says Graham. "Plus I got it cheap for only about $4,000. And I have fishing rights in a river in England." He opened a showroom in New York City's fashion district called the Manor of the Lord of Balls, which sported giant chairs with wigs, an eight-foot-tall banana sculpture and a conference table imprinted with the words "Blah, Blah, Blah." He also opened a restaurant in San Francisco's Japantown called DOT (dotrestaurant.com), complete with a virtual hostess, holographic fireplace, wingback chairs to snooze in, and the Lord of Balls lounge.

But the one marketing exercise they still talk about occurred in 1997, when the eccentric underwear designer managed to get more than 100 fashion editors, weary from a week of viewing the New York collections at the annual "7th on Sixth" show, to fly to Iceland to view men's underwear. "We took over the country for 48 hours," says Graham of the exotic promotion that featured a weekend of salmon fishing, glacier snowmobiling and, of course, a fashion show starring the company's new collection and an all-Icelandic cast, including a few sheep. Ironically (a Graham trademark), "It was cheaper to fly to Iceland than to do a show in New York City, and we got 10 to 20 times the publicity kick," he points out.

Co-branding also worked some magic. Graham tapped Warner Bros. to create a new line of cartoon-emblazoned sleepwear and underwear that featured classic cartoon characters—with a twist, of course. Bugs Bunny cavorted with Mr. Licky, the Joe Boxer logo that features a smiley face with a giant tongue, and Scooby Doo took a bite out of it. The company also partnered with Motorola on the Joe Boxer Cyberscooter, a rebuilt Vespa scooter that came fully equipped for fast cruising and which was featured in the Neiman Marcus Christmas catalogue.

This informal approach to building the Joe Boxer brand name worked. (Necessity is definitely the mother of invention, and mother always told you to wear clean underwear.) According to Graham's estimates, Joe Boxer has 77 percent brand-name recognition, close to competitor and marketing icon Tommy Hilfiger, who has 80 percent brand recognition. Advertising giant Coca-Cola has 99 percent, but Graham points out, "Tommy and Coke spend a lot of money to achieve that recognition. We did well with the teeny-weeny amount we spent on marketing and advertising, typically about half a percent of annual revenues." And even for that small amount he managed to win a coveted CLIO award, the ad industry's highest honour.

Were all these guerrilla marketing stunts mapped out in some strategic planning session? Hardly. Nick Graham is a guy who firmly believes in flying by the seat of his (under)pants—but he knows where he's flying to. Like his friend and hero Richard Branson, head of the Virgin conglomerate, Graham recognized instinctively that marketing in an oversupplied (which leads to lower-priced) world is all about personal branding. A company has to stand for something or it won't stand out at all. Ultimately, what Graham did was turn Joe Boxer from an underwear maker to an entertainment company that utilized a product as its primary medium.

BE AN ENTERTAINER

Business is an amusement park and the actual product is merely the souvenir, says Graham, who ensured that his Joe Boxer line of products—and his marketing methods—always entertained the buyer.

Says Graham, "I like to say the brand is an amusement park and the product is the souvenir. You need to entertain the customer. Think of it as a party, like an amusement park. When you buy this brand, you're going to be entering another world and it's going to be really exciting and cool. It's that emotional thing. All we were doing was filling another emotional part of the consumer, who said, 'I don't want to wear Stanfield's underwear because that's not me,' but that's all that was on the market. Anyone can make underpants, but what do they stand for? And what do they represent in that person's life? Once you get that defined, and if it's relevant and large enough, then that becomes a business."

Graham gets many of his ideas from Branson, an acknowledged brand master who operates a widely diversified consortium of businesses under the Virgin label. Globally, Virgin's 350 companies provide air travel, telecommunications, trains, cosmetics, credit cards, music, and several other services. "Virgin is an unusual brand," Branson told Wharton School of Publishing, because it is a "way-of-life" brand, unlike Western brands such as Coca-Cola or Nike that focus on one type of product.

Says Branson: "In Nigeria, we've been asked to set up a national airline. In India, we're going to build a phone company. In South Africa, the financial services industry is still stuck 30 years back with incredibly high prices. We're looking at getting in there and shaking up the industry. In America, we're looking at space travel. Around the world we're looking at taking the brand into a number of different industries. Our criterion is: Will it fulfill the Virgin yardstick of being good value for the money? Will it enhance the brand by bringing great quality? Will we have fun doing it and can we make it profitable? If those criteria work, then we'll seriously look at a new industry."[1]

It's on the will-we-have-fun-doing-it factor that Branson and Graham meet. The two clicked instantly when they first worked together, recognizing kindred spirits in each other. The fun factor was obvious when they were promoting a joint venture in 1995 in Times Square. Says Graham: "We did this promotion where if you buy five pairs of Joe Boxers, you got a free companion ticket on Virgin. I was dressed as the Queen of England and Richard was dressed as Prince Charles and we were in a bucket with a crane in Times Square, 200 feet

---

1   Knowledge@Wharton, December, 2004.

above, throwing bagels down on the homeless people. It was really at that moment that I thought, 'This is what I want to be doing when I grow up.'" That is, if he ever grows up.

FIND THE EMOTIONAL GROWTH MARGIN

There is a delta between what some products are worth and the higher price some people are willing to pay for them. This gap is filled by fervour injected by the seller (and by the revitalized buyer). There's a new enthusiasm in the purchasing process. Graham calls this the "Emotional Growth Margin."

Graham believes that the emotional connection a brand delivers is essential in a world over-hyped with advertising. "We're all sold everything 50 million times a day," he explains. "But the consumer has moved beyond all that. Richard's brand completely defines what I'm talking about in terms of the amusement park. When you buy a ticket on a Virgin flight, you're not just buying a ticket; you're buying an experience. When we do these crazy stunts, that has nothing to do with gaining market share—that's a diversionary process—but it leads back to the brand. People think, 'Wow, that company put something in space.'"

According to Graham, the world has run out of new things to sell but it is hungry for new ways to buy. The constant bombardment of selling messages has turned consumers off, and they long to have some emotional touchpoint with vendors. Graham spends time thinking about how to refresh the buyer. It's a common theme when he consults and speaks—he is a sought-after speaker on branding and marketing. To Graham, getting consumers interested in buying is the antithesis of selling to them—the "end of selling in a world that has everything," he says.

Says Graham: "The consumer is saying, 'I want a new way of buying something.' Look at the iPod. The music consumer was saying, 'I want a new way of listening to music,' and that's where the iPod came in; iPods don't have to be sold—they sell themselves. I always say we're not selling anything; we're just giving a choice. If we've made the right decision on what we're offering, well, you're going to buy. If we haven't, well you don't. Either we've done our job up front, or we haven't. And it's your decision now."

Graham calls this the "emotional growth margin," or EGM, a gap between the cost to produce a product, plus markup, and the final price. This often-elastic span is filled with the emotion the manufacturer and a buyer invest in the purchasing process. To illustrate EGM, he points to the automobile world, using Volvo and the new environmentally friendly Toyota Prius gas-electric hybrid cars as his main examples. "It doesn't all have to be fun. Volvo's branding is about safety. People could get the same kind of car for $10,000 less, but the Emotional Growth Margin of Volvo is its safety. Prius is a car with an EGM about doing your bit for the environment."

Although he sold Joe Boxer in 2001, Nick Graham is still its Chief Underwear Officer and primary spokesman. But Graham has branched out from his role as an underwear maker and now consults to large and small companies on branding and the creative process. He is bringing his wildly successful creative philosophy and unconventional business methods to the rest of the world via his new venture, the 100 Minute Company.

At a pivotal time in history when the collective attention span is getting shorter by the minute, people hunger for new ways to consume, he says. Believing that people long to have access to, and to enjoy, everything from fashion to music to travel to books, and everything in between, Graham founded the 100 Minute Company to maximize his theory that brands need to be more expansive in their thinking across multiple platforms—just as their consumers do.

If only underwear could talk.

5 THINGS YOU NEED TO KNOW

Nick Graham's secrets for taking a product from ordinary to extraordinary:

1. The "More" Factor

Understand your buyer and recognize when he or she is tired of the same old thing. Today's sophisticated consumers want more, and you have to keep up with their desires—even when they may not be able to clearly articulate what those are. People gravitate toward things that spice up the mundane.

2. Some Enchanted Evening

Sale of premium products is a seduction process. It's all about establishing a relationship between your brand and the customer. Consumers want a connection to what they buy, and that's what your marketing strategy must achieve. They no longer want to be sold to—they insist on ownership of the buying process.

3. The Medium Is the Message—Go Guerrilla

Even if your product is as ordinary as underwear, find a way to make it stand out and be used as a vehicle for people to express their individualism. Once you have found this x-factor, use extraordinary methods to tell people about it. Unique products deserve creative ways of spreading the word about them.

4. Be an Entertainer

Business is an amusement park and the actual product is merely the souvenir, says Graham, who ensured that his Joe Boxer line of products—and his marketing methods—always entertained the buyer.

5. Find the Emotional Growth Margin

There is a delta between what some products are worth and the higher price some people are willing to pay for them. This gap is filled by fervour injected by the seller (and by the revitalized buyer). There's a new enthusiasm in the purchasing process. Graham calls this the "Emotional Growth Margin."

CHAPTER NINE

Your Host

The Complexity of Being Known for One Thing

FEATURING THE WISDOM OF ISSY SHARP

In 1961, a small hotel opened in Toronto. Located on the outskirts of downtown, the Four Seasons Motor Hotel featured 165 rooms and offered travellers basic amenities for a nightly rate of $12.

The Hotel's restaurant, known for its friendly service, became a popular destination for local business people. The owner, Isadore Sharp, was the son of Polish immigrants who had moved to Toronto in the 1930s. During high school Sharp often helped his father, a plasterer by trade, on his construction projects. He joined the company full time after completing an architecture degree from Ryerson University in 1952.

After working alongside his father for several years, Sharp became eager for a new challenge. The complexity of a hotel offered an intriguing alternative to the houses he was currently working on; he decided to build his own property.

"I can say with a great deal of certainty and truth that there was no vision, there was no grand dream," he has said of his humble beginnings. "The fact is I was just trying to do one small hotel deal. One deal — not a company."

A few decades later, Four Seasons had become one of the biggest hospitality brands in the world, with countries sending entire delegations to persuade him to build Four Seasons properties in their cities.

Today, there are over 81 hotels and resorts in over 34 countries, and more than 31 projects under development. The Four Seasons brand is synonymous with luxury; the company dominates the hospitality market in providing top-of-the-line service. In 2008, 22 Four Seasons proper-ties won the AAA Five Diamond Award. Properties are continually ranked high in excellence and quality by publications like Zagat and Condé Nast Traveller.

In addition, the company has shown a deep commitment to fostering a positive and healthy environment for employees. This year, 2008, for the eleventh consecutive year, Four Seasons was included in Fortune *magazine's "Top 100 Companies to Work For," a title it has earned every year since the launch of the list in 1998, and one of the keys to its remarkable success.*

In 2006, Microsoft founder Bill Gates and Prince Al-Waleed Bin Talal of Saudi Arabia bought out the privately held company for US$3.4 billion dol-lars. Sharp is still the chairman and CEO.

The definition of a brand has evolved to become a symbol of personal philosophy and identity affiliation in the minds of consumers. With the proliferation of social networking tools, brand monitoring compa-nies like Radian6 argue that the very essence of branding is shifting:

> The impact of social media on public relations and advertising is fundamentally changing the profession. Brand ownership is no lon-ger solely the domain of the institution. A brand is now defined as the sum of all conversations taking place among users, and it's happening now regardless of whether or not you are part of these conversations.

In an era when consumers can easily rave (or rant) about their ex-periences with corporations to a mass audience, it has become signifi-cantly more difficult for brand identities across all industries to remain unaffected in the face of such numerous and uncontrolled dialogues.

According to the "2007 Social Media Brand Report," commis-sioned by Tamar, a UK-based interactive agency, travel brands includ-ing hospitality providers are the most at risk from comments generated by online users. The study found 58 percent of respondents indicated that reading negative comments about a brand would influence their purchasing decision enough to abandon the transaction. Findings also revealed that 80 percent of consumers are actively commenting on brands online via discussions, blog posts, online reviews and social networks. The consumer has become tech-savvy, shrewd and adept at searching the web for information about any corporation or brand. For many organizations, the thought of consumers discussing, reviewing or altering their corporate messaging is unsettling; it has unknown implications for the brand.

Consider TripAdvisor.com. As one of the web's most popular travel review sites, it contains over 15 million consumer reviews of vacation destinations and hotel properties worldwide. Consumers upload their own photographs or videos of specific rooms, and they can share their experiences and impressions. The stories (some offering high praise; some horrified) cover every topic from the uniforms worn by staff to the appeal of the art hanging on the wall. Users rate their hotels on everything from the cleanliness of the rooms to the quality of the service.

These reviews have a significant impact on consumer buying behaviour and brand association. A 2007 report fielded by ComScore revealed that a five-star rating on TripAdvisor would entice consumers to increase their lodging spending by 20 percent; 87 percent of users were significantly influenced on their choice of hotel by the reviews they had read. Incidentally, the 2008 Trip Advisor Travelers' Choice Awards recognized Four Seasons as the Best Brand for the second straight year.

Since travel tends to be a high-investment purchase, consumers are more likely to do a fair bit of research before confirming a purchase. For those in the hospitality industry, this means that every consumer interaction counts. Every booking, every check-in and every meal counts, every single time. Even loyal consumers can alter their perceptions of the brand after one terrible experience. This presents a tremendous challenge for hospitality brands, since they must provide a continuous level of excellent service while navigating the corporate challenges of high staff turnover rates, managing costs and operating in a tumultuous industry.

Success in such an industry often requires a highly committed leader who can manage the fine balance between investing in employee development and focusing on the bottom line (while simultaneously building a recognizable brand). If too much focus is on financial performance, service levels may be negatively affected, or morale may suffer. However, if too much emphasis is placed on catering to employees or adding staff, companies may become unprofitable or risk losing their competitive vitality, which will also affect the brand. In a Harvard Business Review article, "An Uncompromising Leader," authors Russell Eisenstat and Michael Beer outlined the practices needed to become a successful leader in high-performance organizations:

- *Earn Trust:* Establishing a policy of openness and transparency in communicating information throughout the organization will create a sense of unity and a feeling of ownership among employees.

- *Engage Directly with Employees:* Demonstrate a genuine concern for the well-being of all employees. This will increase loyalty as well as job satisfaction.

- *Maintain Focus and Consistency of Purpose:* Be particular about the number of change initiatives implemented. Choose a manageable amount to focus on, and then pursue with a relentless tenacity.

- *Build a Collective Leadership Power:* Leaders must find the right balance between their personal involvement and creating the right environment where others are empowered to uphold the company's vision themselves.

- *Foster a Shared Purpose:* Create a culture that revolves around an idea or philosophy that resonates emotionally with employees. In the case of Four Seasons, it's delivering service levels employees can be proud of.

Any traveller who has ever depended on the small bottles of shampoo readily available at most hotels owes Isadore "Issy" Sharp a word of thanks. Sharp was the first hotel owner to offer these amenities in every room in his hotels, an unprecedented move in the industry. The new policy was one tiny step in Sharp's journey to transform Four Seasons into a high-end luxury accommodation.

It was an uphill battle from the outset. Sharp would spend five years unsuccessfully attempting to raise the needed capital to build his first property. "If someone had told me 'Look, you're going to start today and spend the next five years wasting your time trying to get this thing started,' I would have said I can't do that," recalls Sharp. "But you never think about what it's going to take of you."

After recognizing that outside investors would be unwilling to risk financing a project spearheaded by an inexperienced and unknown young man, Sharp considered alternative options. He turned to his family and friends, who agreed to help him. Finally, after years of trying, Sharp was on his way to building his first hotel.

In 1961, the Four Seasons Motor Hotel opened its doors on Jarvis Street in Toronto, on the outskirts of downtown. Focusing on business travellers, the Hotel soon had a reputation for friendly and efficient service at a reasonable price. Sharp's attention to detail ensured that guests enjoyed a pleasant stay at the modest accommodations. To his delight, the venture was profitable, and, sensing the opportunity for expansion, Sharp soon began entertaining the idea of building another property.

"I started just from building one hotel. It worked, so let's build another, and it worked, so three went to four," explains Sharp. He credits these "stepping stones," with allowing him to expand at a steady pace while ensuring he learned from previous experiences.

At the time, the Toronto native wasn't dreaming of global expansion or envisioning a future hospitality empire. His only concern was the satisfaction of his guests and anticipating their needs to ensure an enjoyable experience. His intense and constant focus on the consumer experience has elevated the Four Season brands into a benchmark of luxury around the world. Sharp dreamed of a brand that would create "a reputation for service so clear in people's mind that the Four Seasons name will become an asset of far greater value than bricks and mortar."

Be Obsessively Single-Minded

Sharp's stepping-stone approach allowed him to break his goals down into tasks he could pursue with a singular fervour. He did not aspire to be the largest hotel operator, but aimed instead to deliver the very best service he could. From the modest Four Seasons Motor Hotel to the luxurious George V Hotel in Paris, Sharp strove to ensure each property operated at its fullest potential. He consistently focused on service and was always seeking new ways to deliver a superior experience for his guests.

By breaking down his dream into smaller, more actionable items, he was able to retain his momentum without feeling overwhelmed by the sheer scope of what he one day hoped to accomplish. It also helped him build a solid foundation.

This focus has translated into incredible success for Four Seasons. The company's pricing strategy is to be the premium hotel price for the area by setting their room prices to be 20 percent higher than their closest rival. This strategy succeeds by delivering on a promise: guests are guaranteed a worry-free and exceptional stay. By repeatedly emphasizing exceptional service, Sharp has built a loyal clientele of travellers who are willing to pay a premium price in exchange for the Four Seasons experience. "A company is eager to pay the extra $50 to ensure a hassle-free trip for an executive who might be working on a $50 million deal," explains Sharp. He has made certain that the standards of service are consistent across all properties, so guests can choose Four Seasons properties with confidence whether they are staying in France or Egypt.

So, what kind of personality does it take to lead such an organization? Niel Nicholson, a researcher at the London Business School who studied commonalities between personality and entrepreneurial leadership, concluded that contrary to popular belief entrepreneurs are not "open-minded risk takers so much as single-minded, thick-skinned, dominating individuals." From rebounding after recurring rejection to focusing all his attention on one task at a time, Sharp clearly embodies this profile.

He consciously limited the number of competitive advantages to pursue, allowing his organization to excel beyond his competitors on one particular value axis rather than to be comparable on several. By prioritizing outstanding service, he has carved out a niche for Four Seasons that is unmatched by competitors.

BE OBSESSIVELY SINGLE-MINDED

Be selective in the number of initiatives you pursue, but once you focus on something in particular, be it a consumer segment, a product or a brand value, pursue that goal with a relentless single-mindedness until it is achieved. By breaking down larger goals into smaller more manageable action items, tasks become more actionable and easier to concentrate on.

Understand What You Want to Be and Then Be the Best at It

During his successes with his first hotels, Sharp honed his approach to the company's core capability: providing unmatched service for consumers. "The essential question for us in the early days was: 'What did guests value most?'" says Sharp. "Market research said luxury, not necessarily elegant surroundings and gourmet meals. The greatest luxury is time, and service can help you make the most that. Give greater productivity, greater enjoyment; what better luxury can there be?"

His commitment to understanding consumer needs and introducing services designed to fulfill them would help the Four Seasons brand become synonymous with quality service (and prove to be vastly profitable). He looked past what many might have thought would be the competitive advantage — a fancy lobby — and focused instead on what really mattered to the customer base: seamless service and exceptional comfort. These core principles were then wrapped in a luxurious exterior which ensured the package was complete.

Sharp instinctively worked on building the brand's reputation instead of being swayed by short-term profitability figures. "Profits direct our focus toward short-term market gains," he explains. "As long as we can keep on creating customer value, profit is unlikely to be a concern."

This was counterintuitive to an industry that was responding to the increased cost of travel and a decline in tourism by offering price discounts. While this provided the needed short-term revenue, ultimately it eroded the consumer's perception of the brand's value. Authors Leonard M. Lodish and Carl F. Mela explored some of these issues and argued that such promotions can "hurt a brand's long term health." Consumers will be more likely to forgo purchasing goods and services until another promotion comes along, which ultimately translates into sinking profits for organizations that find themselves continually resorting to this tactic. Sharp established an unspoken agreement with guests that they would receive unparalleled service in exchange for a consistent price.

His focus on delivering superior service would yield another surprising discovery: Sharp realized that the ownership issues surrounding hotels were only detracting him from providing the level of service he envisioned. He introduced a radical new model where Four Seasons would give up ownership of the property, and instead manage it in exchange for a fee. The fee was comprised of a base amount derived from a percentage of each hotel's gross revenues, an incentive fee based on the operational management of Four Seasons' properties and a charge for sales, marketing and reservation services. By eliminating these time-consuming tasks, Sharp was able to concentrate on the methods through which Four Seasons would continue to deliver on its brand promise of luxury as a service.

His instincts in identifying service as a competitive advantage instead of owning real estate would prove to be correct: in the past years ownership operations have declined, while management earnings have been on the rise. Four Seasons makes the majority of its profits from the management fees.

Sharp's decision also insulated the brand from the cyclical nature of the hotel business by passing the costs of renovations and maintenance to owners. This allowed Four Seasons to focus on building the brand, rather than being jostled by macroeconomic factors such as economic downturns, rising oil costs and travel disruptions, which can have a severe impact on profits.

UNDERSTAND WHAT YOU WANT TO BE, AND THEN BE THE BEST AT IT

It is better to be excellent at one thing than just average at many. Determine what will distinguish your company, and then focus on delivering on that better than anyone else. Build everything, from branding to hiring policies to corporate culture, to support that objective.

Dare to Redefine

Providing customers with a luxurious hotel experience was not a new or revolutionary idea. When he entered the hospitality industry there were plenty of competitors who were offering guests opulent accommodations. "How important are those to our customers?" Sharp wondered. "They are mostly executives, often under pressure, fighting jet lag, stress and the clock." They wanted to conduct their business deals in the most efficient way possible, and return home to their families.

Sharp recognized the need for a hotel that could replicate the comfort of being at home combined with the functionality of the office.

"We set out to redefine luxury as a service, and to provide a support system at our hotels to replace the one left behind at home or at the office," says Sharp. The decision to upgrade Four Seasons' properties to Five Star standards soon followed. From the installation of the quietest plumbing to the use of the softest linens and towels, no detail was forgotten. From two-line phone jacks and well-lit desks to irons, bathrobes, hair dryers and free shoe-shining services, Sharp transformed his hotel into a business traveller's haven. Four Seasons continued to lead the industry by being the first hotel to provide 24-hour secretarial services. Once again, his attention to detail and single-minded focus ensured that a traveller's every possible need was anticipated.

Tom Kelley, the CEO of IDEO and global expert on innovation strategies, describes the same methods that Sharp instinctively applied in his book *The Ten Faces of Innovation*. Sharp played the role Kelly calls "the anthropologist."

"The Anthropologist is rarely stationary. Rather, this is the person who ventures into the field to observe how people interact with products, services, and experiences in order to come up with new innovations. The Anthropologist is extremely good at reframing a problem in a new way, humanizing the scientific method to apply it to daily life. Anthropologists share such distinguishing characteristics as the wisdom to observe with a truly open mind; empathy; intuition; the ability to 'see' things that have gone unnoticed; a tendency to keep running lists of innovative concepts worth emulating and problems that need solving; and a way of seeking inspiration in unusual places."

By identifying this latent customer need and being the first company in the marketplace to adequately address it, he was able to capture a large part of the market. As pioneers, Four Seasons could stand out and enjoy the generated media buzz while consumers associated the brand with luxury and high standards of service. While competitors were quick to imitate these services, Four Seasons had already earned the reputation of high quality luxury service.

DARE TO REDEFINE

Take a step back and challenge industry assumptions with an un-biased eye. Talk to your customers and find out what is really important to them, not what you think is important to them. Your findings might surprise you, or reveal an unmet consumer need that your competitors have overlooked. Dare to examine things in unique and different ways to uncover opportunities you otherwise would have missed.

Be Flexible

While remaining consistent to his branding, Sharp did not adhere to a one-size-fits-all approach when building his hotels. Instead of establishing rigid internal standards across all properties, he insisted that hotels in different cities have varying styles, feels and atmospheres; the definition of quality would have to be tied to a local context. It took effort to properly research the various markets and to agree on the right atmosphere for each hotel. The additional managerial preparation paid off; the strategy ensured that Four Seasons pricing would be aligned with local market and consumer expectations. Furthermore, it allowed the brand the flexibility to adapt to the different mindset of those in varying geographical and cultural locales without losing the emphasis on luxury service. Once again, Sharp's instincts were dead on: Zagat rated the Four Seasons George V Hotel in Paris as the best hotel in the world due to its complete embodiment of Parisian luxury standards. In 2008, the readers of Condé Nast Traveler named Four Seasons Tented Camp Golden Triangle—the company's first all-inclusive jungle experience—the number one travel experience in the world. It's the fourth time the company has garnered the "best of the best" distinction.

Consumers associated Four Seasons with luxury, however it happened to be packaged.

Yvez Doz and Mikko Kosonen, authors of Strategic Agility, describe strategic agility as "the ability to continuously adjust and adapt strategic direction in core business, as a function of strategic ambitions and changing circumstances, and create not just new product and services, but also new business models and innovative ways to create value for a company." Sharp's methodology of adapting each hotel to its local geography, while maintaining a consistently high standard throughout the chain, was strategically agile to say the least.

BE FLEXIBLE

While it is important to stay focused and true to your values, remember that things change, and context may require flexibility. It is easy to treat corporate strategy as though it is set in stone and organizations that do so may find themselves in a vulnerable position. By retaining strategic agility, entrepreneurs are able to quickly adapt to changing or different market conditions and take advantage of emerging opportunities quickly and efficiently.

Walk the Talk

The hospitality industry is notorious for high staff turnover. In a market where employees are the most important brand ambassadors, how did Sharp attain the level of service and dedication required by hotel staff to deliver the promise of unparalleled "luxury as a service?" He recognized the causality between the way a hotel treated its own staff and the way those staff treated guests. He established one core managerial credo that was applied to the entire organization. The "Golden Rule" encouraged all employees to deal with guests, partners and co-workers in the same manner that they wished to be treated.

"That set in place the culture of the company, which gave us service, which allowed us to become the best," says Sharp. His vision was a cornerstone of Four Seasons' philosophy and encompassed everyone who interacted with the brand. This resulted in a philosophy of extraordinary service that was diligently applied to each aspect of hotel operations.

"Senior managers who couldn't or wouldn't walk the talk were all whittled out within a few years. It was a painful process and personally distressing — perhaps the hardest thing I ever did. But the fastest way for management to destroy its credibility is to say employees come first and then to be seen putting them last," he says. "Better not to profess any values than not to live up to them."

In an industry where one bad experience can tarnish a hotel's reputation in the eyes of a guest, Sharp knew his only defence lay with happy and motivated employees. Sharp initiated several programs to improve morale, including a profit-sharing plan and complimentary room nights for all staff as well as giving employees two "stress breaks" every day. These 15-minute breaks allowed staff, the opportunity to take a breather after dealing with challenging situations in order to regroup and return to their duties calm and refreshed.

In addition, Four Seasons' front desk staff averaged a salary that was twice the industry rate. This allowed employees to focus on delivering the luxurious service Four Seasons is known for. "A company's ability to provide that type of experience depends on its employees," Sharp says. These actions reinforce the value the organization places on all members of its staff, and Sharp believes it produces excellent results. "By nurturing the full potential of every willing worker from top to bottom, I believe that businesses can tap a unique source of leadership and success for the twenty-first century." Four Seasons has been the only Canadian participant in *Fortune* magazine's "Top 100 Best Companies to Work For" every year since the list's inception. When Sharp opened Four Seasons Hotel New York in 1993, the organization received more than 30,000 applications for the 400 available positions.

As for Sharp, he looks to himself to set an example. "Leaders have to set a pattern of behaviour for others to follow," he says. That can be challenging when times are rough. However, when faced with adverse conditions, Sharp has repeatedly proven his commitment to his employees. He upheld the company's dedication to staff during several turbulent market crises. In the market downturn that followed September 11, 2001, many hotels were laying off staff in an attempt to reduce costs; Sharp refused. He was willing to incur some losses if it meant ensuring the livelihood of people that were depending on him.

When the tsunami crisis ravaged Southeast Asia, the company was forced to evacuate and close its Maldives Resorts. Suddenly, hundreds of hotel staff were without jobs, at a critical time when they needed income to rebuild the damage to their communities. Sharp sent all Maldives staff to other Four Season hotels around the world in order for them to keep their jobs. "In true Four Seasons fashion," he says, "they have become a dynamic part of the teams at these hotels, embracing our guests with their caring service."

These actions have built a strong relationship between employees and employer. The respect is reciprocated and demonstrated. There is the legendary tale of a bellboy who purchased a plane ticket with his own money to fly to another city and deliver a forgotten briefcase that was urgently needed at a meeting. It is these stories of dedication to the brand value that have allowed Four Seasons to excel at delivering an excellent experience for guests.

By infusing the principles of the Four Season brands into every aspect of his operations, Sharp and his organization ensure that each employee believes and supports their overall vision, resulting in a unified effort to execute and uphold the company's reputation.

WALK THE TALK

Organizations must embody the characteristics they want their brands to be. Slick marketing and public relation campaigns are not sufficient in convincing employees and consumers. Authenticity is key, and organizations have to be ready to stand up for their values, especially in challenging times.

Conclusion

Today, the Polish boy who started as the son of a contractor is a globally respected businessman with a net worth of $460 million. He remains surprised at his accomplishments, considering he started out with the dream to open "just one hotel."

He humbly credits the efforts of those who helped him along his way. "Long-term success is never achieved on our own," he says. "The phrase 'a self-made man' is a myth—all along the way we need support." The respect he incites in his employees is a testament to his authenticity in embodying the values of the Four Seasons brand.

"Usually, when you understand something and feel good, it gives you the will to persevere, overcome the scepticism and see through the negative side people present," he says. "Whatever you do, don't ever use a crutch, and don't ever think of having an excuse for not having said, 'Yeah, I did my best.'" Sharp is a believer of living a life with no regrets. Pursue your dreams wholeheartedly, act in a respectful and authentic way, and victory will be your reward.

5 THINGS YOU NEED TO KNOW

1. Be Obsessively Single-Minded

Be selective in the number of initiatives you pursue, but once you focus on something in particular, be it a consumer segment, a product or a brand value, pursue that goal with a relentless single-mindedness until it is achieved. By breaking down larger goals into smaller more manageable action items, tasks become more actionable and easier to concentrate on.

2. Understand What you Want to Be, and Then be the Best at It

It is better to be excellent at one thing than just average at many. Determine what will distinguish your company, and then focus on delivering on that better than anyone else. Build everything, from branding to hiring policies to corporate culture, to support that objective.

3. Dare to Redefine

Take a step back and challenge industry assumptions with an unbiased eye. Talk to your customers and find out what is really important to them, not what you *think* is important to them. Your findings might surprise you, or reveal an unmet consumer need that your competitors have overlooked. Dare to examine things in unique and different ways to uncover opportunities you otherwise would have missed.

4. Be Flexible

While it is important to stay focused and true to your values, remember that things change, and context may require flexibility. It is easy to treat corporate strategy as though it is set in stone and organizations that do so may find themselves in a vulnerable position. By retaining strategic agility, entrepreneurs are able to quickly adapt to changing or different market conditions and take advantage of emerging opportunities quickly and efficiently.

5. Walk the Talk

Organizations must embody the characteristics they want their brands to be. Slick marketing and public relation campaigns are not sufficient for convincing employees and consumers. Authenticity is key, and organizations have to be ready to stand up for their values, especially in challenging times.

CHAPTER TEN

What's Next:
The Uncontrollable Brand

FEATURING THE WISDOM OF STEWART BUTTERFIELD, FOUNDER, FLICKR

Photographs used to live in shoeboxes, haphazardly jammed in the back of the closet or under the bed. Finding one particular print was difficult and took forever. With the advent of digital photography, users turned to their computers for storage, but they were left with the same problem: how could they organize and share photos without having to search through hundreds of files?

That's the question Victoria, B.C. based husband-and-wife team Stewart Butterfield and Caterina Fake addressed when they came up with Flickr, a photo-sharing website that has become a staple application for all on-line fanatics. "Part of the idea was encouraging users to add tags, titles and descriptions to their photos, to make it as easy as possible for them to organize and share them with others," Butterfield says.

The application was originally created as a peripheral feature to an online game they were developing through their company, Ludicorp, but it soon evolved into a stand-alone project. When they launched Flickr in 2004, the site quickly became one of the richest repositories of digital images on the web.

In 2005, Yahoo acquired Flickr for $35 million. Embraced by photography professionals and amateurs alike, today the site has over 20 million users and is home to more than two billion images. Just the way Google now "owns" online searches, Flickr has become synonymous with digital photographs on the web.

I AM FLICKR

Traditionally, brands were restricted to corporations and their products; the concept of a personal brand was limited mostly to job seekers. But with the advent of the Internet, brands became a new way for individuals to define their own identities. More than just a company's call sign, a brand is a reflection of the needs and feelings of a particular demographic that the company is pursuing, or building community with. According to Butterfield, this new aspect of the brand is a natural reaction to an increasingly globalized world. "In North America, most people are immigrants or the descendants of immigrants," he says. "There isn't a fierce type of culture that they inherit, so people get to choose who they are by what they buy and the brands they associate with." Their identity, and especially their online identity, is a construct of the brands they associate with and the one they build online.

Successful companies will use their brands to forge emotional bonds around ideals and philosophies that are highly meaningful to their consumers. "You have to choose a particular group of people who have a well defined set of needs; in our case it was photographers, bloggers and Internet enthusiasts," explains Butterfield. "And then you have to make something that appeals exactly to them." By filling a group's particular needs, you become, in effect, an extension of who they are. And by bonding with that particular group, you build your own brand and the business that it serves.

WE, THE PEOPLE

Flickr exists in a market where there are several competitors offering similar services. And yet, Flickr's membership keeps growing, along with the number of pictures being hosted. Why? The secret to this growth is creating a brand where people are encouraged to invest something of utmost value—in this case, pieces of themselves. Moreover, the pieces they offer are their photos. It's a very intimate sharing experience, which makes it personal and meaningful to the online users.

Butterfield understood the significance of allowing users the utmost flexibility in grouping pictures, labelling them and sharing images within their network. "It wasn't that people just used Flickr; a lot of people came to love it, and talked about it to all of their friends. Some people even composed songs about it," he says, laughing. "At that point, it wasn't about Flickr anymore; it became about the people."

Butterfield recognized the intrinsic importance of the data created in Flickr over time, including statistics about how many times the photos had been viewed, comments from friends and tags they had created. "We wanted to capture as much social context around photographs as we could," says Butterfield.

HELP THEM, HELP YOU

Technology has revolutionized the ways groups form, as well as the power of the group to exert influence. Butterfield credits the Flickr community for growing the brand both online and off. "A lot of spontaneous stuff happened that we weren't driving," he says. "For example, people started having Flickr meet-ups, where they would physically gather. When we heard about this we were quick to encourage it."

Today Flickr meet-ups are happening all over the world, and the site has become a popular way to connect with others who share a love of photography. Butterfield used these meet-ups as a way to reward brand users who liked the service and were evangelizing it. "If you're organizing a gathering let us know," he told brand enthusiasts. "We'll send you a gift bag with stickers and buttons and other Flickr-branded stuff."

Flickr also rewarded users who recruited others into the community. "We told users that if they invited three friends who signed up, they would get six months of Flickr's premium account service for free. That drove a lot of traffic."

The campaign was a bigger success than anyone had anticipated. "We originally did it because hooking up Flickr's payment system was a low priority for us at that point," Butterfield explains. "But then people who wanted to pay for a Pro account couldn't do that yet, so instead they set out and convinced their friends to join."

This also leveraged what Butterfield calls the network effect. "The more people you know who use Flickr, the more valuable it is for you, and the less likely you are to go randomly switching to another site that offers similar services."

SPIRITUALITY 2.0

Flickr continues to grow and has added video uploading and sharing capabilities, as well the ability to tag pictures with a geographic location. As for Butterfield, when asked about his future he is a little less sure. "Maybe I'll go to India and live in an Ashram for a while," he jokes. "Then I'll come back and start another Internet company."

PART THREE

Third Period

The Elusiveness of Change and Time

CHAPTER ELEVEN

Magnificent Obsession

How the Relentless Persuit of Vision Can Change the World

FEATURING THE WISDOM OF GEOFFREY BALLARD

In 1983, geophysicist Geoffrey Ballard, a former oil patch scientist and conservation advisor to the U.S. government, moved a small company with a radical vision to the unlikely spot of Vancouver, B.C. Ballard aimed to replace the automobile's internal combustion engine—and its resulting pollution—with something that would revolutionize the world's transportation industry.

That something eventually became the fuel cell, an electrochemical device that combines hydrogen with oxygen to create electricity. Today, early versions of Ballard Power's fuel cell are now powering buses in major North American cities, as well as some test cars. Further versions will (probably over the next two decades) be standard operating equipment in the world's automobiles.

Large oil producers and automobile manufacturers dismissed Ballard's original vision; they, of course, had billions of dollars invested in the very systems Ballard wanted to replace. The concept did not play particularly well with a car-owning population that was accustomed to a wide selection of fuel-inefficient, but high-performance, automobiles. Anything less was unimaginable. The idea did not register with his colleagues in the energy industry either, who believed in improvement by slow incremental innovation, rather than disruptive or transformative technologies. In fact, just about everybody scoffed at Geoff Ballard and his little company that was not looking for a base hit, but openly swinging for the fences. Most dismissed his quest as sweeping fantasy, a faulty fixation that was consuming his life.

But Ballard's stubborn pursuit of his dream eventually convinced the world that the dominance of the gasoline-powered, pollution-producing automobile was ending. His vision made him a multimillionaire and a fêted figure in the scientific community and earned him the label "Hero of Our Planet" from Time magazine. He put in motion a movement that will no doubt change our world.

—⁓—

Update: *It is with regret that we report the sudden passing of Geoffrey Ballard on August 2, 2008 in Vancouver, Canada. He was 76 years old. The cause of his death is unknown at the time of this writing. He will always be remembered for championing the development of non-polluting energy sources. A true hero of the planet, his vision and foresight will be greatly missed. Plug Power Inc. purchased General Hydrogen in 2007 for US $10 million.*

Innovation is a term that everyone innately understands. There are entire armies of researchers and theorists that spend their lives attempting to wrap a ribbon around the term *innovation* and give it some semblance of a common, articulated understanding. Regardless of which interpretation you look at, all paths essentially lead to the same basic premise—innovation is simply the process of designing better ways of doing things.

From the perspective of a scientific process, innovation is the development of new knowledge to serve a market demand in a way that was not previously being done. Often this process is described as a sequence of stages known as RDD&D—Research, Development, Demonstration and Deployment. This traditional model features development that evolves basic research to perfect a new technology, tests it on a small scale, and then demonstrates its usefulness with full-scale experimentation. If this demonstration is successful, the technology is adopted more widely.

This model, *incrementalism*, is the most common methodology around innovation used today. It involves building on a foundation; an improvement process that makes an existing technology or system work better. Another model, at the core of many industries (the technology sector in particular) is *disruptive innovation*. This market-oriented theory suggests there is an ongoing battle between established companies using incremental innovation to bring better solutions to leading customers, and smaller, newer companies offering competitive but different solutions. While the latter may offer something entirely new, it is still usually just a variation on a theme—a better way to do something already done before. A different train on the same set of tracks. An example of this is the challenge that Skype has recently posed to the legacy telecom companies. Skype uses the revolution of the Internet to change the very delivery of phone service from cable and fibre optics to broadband, thereby allowing much lower cost to end users and higher quality features.

There is a third innovation process that is little known, and practiced even less, outside extreme science. It is not just a new way to do something, but a revolution that alters the way we live. This procedure of research and discovery leads to groundbreaking transformation of entrenched systems. These transformative, or revolutionary, innovations often lead to the wholesale overthrow of traditional systems. Take the Internet; it has fundamentally changed the way we communicate and interact. Many of the great developments in physics, such as Einstein's Theory of Relativity, provide other examples. Fundamentally they changed the way we live and the means by which we moved forward to new discoveries. They sent us down a multitude of new paths from which there is no turning back.

A recent example of revolutionary innovation took place in Vancouver, B.C., in the 1980s and '90s. After a failed attempt in the U.S. to create a better battery, Dr. Geoffrey Ballard moved Ballard Research, which later became Ballard Power Systems, to the region, then known more for its harvesting of natural resources than its dedication to innovation. In Vancouver, Ballard and his team worked quietly, and at first relatively anonymously, to develop an electrochemical device that combined hydrogen with oxygen to make electricity. This so-called "fuel cell" would replace the gasoline-burning internal combustion engine that is currently the backbone of the world's transportation systems—and much of its consequent pollution problem.

Ballard and partners Paul Howard and Keith Prater aspired to stop the auto-caused pollution they believed was ruining the environment. In 1993, in a spectacular demonstration of his new pollution-free power system, Ballard put some of those fuel cells in a bus—dubbed the "magic bus"—and drove it around in front of startled government officials who had grudgingly supplied some funding for his work. He then sipped from a fluted glass the only emissions the fuel-cell engine released out of its tailpipe—water.

The Ontario-raised, U.S.-educated geophysicist stunned the world with this and subsequent demonstrations. He sparked a rush to apply what had once been an outlandish idea to everyday use in the atmosphere-defiling automobile. Car manufacturers, increasingly under the gun from regulators to stop this contamination, poured more than $1 billion into Ballard Power Systems, hoping its fuel cell would alleviate their problem. To date, it hasn't, mainly because of its high cost. However, work continues on how to deliver it more cheaply and most believe they will find a way in the not-too-distant future. Meanwhile, Ballard, who retired a multimillionaire in 1997, started a new company called General Hydrogen. Its goal is to create an infrastructure to supply drivers with the hydrogen they need to power the fuel cells.

After a lifetime pursuing what many thought was impossible, Dr. Geoffrey Ballard has been recognized for his vision and perseverance. In 1999, *Time* magazine named him a "Hero of Our Planet," and *Scientific American* magazine voted him a business leader of the year in 2002. Chiefs of the energy industry, who once saw him as a threat, or a harmless idealist not to be taken seriously, now ask him to discuss the future of their industry. Several universities have awarded him honorary degrees, and scientific colleagues who once shunned him at professional gatherings now invite him to lecture at their institutions.

Ballard, once considered an oddball fixated on a bizarre idea, has become a doyen of grand visions, of glorious thinking, of magnificent obsession. Like the fictional Don Quixote, the Man of La Mancha, to whom he has occasionally (and usually pejoratively) been compared, he dreams impossible dreams. More significantly, Ballard, who candidly admits that he has "never followed the herd," has had the courage to chase those dreams. "Be impatient," this now 72-year-old archetype of visioning once told a group of university students. "Challenge the normal. Dare to be in a hurry to change things for the better."

Geoffrey Ballard reached this pinnacle of achievement because he was able to form a big vision and convince a select few acolytes of its value. He then obsessively pursued that vision in the face of financial limitations, isolation by colleagues, opposition by huge, entrenched industries, and disapproval by a society that just didn't get it. This behaviour did not surprise those who know Ballard. He is the kind of innovator who has always thought in grand, sweeping—and often defiant—terms.

Ballard first developed the vision that was to take over his life in 1974 when he was an advisor to the U.S. government on energy conservation. This was the time of the Arab oil embargo, when gasoline supplies were restricted, lineups were a daily feature at every gas station, and prices soared. The government convened a panel, which included Ballard, to study how oil could be conserved. Looking for sustainable solutions, most on the panel concluded that the American automobile as it was configured was at fault because of its inefficient use of fuel. They recommended that more efficient methods be developed to burn gasoline and convert it to energy. In essence, they were looking for an incremental innovation: create a more efficient power plant. They also advocated, and many still do, getting people out of their cars and on to more efficient mass transit.

Ballard knew that more radical innovations would be needed to solve the automobile-pollution problem, that conservation alone would not be enough to prevent the world from choking on its own exhaust. Not only would this new system have to provide the freedom the automobile now provides, it would have to do it cleanly.

The statistics were daunting. In 1997, the world consumed about 9,521 million tonnes of oil equivalent (Mtoe) of primary energy supply. Many authorities believe that by 2020 consumption will grow a further 60 percent. Growing car ownership will exacerbate this. There are currently 850 million automobiles on the planet, and manufacturers are cranking out millions more every year. Less than 20 percent of the world—primarily in the developed world of North America and Europe—currently has access to a private automobile. As modern communications bring the western world's image of private car ownership—a symbol of personal freedom and success—to the developing world, demand is guaranteed to grow, as will the resulting contamination that goes with it. Think of China, the world's most populous country, where the love affair with the car has only just begun, and emission standards barely exist.

This increasing use of cars and mass transit vehicles is creating another looming problem. Their use of the internal combustion engine to supply power means the requirement for fuel is also guaranteed to grow. However, the current method of creating that fuel—

gasoline produced from oil—is running up against capacity problems. Oil companies have improved their techniques for finding new supply, and auto manufacturers have made their engines more efficient users of fuel—their latest method is the development of the "hybrid," a vehicle that uses an internal combustion engine to generate electricity to power a car—but this will not be enough to keep up with increasing demand. The freedom that the personal vehicle provides is extremely addictive.

"You have to understand the mission profile of the automobile buyer," Ballard explains. "If you have two people walking into an automobile showroom, one might be a young 18-year-old guy who wants a car to drive down Main Street and get girls. He's going to drive around the block and fill the gas tank whenever he has to so he can roar up Main Street. But someone like myself might want to drive to Alberta to see my grandchildren, so I'll choose something with a large fuel tank and a very efficient power plant. There's a different mission profile, or requirement, for each of us. The automobile with the internal combustion engine currently serves both those profiles. It's a difficult combination to beat."

BE CLEAR ON THE PROBLEM; LET YOUR DATA GUIDE YOU TO THE SOLUTION

If you're going to innovate, you have to be clear on your objective, which should be something fundamentally more than a fishing expedition in the name of discovery. Ballard understood the potential of the fuel cell and made sure he drove his innovation in that direction. But it wasn't obvious to anyone, him included, at first. His success was the result of years of trial and error, with incredible attention spent on his data and what it told him about his mistaken assumptions.

Movement is an atavistic urge: anyone who attempts to hinder freedom of movement is doomed to failure. Humans have been trying to perfect better methods of moving from place to place since they first climbed down out of trees and started hunting on the plains of Africa. From foot to horse to steam-powered trains, jet-fuelled planes, and gas-fed cars, they have always hunted for transportation methods that would move them faster, and to more destinations. With his understanding of the psychological benefits of the automobile, Geoffrey Ballard realized the ultimate problem he was facing, which was simply that as long as the car, as it was configured, represented freedom of movement to a human being it would be impossible to eradicate it as a favoured means of transportation. That understanding of the problem created a solution—don't eliminate the car; eliminate the engine. Find a cleaner source of power.

Ballard moved to Arizona and started to investigate the battery, that storehouse of electricity that can be recharged in order to continue to provide power. He found a private backer who shared his dream and started a business that aimed at developing a lithium-based superbattery that would replace the internal combustion engine. But his investigation almost killed the dream: the battery simply couldn't do the job. After seven years, with his company in bankruptcy and now in Vancouver, he realized he was on the wrong trail. The battery might work to power single-purpose vehicles like golf carts or delivery vehicles, but it wouldn't work for the automobile because it could not escalate fuel and power supplies like the fuel tank/combustion engine combination.

Once he clearly understood the needs of the car owner, Ballard knew where he had to go next—find a power/energy system that matched those needs to those of society at large. He eventually chose the fuel cell, which works by forcing oxygen and hydrogen together, creating an electrochemical reaction that produces water, and capturing the resulting energy. This fuel cell eliminated the harmful pollutants created by burning gasoline; it maintained the ability to escalate fuel and power systems; and it helped tailor the adaptation of various power/energy permutations to individual need. This point was vital, given that it is just this freedom-granting appeal that makes the gas-burning automobile so attractive. Hydrogen/oxygen fuel cells had been around for 150 years—they were used in the Gemini space program—but were considered too cumbersome and expensive for practical use. Ballard's mission was to make the fuel cell lighter, smaller, cheaper and powerful enough for ordinary vehicles.

DON'T SHOOT FOR THE MIDDLE

Dare to think big. Disrupt. Revolutionize. Don't be afraid to form a sweeping dream that inspires, not only others, but yourself as well. Incremental innovation will not lead to real change—it only improves something slightly. Look for breakthrough innovations, changes that will make a difference.

The Ballard fuel cell's ability to provide different ratios of power and energy without reliance on the internal combustion engine is a true revolutionary innovation. It will create a radically different system that will achieve results similar to those of the legacy oil-based system still in use. But could this innovation indeed be called a success? There are still no fuel cell-powered cars cruising along Main Street.

Revolutionary innovation can take a long time to play out—the personal computer was invented in the 1970s but took 20 years to revolutionize modern life. True evidence of the fuel cell's transformative power will likely not be obvious for several decades, when fuel cell–powered automobiles become common in garages and there is a hydrogen refuelling station on every corner. Before that happens, however, this revolution in the making will have to overcome one other enormous obstacle: it challenges the very existence of some of the largest corporations and oligopolies in the world.

When Ballard started talking about replacing the internal combustion engine, most people just laughed or thought of him as a "mad scientist." It was inconceivable that anything might replace the modern engine. Because the revolution is still underway, many still think that way.

Says Ballard: "People thought that oil would be there forever, and they'll find a way around its problems: they'd say to me, 'You're crazy, crazy.' They thought, 'We'll just make cars more efficient, we'll develop techniques of using less oil, of using it more efficiently.' Very few people still believe that today.

"Those who did have an inkling of a combustion-free future said it's going to be solved by someone like General Motors, not an unknown like you who thinks he knows something. Major world problems are not solved by small people in Podunk."

In fact, an executive of GM once delivered this very statement at a meeting of Canada's provincial energy ministers. As Ballard recalls it, after he had outlined his vision to the ministers, the vice-president of General Motors Canada followed him to the podium, chuckled about the preceding speech, and declared, "Let me tell you, when there is something worthwhile for you to consider that will change the way we're doing business, General Motors Canada will tell you what to do."

What Ballard has proven is that small people in Podunk can instigate revolutions. But because acceptance of scientific discovery is often social rather than scientific, such individuals might only be able to succeed if they have the skills to deal with the communal censure that comes with revolutionary innovation. They must be used to being outside the norm, familiar with isolation, and comfortable with marching out of step with the procession. Geoff Ballard fit this description to a T. He has been an independent thinker and an outsider for most of his life.

As a child during the Second World War, he lived near Niagara Falls, Ontario. When everybody was too busy to bother with him, he roamed nearby fields and rivers alone, dreaming of knights and castles, sailing the Mediterranean with Ulysses, or imagining digging for gold in the Yukon with Robert Service. A young Geoff Ballard had a lot of time on his hands to think what he wanted and to learn self-reliance. But as he grew older, this became a problem. At engineering school at Queen's University in Kingston, Ontario, he was drawing from both science and classical literature to come to radical conclusions, which he occasionally noted in a column he wrote for the campus newspaper. This was much to the consternation of some of the university's academics, who didn't like a student horning in on what they considered their territory. In a foreshadowing of what was to come later, Ballard was chastised and occasionally vilified for his uppity and inappropriate thinking.

Later, when he was working as a data analyst for oil companies in the Middle East, he questioned why they were exploring in one area, when it was clear to him that another nearby area was a better bet. He was firmly told to stick to his own job and that the people running the project knew better. He did, but not for long. Ballard left the oil company, just as he was to leave most other jobs in his life, because they restricted his thought. (Incidentally, his hypothesis on the oil patch was later proved correct.) Enveloped in routine and incremental thinking, his employers couldn't imagine the bigger picture, the one that reveals the completely different big idea. Ballard became an itinerant intellectual, a visionary without a vision, until he found the big idea that was to consume the last half of his life.

PROCESS & PAVING

Innovation requires careful management. Too much control may stifle creativity, but there must be enough to ensure that the path is consistent among team members. When you find the right people to work with you, empower them and turn them loose. It is, however, important to re-pave the path regularly to keep from becoming complacent.

"When we cease to grow we cease to create," Ballard now muses. "For a long time I paved over my own life every two years. [After that time] I had made enough mistakes that I had to start again in order to get rid of the baggage that experimenting with life had burdened me with. I once advocated that U.S. Army laboratories should be 'paved over' every 10 years to assure innovation would not succumb to incremental uselessness. Startup companies are very similar. Small new companies need to be reinvented every few years because so many of the expedient decisions involved with survival are not useful baggage to carry later on as the company tries to mature. Paving over, or reinventing, is essential to growth and survival."

THREE O'CLOCK IN THE MORNING IS A VERY DIFFICULT TIME

Leading edge thought will always incite ridicule and resistance. Listen to those who can offer valuable insights, but do not be swayed by small minds. Following traditional thinking will win you companionship, but may not achieve your goal. It can be a lonely life, but if your vision is large and clear enough, other visionaries and team mates will be drawn to you.

However, "paving over," or wiping the mental slate clean in order to innovate, has its hazards. There is a price to pay when pursuing visions and that price is usually social isolation. People are social animals and will always be with you when you walk the path that is placed before you. But carve one of your own, and it can be very lonely walking it. It takes a strong will to pursue a vision when no one else can see it.

Says Ballard: "When I look back at my life, I am amazed that I survived and find it incredible that my wife stayed with me and did not leave for an easier life with a normal person. I am also amazed that I am good friends with my sons, when I was really a very neglectful father. The sense of superiority I always had, which was quite unfounded, I think led me to assume that I could do anything I put my mind to and left me with very few doubts that I could change the world if I really wanted to change it. I always felt I knew what was right and what needed to be done, and how the future would unfold.

"But I was also plagued with insecurities that I might be wrong. Three o'clock in the morning is often a very difficult time for me."

Insecurities or not, and despite various setbacks, Ballard continued moving toward his envisioned future and proceeded to study the fuel cell's possibilities. To do that, he had to become a communicator who could convince others to share his vision. Isolation can be endured, perhaps, but it doesn't pay very well. One needs money to conduct research, so Ballard became a salesman, a hawker of his own vision who could be flexible enough to turn it to whatever was required to make a sale. But he had to target his salesmanship, because the ordinary world of financing was outside his scope: his idea was just too outlandish.

Ballard's original funding for fuel cell research came from the Canadian military, which wanted to examine proton-exchange membrane fuel cells. Ballard's failed battery company, Ballard Research—"three guys and a prayer" is how he describes it—won the contract and set up a lab in the back of a warehouse in North Vancouver, B.C., in 1983. Soon, as other researchers flocked to the interesting experiment, they were increasing the cell's power from tens of watts to more than three times what was needed to power a strong light bulb. By 1986, they could melt a thick copper cable with the electricity generated by the cells.

SELLING TO PREPARE FOR DOUBLE OVERTIME

Big visions mean very long-term goals, so finding people to work with you, financiers to stand beside you, and partners to align with you will be difficult. If you are passionate enough about your vision and not afraid to articulate it, the right business partners will find you. You have to be flexible enough to sell the vision to whoever is willing to listen, in the manner in which they want to hear it. Once sold, keep them focused not just on the long game, but the inevitability of overtime.

It was all done on a shoestring budget, because money was hard to come by. The military contract had ended, and they were now on their own. There weren't many venture capitalists or other large investors, let alone bankers, who wanted to go near the shoebox-sized fuel cell that had "weird science" written all over it. They couldn't see any near-term upside in it.

"One potential investor said Ballard Research was really a family-run company that was expressing Geoff Ballard's social responsibilities," said journalist Tom Koppel in his 1999 book *Powering the Future: The Ballard Fuel Cell and the Race to Change the World*. "And as such it did not have the proper attitude to compete effectively in the give and take of modern business."

Ballard's stock eventually climbed into the stratosphere because of interest from automobile companies. But early on, the company survived on a few small investments from individual private investors, a private Vancouver venture capital firm, and individual stockholders who just wanted to make the world a better place. "People were buying shares in the company who had never bought stock before, because they thought the research was important," Koppel wrote. "I think there is a sense of wanting to be on the side of angels."

Ballard's greatest sale came one day when he was sitting in a hot tub after a tennis game with the late British Columbia energy minister Jack Davis, an engineer himself. Ballard began expounding on his concept. Then he tossed out a visual illustration: what if he could build a fuel cell collection that would power a bus, and the only result of that power generation would be water? Davis, who saw one part of his job at the time as providing attention-grabbing headlines for his own boss, then Premier Bill Vander Zalm, bit immediately. It would be a great photo opportunity.

"We talked about it some more and put together a proposal for a couple of million dollars," Ballard recalls with some amusement. "We created a package that had slides of [Vander Zalm] receiving accolades from the United Nations, of him visiting the White House. We really sold it. And we got the money."

It also generated more money. Not right away, of course. But after he demonstrated his "magic bus" to government officials and the energy industry in general, car companies and other investors started to figure out that this fuel cell might really revolutionize the transportation industries and they began to fall over themselves to put money into the project. Although sceptics—"pistonheads" as Ballard calls them—insisted the company was decades away from making fuel-cell cars affordable, auto manufacturers like DaimlerChrysler had put $750 million into the company by 1999. Thousands of small investors joined the rush and Ballard stock skyrocketed.

Looking back on the early days, Ballard is almost astonished at the dichotomy between the small know-nothing investors and the so-called professionals. "Before the demonstrations, the venture capital people kept saying that the way to grow was to put new directors on the board," he says, slightly embittered from his wars with the money people. "And I said we're unknown, in a province that isn't known for technological developments, and we have to do something to draw attention to ourselves and point out that we have an innovative idea here that's going to change the world. The thing to do is build a bus and drive it down to the energy show. And everybody panicked. They said 'You can't do that, you can't build a bus, you're not an automotive engineer, you don't know what turns the wheels.'

"In the end, I did it anyway. I went against the venture capitalists. Most business people won't take risks, are notoriously conservative. Early investors in revolutionary technology are usually strategic in nature rather than shorter-term economic in nature. Economic investment usually plays out as 'hope into greed' and soon becomes discouraged with the cost."

With the 1993 demonstration of the magic bus, Ballard proved he was right and the Venture Capitalists were wrong. But that wasn't always the case. Ballard had been wrong before, and often. There were the seven years he wasted after he and his partners met in an Arizona motel and planned the superbattery, the quest that landed him briefly in bankruptcy. And there were several twists and turns in the development of the fuel cell that eventually energized the automotive industry—and his company's stock.

Ballard recognizes that innovation is never the linear process of incremental innovation that is often laid out in textbooks. The innovation management model usually refers to "idea generators, champions or sponsors, and orchestrators," with the emphasis apparently put on the last two in order to steer an innovation through an organization. But Ballard knows that adjustments must always be made. Any innovator, especially one who is attempting to create a revolution, must be flexible, and go where the research and the support tell him to go. The vision, or objective, remains paramount, but the road to that vision can have many curves.

Says Ballard: "If your vision is very early, you start down a path with it, like I did with the battery. Eventually you have enough data to tell you if the path is wrong. The person who doesn't make it is the person who ignores the vision. If you really have the vision that something is going to change, but you don't insist on being right, if you don't let your ego get in the way, you start down another path. You're going to be called an idiot, and they're going to say you changed your horses in mid-stream, and last year you said one thing, and now it's different. If you don't let those things bother you, and know your data clearly, you have a chance at succeeding."

One way Ballard improved his chances was to attract the best researchers he could find, inspire them, and then reward them well. Good scientists, he says, will always be willing to chase a dream: it's the bad, or worse, the comfortable ones who prefer to innovate in calculated stages.

"Most really good engineers and scientists want to do something, to apply their brains, and all you really have to do is offer them freedom," he explains. "If you do, they'll flock to you. Most research is conducted in North America and Europe by somebody who is elected director of research, and that somebody decides the directions and assigns little incremental bits to people to get the data so they can all walk down the same path. That's not very exciting for somebody who has dreams. But if you pull together half a dozen people and say, 'I would like to devise a system that will replace the internal combustion engine, and I've got some backers, and here are some suggestions I have, but let's see where you guys can take it, let's see what we can find,' they'll back you."

As an example of this spirit, Ballard points to the time when the president of General Motors, who was an investor with Ballard's new company, General Hydrogen, had a television interview coming up and wanted a hydrogen-powered forklift to show off how his company was investigating alternative energies. The vehicle had to be in Detroit within five weeks, and it had to be operational.

Says Ballard: "We said, 'Okay, this is important to us financially, so I want everyone to drop everything. We're going to design and build a forklift with an electricity pack that we can deliver to GM in Detroit, and it has to be so good that anyone can drive it. It has to do the job and you have 30 days to put it on a truck for Detroit.' They delivered it in 22 days—any other company would have taken years—because it was their company. They were part of the whole thing. When you needed something, they were there."

But while offering intellectual freedom is laudable, it has to be managed to ensure that the operation doesn't descend into anarchy. Mad science and financial reality must be balanced in the research business. Scientists and managers at Ballard met in town hall-style meetings in which management would fill them in on what was going on behind the scenes financially and where they thought the research should go. Then together they would set goals. "The staff quickly gets the knowledge that you have to be successful as a company in order for them to continue to get paid," Ballard says. "They're not guessing what you want from them because they're helping set the goals."

Ballard also managed to keep investors away from the process. "If you want your researchers to have freedom, you can't afford to have somebody else in control. You need the control because you're giving it to your employees. You solicit them to work with you. You share the wealth."

Geoff Ballard points to one more intangible in bringing about a revolutionary innovation: luck. Ballard recognizes that concerns over global warming and its connection to pollution from burning fossil fuels became a universal driver in the search for alternative means to power transportation, as did the energy crisis of the 1970s, when he first conceived of his innovation. Eventually, the U.S. drive for homeland security and independence from OPEC after September 11 will add to the urgent end of the oil-driven automobile. Hydrogen and electricity—"hydricity"—will become the dominant energy sources of the future, he says, reducing oil to a supply source for the chemical industry instead of the automotive industry.

Perhaps Ballard is right. Already, an entire power technology cluster has formed in Vancouver. Once the bastion of "hewers of wood and drawers of water," the city is now a world centre for developers of alternative energy, in no small part because of Ballard's stewardship. Certainly he is making a bet on this future with General Hydrogen, which is trying to create a simple method of furthering the hydrogen economy by making the fuel delivery mechanism available commercially. Then again, perhaps he is wrong, as many sceptical financial analysts and technology mavens currently believe.

Either way, it really doesn't matter. Ballard has shown the world that a man with a vision and the will to follow it can spark a revolution that in one form or other changes the world. Surely that is enough for one person's lifetime.

When Geoffrey Ballard went off to university some 50 years ago, his mother gave him a copy of Ralph Waldo Emerson's Essays. He reads it still, especially on long trips. His favourite quote is from the second essay, "Self Reliance":

"A foolish consistency is the hobgoblin of little minds, adored by little statesmen and philosophers and divines."

5 THINGS YOU NEED TO KNOW

Dr. Ballard has several pieces of advice for would-be visionary innovators. Though some of them are harsh, all arise out of experience gained as he inexorably pursued his obsession.

1. Be Clear on the Problem; Let Your Data Guide You to the Solution

If you're going to innovate, you have to be clear on your objective, which should be something fundamentally more than a fishing expedition in the name of discovery. Ballard understood the potential of the fuel cell and made sure he drove his innovation in that direction. But it wasn't obvious to anyone, him included, at first. His success was the result of years of trial and error, with incredible attention spent on his data and what it told him about his mistaken assumptions.

2. Don't Shoot for the Middle

Dare to think big. Disrupt. Revolutionize. Don't be afraid to form a sweeping dream that inspires, not only others, but yourself as well. Incremental innovation will not lead to real change—it only improves something slightly. Look for breakthrough innovations, changes that will make a difference.

3. Process & Paving

Innovation requires careful management. Too much control may stifle creativity, but there must be enough to ensure that the path is consistent among team members. When you find the right people to work with you, empower them and turn them loose. It is, however, important to re-pave the path regularly to keep from becoming complacent.

4. Three O'Clock in the Morning Is a Very Difficult Time

Leading edge thought will always incite ridicule and resistance. Listen to those who can offer valuable insights, but do not be swayed by small minds. Following traditional thinking will win you companionship, but may not achieve your goal. It can be a lonely life, but if your vision is large and clear enough, other visionaries and team mates will be drawn to you.

5. Selling to Prepare for Double Overtime

Big visions mean very long-term goals, so finding people to work with you, financiers to stand beside you, and partners to align with you will be difficult. If you are passionate enough about your vision and not afraid to articulate it, the right business partners will find you. You have to be flexible enough to sell the vision to whoever is willing to listen, in the manner in which they want to hear it. Once sold, keep them focused not just on the long game, but the inevitability of overtime.

CHAPTER TWELVE

While the World Was Stacking

Convergence—Success and Exploration in the Second Period

FEATURING THE WISDOM OF LEONARD ASPER

The relatively recent concept of media convergence—the intermarriage of all forms of information delivery—has opened up a vast new universe of possibilities for content producers. We are now starting to witness the intertwining of traditional information delivery devices such as print, radio and TV, combined with the multiplicative power of the web. To date, however, most media companies have merely paid lip service in their attempts to penetrate this bold new reality.

CanWest Global Communications, under the leadership of CEO Leonard Asper, is one exception. Asper is willing to take CanWest where no company has gone before in order to tap into the potential of this emerging opportunity. He is building the company into an example for media empires around the world on how it should be done.

Founded as a single television station in 1974 by Leonard's father, Israel H. (Izzy) Asper, CanWest has grown to become one of Canada's most significant broadcasters, its largest newspaper publisher, and the owner of significant media interests around the globe. As the delivery vehicles for information have exponentially increased over the past three decades, CanWest has steadily built up its fleet in response.

Asper the younger believes it is time to use the company's presence to exploit the market created by an environment plagued with fragmenting audiences, the emergence of multiple delivery technologies and an ever-widening choice of media to consume. Even though his industry includes many old-world thinkers who can't understand where he's going, he is determined to continue driving forward.

Asper, a careful captain with a well-thought-out vision that extends beyond what most can see in plain sight, is ready to embark on a journey that most of his peers around the world have only talked about. From his unlikely base in Winnipeg, Manitoba, he is determined to explore this universe of new technologies and dense media channels, and to see CanWest standing on top of a very profitable summit.

—៣—

Update: *In 2007, Asper was the executive co-producer of the documentary* My Opposition: The Diaries of Friedrich Kellner. *The film followed an American orphan, who discovers a diary written during the Third Reich while searching for his German grandfather. That same year, CanWest Global Communication partnered with investment bank Goldman Sachs to acquire Alliance Atlantis, a leading Canadian company that owns 13 specialty branded television channels. While the deal was closed in August of 2007, the transaction is still awaiting CRTC approval.*

From the beginning, humankind has sought out new territories to exploit for economic gain. Early European explorers hugged the coasts of Africa to find trade routes to China. Their followers from Spain, Portugal and Britain, ignoring warnings that the earth was flat, sailed westward until they found the Americas and their plenty. French voyageurs travelled the rivers of the new continent making contact with native people and developing the grandfather of North American industry—the fur trade.

Often these expeditions resulted in more than just fiscal gain. In the late 1800s, for example, the development of the railway and its ability to move people and goods long distances relatively quickly brought tremendous social change in its wake. People began to see their place in the world differently when a major barrier to the physical movement of labour, goods and capital was diminished. As management guru Peter Drucker put it, "The railway changed every nation's economy and workforce; it changed humanity's mindset, its mental geography."[1]

The new development that promises just as profound a revolution in the way people interact is the convergence of telecommunications and computer technology, enabling electronic commerce and

---

1   Peter F. Drucker, Beyond the Information Revolution, *Atlantic Monthly*, 1999.

community building via the Internet. In 1999, at the turn of the new century, Arthur Carty, then president of the National Research Council of Canada, insisted that the Internet's power for social and economic change would eclipse that of the computer itself.

"New technologies will be created as a result of the process of convergence that made the Internet," he said. "We live in an age of convergence, where the traditional boundaries between disciplines, technologies and sectors are being erased."[2]

This convergence of new technologies, information and knowledge has altered almost everything in its path—from transportation to medical services to education. Nowhere has the impact been more profoundly felt, however, than in the media, where convergence was all but inevitable as the digital revolution changed the very foundation of information delivery. Voice, images and the written word became indistinguishable from one another, a series of ones and zeros moving at the speed of light through fibre optics, cellular networks and even old-fashioned twisted copper wires.

Publishing, broadcasting, entertainment, cable and telephony— once distinct and separate silos—have become part of a sprawling ecosystem of specialized sub-industries dedicated to delivering content to audiences watching conventional TV, working on computers, or carrying a mobile device.

In its early days, this media revolution spawned a frenzy of corporate mergers and acquisitions as companies in various sectors of communications positioned themselves to gain access to this new, unmapped territory. In 1990, in the United States, Warner Communications and Time combined to create the world's largest media conglomerate, Time Warner, which subsequently snapped up Turner Broadcasting. Just four years later, Internet service provider AOL, its market capitalization inflated by the tech bubble, merged with Time Warner. Meanwhile, Walt Disney Co. bought Capital Cities/ABC; cable provider Viacom bought video retailer Blockbuster Entertainment and movie producer Paramount Communications. A former French water utility transformed into Vivendi, a major entertainment empire, when it merged with Seagram, which owned Universal Studios, and TV broadcaster Canal+.

In Canada, telephone giant BCE acquired the CTV television

---

2 Arthur Carty, The Age of Convergence, speech, *Technology for Success Conference*, Edmonton, 1999.

network and six months later scooped up the national daily newspaper *The Globe and Mail*. It also established a satellite service, Bell ExpressVu, and launched the Internet portal Sympatico-Lycos. Printer and newspaper publisher Quebecor bought Videotron, the largest cable company in the province of Quebec. It also operates web publisher *canoe.ca*. Rogers Communications added wireless products, specialty channels, publications and even sports teams to the foundation of its cable business. CanWest Global Communications, which owned one of Canada's leading television networks, acquired the country's largest newspaper chain, Southam Inc.

Unfortunately, many of these early acquisition strategies under-delivered on their promises. In some cases, the transactions were simply too early and had to wait for consumer behaviours to catch up; in others, they chose the wrong routes and vehicles altogether. Like any explorer, they were taking risks by travelling where few had set foot before and many were unable to sustain their own momentum. Rooted in old thinking and hampered by corporate structures that demanded instant returns, many of these companies abandoned the vision and re-treated back to what they knew. Yet, quietly, the market has continued to evolve despite corporate manoeuvring.

Print, television and radio have converged and the very technology that made it possible also appears to have made it a necessity. But while media companies have adopted convergence strategies to pursue their disparate audiences, questions still remain as to how they will properly execute on them. Except for the first tentative attempts to access this sphere—akin to the early Apollo flights into the vast territory of space—this expanse remains virgin territory. "What will consumers buy, and how will advertisers use this new cross-media capability?" asked author Gordon Pitts. "What will people want to watch, in what form, at what cost and on what devices?"[3]

These are the very questions that occupy the majority of Leonard Asper's day, and he thinks he has some of the answers. The youngest son of CanWest's founder, the legendary entrepreneur Israel H. (Izzy) Asper, is a family man who grew up in Winnipeg, Manitoba, and inherited the CanWest mantle, for which he had been groomed from childhood. Leonard has described the family dinner table as being "like a boardroom."

---

3   Gordon Pitts, *Kings of Convergence*, Doubleday Canada, 2002.

Asper, who took his seat alone at the controls when he was appointed President and CEO in 1999, received a B.A. from Brandeis University in Boston, attended law school at the University of Toronto, and articled at a top Bay Street law firm before joining his father's company. Since then he has become a globe-trotting media mogul who remains rooted in the Canadian city of Winnipeg, set in the centre of the country between the forest- and lake-filled Canadian Shield to the east and the grassland prairies to the west.

"Izzy was one way, Leonard is another," says his older brother, David, who also works at CanWest and is a lawyer celebrated for the high-profile freeing of David Milgaard, who was wrongfully convicted of murder. "In a way, his style is reflective of the life cycle of the company. It's past the go-go-go founding stage into a more process-oriented dynamic. I think Leonard marries that process style excellently with an entrepreneurial drive." [4]

This dynamic has opened up a new world for Asper that is a long way from his Winnipeg neighbourhood of River Heights. When he took the captain's chair at CanWest, he was immediately thrown into negotiations that ultimately led to the company's $3.2 billion purchase of Southam Inc. from Hollinger. Canada's largest newspaper chain, Southam included 14 major metro papers, a 50-percent interest in the flagship National Post (subsequently increased to 100-percent owner-ship), 200 small papers and trade publications, and related Internet properties.

The deal was just one result of an earlier strategy to diversify the company by building on five media pillars: print, television, radio, the Internet and outdoor advertising. If a strategy is simply a corporate road map formed in reaction to outside and inside business forces, it usually begins with some recognition of the changing market landscape. Like many other media companies, CanWest surveyed its environment and recognized that it was at the mercy of technological advance. Can-West's core business was selling advertising space on television, but that traditional market was facing inherent challenges. In reply to this problem, it decided to diversify—it would not restrict itself and would instead broaden its reach across multiple channels of information de-livery. If media convergence was to become the norm, then CanWest

---

4 Martin Cash, CanWest CEO Leonard Asper mixes corporate, family life, *Winnipeg Free Press*, Aug. 2, 2000.

would meet the challenge by diversifying its media holdings and push full steam in that direction.

This diversification of advertising and content delivery channels has been a strategy CanWest has continued to pursue even more aggressively under Leonard's stewardship, especially now that market conditions have made it more than just a pipe dream. It may turn out that Asper's solution to the problem of fragmenting markets is actually the convergence model everyone has been struggling to find. Why? Because diversification of media ownership is not some one-shot exploratory foray into foreign territory, but a long-term strategic combination of defence and offence.

Convergence does not suddenly create a brand new media entity. Instead, it forces companies that had owned one type of media vehicle to evolve in order to carry on their native business. As audiences fragment, which affects advertising rates, a media company must spread its services over several channels. Just as many new shores were discovered by settlers out of necessity due to social, economic or political change, the new world of convergence is being explored by CanWest as a method of coping with a market that is simply not the same as it was when the company started with one television station.

That change is indeed profound. The media world is now a collection of realms that overlap continually because of the web and other digital communications technologies. Newspapers and broadcasters are producing content online; the web hosts a vast universe of video, audio and text. People now consume multiple media simultaneously— a process known as "stacking." For media companies, whose top line relies on selling advertising space and content, this delivery overlap has acute effects. Multiplication of delivery channels means the advertising market has become commoditized—high volumes of inventory are available at low cost. Therefore, only the best "product" draws a premium. It is much harder now to reach a large audience easily, and any company that can deliver large numbers of readers, viewers and listeners can sell the service at a premium price and therefore derive more profit. If real estate is all about location, location, location, media is all about eyeballs, eyeballs, eyeballs.

Meanwhile, behavioural patterns of media use are changing. TV viewership is fragmenting among channels, newspaper readership has been declining for years, and the web is capturing a significant share of the market. A 2004 media usage survey highlighted by the Media Center, a division of the American Press Institute, showed that 62.9 percent of those polled watch TV while also online. Also, the younger generation is increasingly combining traditional media usage with newer forms such as blogs, instant messaging, PDAs and picture phones. For example, 21 percent of those aged 35 to 44 use all these new media options regularly.[5]

Advertisers are shifting strategies to take advantage of this newer pattern of media usage. The Wall Street brokerage Merrill Lynch estimates that online advertising will reach $11.5 billion in 2005, representing 4.2 percent of U.S. ad expenditures, which is significantly higher than was the case only three years ago.[6] Jupiter research reports that online advertising is growing at three times the rate of other advertising, and will overtake total magazine advertising by 2007.[7] Meanwhile, at the end of 2004, 27 percent of Internet users reported that they regularly read blogs—a 58 percent increase from the previous year. This translates to 32 million American blog readers.[8]

"It's no longer a valid strategy to operate one conventional over-the-air TV channel in a sea of 300 or 500 or whatever numbers of channels there are," Asper observes. "We want to have many 'channels,' whether they be websites or newspapers or TV stations. In the end it all becomes about market share."

In the pre-convergence world, advertising was linear: an advertising agency would buy time on a television channel, and then purchase space separately in a newspaper. But in the new world of convergence, this advertising can be co-ordinated by the media supplier itself. As an example, Asper cites a recent campaign by the cosmetic company L'Oreal, which wanted to advertise its products in conjunction with International Women's Day. CanWest created a special magazine as well as a television program that referred to the magazine. It ran both print and TV advertising, developed a special website and produced vignettes that were inserted into news shows that cross-referenced the print ads. To cap it all off, L'Oreal sponsored a commercial-free night on one of CanWest's specialty channels. "They could never get that if

5   *Meet Generation 'C'*, SIMM IV, mediacenter.org, Dec., 2004.
6   Joe Mandese, *Wall Street: Ad Share Shift "Faster than We Realized," Print, TV Budgets Move To Cable, Online*, MediaPost, Jan 21, 2005.
7   *Online Advertising Through 2009*, Jupiterresearch, www.jupiterresearch.com, 2004.
8   *Pew Internet & American Life Project*, Pew Research Center, January, 2005.

they tried to go with a bunch of digital channels, a TV network and a newspaper group," says Asper.

The supply side of the CanWest convergence strategy as described above forms the basis of a backstop, but Asper knows it is really all about a strong offence. Therefore, CanWest is moving on the demand side as well, by chasing the new information consumer wherever he or she resides physically or virtually. This shifting pattern of information access means the viewer or reader is now "king" when it comes to demand, says Asper. With 300-plus television stations, hundreds of radio stations, even more print and online newspapers, and millions of websites to choose from, content can be obtained whenever, wherever or however a consumer wants. The chain of control has passed from the supplier to the audience. For the first time perhaps in its existence, media is now a buyer's market.

Therefore, part of CanWest's convergence strategy is rooted in the recognition that consumers are now in the driver's seat and that they want content—quality information and entertainment—above all. Thirty years ago, a network offered a TV program only once; if you couldn't watch it then, you missed it. Now, with the push of a button on a Personal Video Recorder (PVR) such as TiVO, "king" consumer can watch that show anytime, pause live television and even, dare we say, skip the commercials altogether.

"That's a different world," says Asper. "The consumer has never been ignored but was maybe only the 'prince' before because he didn't have nearly the same power to influence media companies that he does now because of competition. If I don't give it to you when you want it, someone else will."

SPEND TIME IN THE ENGINE ROOM

CanWest is converging five media channels—TV, radio, print, Internet and outdoor signage—in order to best position its underlying business, which is selling advertising and, increasingly, content. In fact, in the changing media universe, content is king and offers the best opportunity for media companies to generate new revenue sources. In this model, broadcasting ceases to be the sole engine and evolves to serve as both a line of business unto itself and the distribution channel for an entirely new income stream.

Another aspect of media convergence is that it offers an opportunity to leverage the content in a company's arsenal. In fact, one might argue that content has now, or at least will become, the primary product, with the medium becoming just the delivery channel. This focus on content is fundamentally changing the media business, as the revenue mix shifts from complete reliance on advertising sales to a more balanced diet of advertising, subscription revenues and income from the ownership and exploitation of content.

CanWest has adapted to these new conditions by beefing up its content production capacity. In fact, to CanWest, convergence means an ability to leverage from its traditional advertising sales model to a corollary model—the publishing of content across multiple channels in order to increase top-line revenue. Asper believes, for example, that content production will someday generate bigger revenue streams than those generated by distributing that content through the veins of the company itself.

BROADEN THE FLEET

Today, the consumer of information has access to television and radio stations, on- and off-line newspapers, and millions of websites. The power has shifted from the media lords to the user. Because these companies can no longer dictate how and what a consumer sees, hears and reads, they have no choice but to operate across a wide spectrum of channels if they wish to keep the mindshare of their audience.

Says Asper: "The shift in the value chain is moving toward content, away from the retail or the broadcast or the newspaper. If I make coats and I own The Bay, I know I can sell those coats in a lot more places than The Bay. Take a TV program. I manufacture it and I sell it in my store—Global TV. Now I also create the DVD, I create the soundtrack, I repurpose it into 'webisodes' for RealNetworks, I put it on Rogers cell phones, I create the book that goes along with the show, I create an event. I've got all these other revenue streams from that content."

However, the move toward content ownership is not only aimed at exploitation of new opportunities, it is also partly a defensive move. Coupled with the changing access patterns of consumers has been a concern that traditional content suppliers might not make their programming available for delivery by third parties like CanWest. When Fox Network owner Rupert Murdoch bought a 15-percent stake in Australia's Channel 7, the first thing he did was to cease selling Fox programming to CanWest's Network Ten. For a content deliverer, the move was a strong warning of rough times ahead.

"We started to feel exposed, that if we didn't own our own content, we may lose supply," explains Asper. "We had to protect our supply lines. That's what we like about newspapers. You don't have that situation where someone can take away your content every day."

SAIL TO UNSEEN SHORES

A successful convergence strategy also serves as an effective means of divergence. A media company wishing to diversify geographically can bolster each foray into new territory by convening distribution in that region to establish market position. Relying on the synergies of these multimedia channels, the company can more quickly acquire market share.

CanWest is further protecting itself by diversifying its operations geographically, continuing a pattern it has been employing for some time. Currently, it owns media properties in Australia, New Zealand, Ireland and the United States, and is reportedly studying opportunities elsewhere in the world. Meanwhile, this divergence strategy is also another opportunity to spread convergence, particularly in the five-pillar model CanWest has chosen—TV, radio, print, Internet and outside advertising.

In the U.S., CanWest has a stake in Internet Broadcasting Systems, a supplier of websites to television stations. In Ireland, it launched and is the founding partner in TV3, the country's first private television network. In Australia, it owns Network Ten, the national television network, and Eye Corp., a supplier of "out-of-home" advertising space such as billboards. Eye Corp. also has properties in New Zealand, Malaysia and Indonesia. And in New Zealand, it operates two television channels, four national radio networks and 27 local radio stations.

Currently this regional diversification of media ownership has not provided much in the way of cost synergies; many of the properties serve different markets, so can't share content. As well, advertising climates differ from country to country. For example, in Australia brand advertising is currently stronger so the TV advertising market is good, while in Canada there has been a move to more tactical advertising in radio and newspapers, so national TV branding campaigns are less prominent. Because these trends are local in nature, they provide good counterbalancing effects for the company.

"I think there are synergies in these converged companies but they're not nearly as pronounced as people have claimed, if only from a timing perspective," says Asper. "Drawing out the synergies will be a longer game than people assumed but there is no doubt that they are there in every aspect of the business—from sales to promotion to marketing to content creation to content selling, including the back office operations like IT, accounting and even content management systems."

Also, Asper says executive transfers have been effective and that Canadians running Global television properties have made successes of the TV operations in Australia, New Zealand and Ireland. On the flip side, the executive group in Australia has undergone a complete conversion to digital over-the-air signal delivery, which hasn't yet happened in Canada. "We now have a body of expertise in Australia that can help us in New Zealand and Canada if and when we decide to go there," Asper explains. "Our company is better off from a diversification point of view and from a knowledge-transfer point of view by having a wider group of assets rather than being confined to one market."

This diversification strategy may be a response to a new market reality and technological capabilities, but it is also almost classically typical of companies that have reached a particular size and stage of their life cycle, say organizational development researchers. In fact, diversification of product offerings, or delivery methods, is a distinct stage in the lifecycle of any organization, say UCLA business professors Eric G. Flamholtz and Yvonne Randle.

"Over time [a company's] product will inevitably play itself out," they say. "When a firm builds up its organizational and management infrastructure, it usually does so with the intention of remaining a going concern. This means that if it is to continue to exist, it must find other products."[9]

---

9 Eric G. Flamholtz and Yvonne Randle, *Growing Pains: Transitioning from an entrepreneurship to a professionally managed firm*, Jossey-Bass, A Wiley Company, 2000.

THE STARS AREN'T RELIABLE—USE A COMPASS

Many previous attempts at media convergence failed because they were mere escapades in mergers and acquisitions without a clear business purpose and strategy behind them. Convergence is more than just a consolidation play—the company that succeeds will have a clear plan of what to piece together and why, where the synergies are, how to merge the distinct cultures and why the new entity will be greater than the sum of its parts.

While CanWest's diversification strategy may be in the classic mould, the landscape it is operating in is not. New technology and changing consumer habits mean that a company that pursues convergence of diverse media properties faces some unique problems. That may be why others' earlier attempts have met with mixed success.

In the first wave of convergence strategies, equipment sellers and telecommunications companies invaded each other's turf. The U.S. telephone giant AT&T bought computer company NCR, only to sell it four years later. IBM bought ROLM, which made PBX switches, and sold it within five years. Later, Matsushita, parent of Panasonic, bought MCA and Universal Pictures, but sold out after several years of losses. Another consumer electronics manufacturer, Sony Corp., has retained the entertainment assets it acquired, including CBS Records and Columbia Pictures, but is incurring heavy losses.

Not surprisingly, these failures have prompted a barrage of warnings and naysaying about the dangers of convergence as well as corresponding advice that any company attempting to explore these uncharted areas be very, very careful. Unknown dangers may lie in wait beyond the known universe, pundits say, echoing early European mapmakers who marked unknown oceans with the simple but dire warning: "Out There Be Monsters."

"Convergence seems to be either a useless epi-phenomena deluding business management to pursue bad strategies, or an interesting concept yet to be analyzed by economic theory," says Stockholm economist Jonas Lind. Though his prose is more eloquent, he is essentially still warning of monsters.[10]

This fear has been reflected by market analysts and investors who cooled on convergence after touted profits failed to materialize, and

---

10 Jonas Lind, Speech, Center for Information and Communications Research, Stockholm School of Economics, 2004.

sometimes were replaced by losses, as was the case with the AOL–Time Warner union. Every media convergence acquisition announcement was greeted with a sell signal and flight from the host company's stock. "Convergence" joined "dot-com" as dirty word for investors.

Sweden's Lind postulated that many of the failed mergers were motivated by a strategy of vertical consolidation, in which a company attempts to own all aspects of a business, from production to wholesale to retail. However, Asper says convergence along vertical lines will likely result in failure. Unlike those of other adventurers in this space, the CanWest plan involves expanding broad and wide rather than narrow and deep.

Under this horizontal strategy, separate media properties focus on one underlying business—advertising sales—with content production and sales forming the fuel that drives profitability. In contrast, many other convergence attempts have approached this emerging media space with a flawed conglomeration mentality, believing that if they put together dissimilar media properties with different business models, they would somehow mesh.

For example, a cable company is, in essence, a utility that provides the infrastructure for digital and television signals, while a television company delivers (usually purchased or rented) content. Merely putting them under one roof presumes that because the two businesses operate in the same field, they must be similar. They are not. In fact they are extremely dissimilar, and it can be difficult to realize any synergies when they are forced into a marriage. This flawed thinking is very similar to the failed conglomeration strategies of the 1970s in which consolidators bought other profitable companies merely because they were there, not because they fit any kind of clearly focused strategy. A company that produces personal products, for instance, may know nothing about operating the retail stores that sell them.

Critics often use the massive AOL–Time Warner merger to argue that the convergence model doesn't work. But they are really arguing against the old vertical conglomeration model instead of a true convergence strategy. Asper points out that AOL–Time Warner was trying to put together a disparate collection of media that included an Internet service provider, a cable company and some specialty channels—a very different proposition from joining newspapers and television stations which are based on similar advertising-based revenue models.

"I don't know what [AOL and Time Warner] got out of [the merger]; it doesn't make sense to me," says Asper. "We put together assets that are in the same business—the selling of advertising—in the two advertising categories that represent 80 percent of all advertising sales." Asper cites as a more appropriate business model a completely different industry and business—the personal products supplier Procter & Gamble, which has multiple product lines it sells at the retail level, rather than one product line that sells up a supply chain.

"I think history shows the vertically integrated plays don't work nearly as well as horizontally integrated plays because up the chain, the retail side of the business doesn't want to be forced to buy from their in-house manufacturer when they might be able to get a better price elsewhere," he says. As an example, he points out that while CanWest provides some programming to its television network, the individual stations still have the right—even the obligation—to choose the best supplier. "If we think we can provide it more cheaply than others, we'll provide our own content. But we won't damage the business at the retail end by forcing a source of supply."

ALL HANDS ON DECK

A media company planning to tackle convergence requires a management team that knows something about the disparate parts that will come together to make up the new whole. There must be a crew in place that understands the distinct peculiarities of each media channel. In addition, there needs to be deep talent at the highest level to ensure that all the moving parts are marching in unison with the master plan.

Asper also suspects the AOL merger's failure to meet expectations had much to do with the combined company's outdated culture and management. "Convergence strategy is impossible without the right people to execute it," he says. "It's a completely different culture. It's a matrix management culture, not a command and control culture. It's dogfights in the air rather than infantry walking in unison. Just as you need a different individual to fly a plane than to be a soldier in the infantry, you need different individuals in these kinds of cultures."

To help lead it further in the direction of convergence, CanWest recently restructured to create a new corporate identity, CanWest

MediaWorks, and recruited several senior media executives from the U.S. who are experienced with television, online strategy, multi-platform integrated sales and marketing, web-based technologies, and the sustaining of profitable web models.

"The old CanWest of 800 employees, which was the seven Global TV stations, was a very innovative culture," Asper says to explain the restructuring and the rash of hires. "We then bought a company called WIC (Vancouver-based Western International Communications), which was another 900 employees but which was slightly less innovative. Then the real dive into innovation came when we purchased the Southam group (the Hollinger newspapers), which has some terrific employees but did not have a culture of innovation, development and growth. So we went from 800 to 8,000 employees in Canada, our major market, of which the vast majority did not have the culture to manage an enterprise that is facing significantly more competition than it had to date."

Asper describes the new management team as a cohesive, integrated executive group that meets often so that everything that happens in the company has a complete multimedia strategy built around it. For example, the TV group doesn't launch a show without knowing how it's going to be promoted in the newspapers and what the web component of that programming is.

While Asper is clear on his strategy, he recognizes that it is really a directional map, not a series of milestones. You may be positioning yourself for new worlds, but it can be difficult to explain to people what they will be like if you haven't been there yourself. He has some advice for media industry watchers confused by this new world: Be patient. "People are critical of convergence because it didn't deliver an instant 25-percent revenue rise, but it was never promised that's what it would do," he says. "We take a very long view of the world."

When he doesn't have his mind wrapped around large subjects such as the future of media, or what lies over the convergence horizon, Asper likes to relax by occasionally playing a pickup game of hockey back in Winnipeg. So, to explain how convergence is evolving, he reaches back to his roots for an analogy all Canadians will understand.

"We're still in the first period, maybe 15 minutes into the first period," he says. "But I think we've scored a few goals and we're winning the game."

5 THINGS YOU NEED TO KNOW

Leonard Asper's suggestions for those who plan to explore uncharted terrain:

1. Spend Time in the Engine Room

CanWest is converging five media channels—TV, radio, print, Internet and outdoor signage—in order to best position its underlying business, which is selling advertising and, increasingly, content. In fact, in the changing media universe, content is king and offers the best opportunity for media companies to generate new revenue sources. In this model, broadcasting ceases to be the sole engine and evolves to serve as both a line of business unto itself and the distribution channel for an entirely new income stream.

2. Broaden the Fleet

Today, the consumer of information has access to television and radio stations, on- and off-line newspapers, and millions of websites. The power has shifted from the media lords to the user. Because these companies can no longer dictate how and what a consumer sees, hears and reads, they have no choice but to operate across a wide spectrum of channels if they wish to keep the mindshare of their audience.

3. Sail to Unseen Shores

A successful convergence strategy also serves as an effective means of divergence. A media company wishing to diversify geographically can bolster each foray into new territory by convening distribution in that region to establish market position. Relying on the synergies of these multimedia channels, the company can more quickly acquire market share.

4. The Stars Aren't Reliable—Use a Compass

Many previous attempts at media convergence failed because they were mere escapades in mergers and acquisitions without a clear business purpose and strategy behind them. Convergence is more than just a consolidation play—the company that succeeds will have a clear plan of what to piece together and why, where the synergies are, how to merge the distinct cultures and why the new entity will be greater than the sum of its parts.

5. All Hands on Deck

A media company planning to tackle convergence requires a management team that knows something about the disparate parts that will come together to make up the new whole. There must be a crew in place that understands the distinct peculiarities of each media channel. In addition, there needs to be deep talent at the highest level to ensure that all the moving parts are marching in unison with the master plan.

CHAPTER THIRTEEN

Moving an Elephant with a Mouse
Changing the Unchangeable

FEATURING THE WISDOM OF ROB MCEWEN

In 2000, Rob McEwen, CEO of Goldcorp Inc., a small Ontario gold mining company, rocked the cloistered mining world by launching what he called the Goldcorp Challenge on the Internet. McEwen posted all his company's proprietary exploration data online, and asked the world to analyze it and tell him where he could find more gold. More than a thousand people partici-pated in the worldwide contest, and from the results the company identified enough additional ore to turn its Red Lake gold mine into one of the world's richest in terms of deposits.

It was an outrageous move that shocked most other companies in what is the most traditional of traditional industries. But it was not unique for McEwen, who had been shaking up the established mining world ever since he inherited, through a company takeover in 1989, a 50-year-old gold mine that its owners believed was all but played out.

McEwen's background was not in mining but in finance, a less process-oriented world and one more responsive to new ideas. His familiarity with that arena enabled him to shift attitudes in the ritual-bound mining com-munity, allowing him to become a catalyst and continually apply the building blocks of change. He viewed the business through the eyes of an outsider and, by trusting his gut, he dragged an ancient industry, kicking and scream-ing, into the twenty-first century.

Update: *In 2005, McEwen received an Honorary Doctor of Laws degree from York University and in 2006* **Canadian Business Magazine** *named him "Most Innovative CEO." In 2007, he was appointed to the Order of Canada, the country's highest civilian tribute. McEwen continues his philanthropic work, particularly supporting Canada's medical community. In 2007, he donated $10 million to the McEwen Centre for Regenerative Medicine at University Health Network. He has cumulatively donated $20 million in support of regenerative medicine and stem cell research, making his contribution the largest of its kind in Canada.*

Change is one of those words that everyone in the business community peppers into conversation. From casual chats around the water cooler to important meetings in the boardroom, the term seems to be a fixture constantly floating in the air. It can be painted as the sole cause for all that ails an organization or the saving grace behind a company's success. Given the challenges the macro business environment has thrown out over the past decade, from too-fast-to-follow technological advances to an aging workforce whose skills are too quickly rendered out of date, it would seem that managing change would be a cornerstone of most corporate agendas. But this is not the case at all. Many see the turmoil, but deny that it affects them—"Not in my industry. Not in my business. If it ain't broke, don't fix it." Some organizations are simply complacent and wrongly believe that the forces that surround them cannot penetrate their shells. But they believe so at their peril.

Resistance to change is often a factor of age and time. Like a couple that has been married for many years, a business that has been operating in the same way for decades will often settle into a static routine. While it may adopt small changes from time to time to make the company function marginally better, often these are just band-aids; the business, at its core, is not really evolving. In the parlance of change management, the business is frozen because the operators believe that consistency and predictability are the end goals.

This state can engulf an entire industry. The mining sector, some 4,000 years old, still functions much the way it always has—look for ore, dig up the ore found, refine the ore dug up, and sell the refined ore to the end user. The metals and minerals sector is one of the world's largest commodity industries, generating billions of dollars' worth of output every year. However, despite its size and global significance, the mining industry has retained fixed processes, systems, mores and attitudes; it also has one of the oldest workforces of any industry on the planet.

However, the wave of change engulfing the rest of the business world has also hit the mining industry, which is finally undergoing an evolution. This movement was enhanced in 2000 when Goldcorp, a small gold mining company listed on the Toronto and New York Stock Exchanges, employed a modern communications method that forever changed how mining companies would analyze the information acquired in their hunt for ore. The CEO of Goldcorp, Rob McEwen, was the engineer behind some of that change when he decided to use the Internet as a tool to unearth gold. And he did it in a way no mining company had dared to try before.

McEwen created the online "Goldcorp Challenge," which offered anyone who was interested a chance to help the company determine the best way to gain access to some six million ounces of gold it believed still lay hidden within its 50-year-old Red Lake mine in Northern Ontario. To help them, it put half a century of proprietary geological, chemical and mining data on a CD-Rom, available through its website. This complete public disclosure of proprietary data was an unheard-of step for a mining company to take. To up the ante, Goldcorp offered $500,000 in prizes for the winners.

More than 1,400 students, professors, mining consultants, prospectors, other mining companies, physicists and mathematicians responded enthusiastically. They downloaded the data, pored over it and then delivered their hypotheses. The eventual winner was a group comprising two rival consulting firms in Australia that had never set foot in North America. But the real winner was Goldcorp, which used the challenge's results to pinpoint where it should dig and very quickly hit the motherlode. Within a couple of years, the almost moribund Red Lake mine became the world's richest gold mine in terms of deposits. After producing roughly three million ounces of gold in its first 50 years, it turned out another 1.85 million ounces in the next four.

When he created the Challenge, Rob McEwen wanted not only to turn the staid mining world on its head, but also to move it into the twenty-first century. Goldcorp, which garnered press coverage around the world because of its novel use of technology, certainly accomplished that. But the Challenge was also risky because it cut across the grain of practices the industry had built up for decades. "This is a very conservative, very private industry," observed Dr. James M. Franklin, former chief geoscientist for the Geological Survey of Canada and a judge in the Goldcorp Challenge. "Confidentiality and secrecy about reserves and exploration have been its watchwords. This was a totally unconventional thing to do."

But McEwen figured there would be more risk in continuing to operate the mine the same way as in the past. When he took over Red Lake, it had been using ancient technology to extract ore, operating with entrenched and complacent management, paying its 180 workers among the highest wages in the industry and spending more to find gold than it was worth. While the Challenge was certainly the most spectacular change, it was only one of a series of changes that also included adding state-of-the-art technology acquired from outside the industry. The result was that the mine later employed only 45 highly paid workers to produce more gold than three times their number had done before.

At the same time, Goldcorp's earnings skyrocketed. Some time before it issued the Challenge, Red Lake was one of the highest-cost producers in the industry, mining about 53,000 ounces annually at a cost of $360 an ounce. After, Goldcorp became one of the lowest-cost producers, turning out 504,000 ounces at $59 an ounce. Profitability increased dramatically. Goldcorp had recorded financial losses for the three years previous to the Challenge, but by year-end 2002, earnings had swollen to $65 million.

Why was McEwen able to take such radical action? Because he was an innovator, not a miner, and because he was able to embrace change. He wasn't constrained by conventional wisdom. As a young man, he had followed his father into the investment business. But his father was also fascinated with gold, and McEwen grew up hearing tales of miners, prospectors and grubstakes at the dinner table. Soon the gold bug bit him too, and he designed a mental template of what he thought a modern gold-mining company should look like. In 1989, as an investor, he stepped into a takeover battle as a white knight and emerged as majority owner of the Red Lake mine, as well as a neighbouring one— both old and underperforming. While he won the first battle, the war had only just begun. The gold market was depressed and the mines' operating costs were high.

TAKE A GOOD LOOK AROUND

You can't fix what you don't understand. Before taking a business through radical, disruptive change, you must first get under the hood and intimately feel for the environment in which it operates. This requires not only a thorough knowledge of the usual metrics and insider know-how of the day-to-day affairs, but a deep, schooled understanding of its processes, thinking, norms and culture. Without this, the business will fragment under the inevitable pressures created by the change process.

Because he was familiar with mining, but not ingrained in it, McEwen had had plenty of time to study the industry before he started instituting radical change. Therefore, when he took over the mines, he was able to move quickly to implement some changes. A curious but logical man, McEwen just couldn't believe the status quo was good enough.

Says McEwen, "I wanted to introduce the urgency of the financial markets to the mining industry. I also saw it as an industry with a lot of opportunity, because everyone was going down the same road and no one was looking anywhere else. What I brought was a different perspective. I could look at the problems from a slightly different angle and in so doing generate alternatives that most of the industry thought were crazy."

The industry, though, was locked in a comfort zone and impervious to change, despite the problems. Yes, it had made some incremental improvements such as new mine site designs, new extraction techniques and better exploration methods. But mining remained in essence an engineering-based process of finding and exploiting metal ore.

At the top of any particular commodity's price cycle, mining brought in enormous wealth. But much of the time, it could be a losing proposition.. "Mining is viewed as risky, because of the exploration involved, but there are very few risk-takers in it," McEwen observes. "It's a very conservative industry. There is this avoidance of bold initiatives."

As for his own company, when McEwen started to introduce some of those initiatives at the mines he had acquired, many of the mines' managers and the boards of directors, steeped in traditional thinking,

refused to budge from their habitual ways of thinking. McEwen fired
the lot of them and brought in people who understood his vision. "It's
a groupthink," he says. "They're trained as engineers to get the job
done and once they set a course, they don't consider other variables.
Even if it would change their assumptions, they'd say 'No, I'm on a
course and I'm going to complete the job,' because that's what they've
been trained to do."

He was also having difficulty changing unionized workers' entrenched attitudes. Throughout the period before and after the Challenge, when he was exploring Red Lake, the mine with the most potential, and as he proceeded to institute operational changes in the
background, his company was involved in a long, occasionally bitter
strike. For almost four years, workers remained off the job, effectively
shutting down the mine. They were not happy at the thought of re-
turning to a job environment that was completely altered from what
they were used to.

But McEwen was bent on creating an efficient and profitable gold
mining company. It was innovation that could not be easily ignored or
halted. It was also the beginning of a path of "change management"
that was required to accompany this innovation.

Change management is a new discipline that is rapidly gaining
currency as a lack of innovation threatens increasing numbers of
businesses and other organizations. A change management regime is
the way an organization puts necessary changes in place, regardless
of whether this need is driven by external or internal stimuli. All
change managers, change agents or change practitioners tend to draw
techniques, tools and skills from a similar pool of knowledge that in
itself is drawn from an array of other disciplines (psychology, economics
and human/organizational behaviour). Which of these techniques and
outlooks forms the dominant approach usually depends on the point
of view of the change agent. Change management consultant Fred
Nickols, senior consultant with the Distance Consulting Company
in New Jersey, insists that a useful framework for thinking about the
change process is to see it as problem solving.

Says Nickols, "Managing change is seen as a matter of moving
from one state to another—specifically, from the problem state to the
solved state. Diagnosis or problem analysis is generally acknowledged
as essential. Goals are set and achieved at various levels and in various

areas or functions. Ends and means are discussed and related to one another. Careful planning is accompanied by efforts to obtain buy-in, support and commitment. Whether we choose to call these situations 'problems' or whether we choose to call them 'opportunities' is immaterial. In both cases, the practical matter is one of identifying and settling on a course of action that will bring about some desired and predetermined change in the situation."[1]

THEN TAKE A GOOD LOOK IN THE MIRROR

Familiarity encourages complacency, and complacency encourages blindness. To be effective, change agents must step outside conventional thinking and view their surroundings from a different perspective. Constantly examining industry norms from first principles—and asking how, what and why is it done that way—will help identify which should be cast aside as having lost their usefulness.

To determine how to change a situation, the change agent must figure out how the problem arose in the first place. One common technique—root causal analysis—is a problem solving method adapted from systems engineering. It can be undertaken in several different ways and with several different tools. The most common one involves restating the problem to differentiate the root from its symptoms, which allows an understanding of cause and effect. Problems can be restated in several ways, but the most useful is simply to ask how, what and why several times.

A problem that requires change is usually expressed initially as a "how" question; this is an action-oriented inquiry. The "what" question expands this thinking to tactical issues, such as "What is to be accomplished?" The "why" question or questions—often called the Five Whys—drill down to the root problem and make it possible to come up with new solutions. Simple whys might be, "Why do we do what we do and why do we do it the way we do it?" Each answer is then questioned again, forming a chain of answers that usually exposes the underlying problem.

Although he did not formally set out to be a change agent, Rob McEwen instinctively employed many change management methods

---

1   Fred Nickols, *Change Management: A Primer*, International Society of Performance Improvement, 1997.

in his line of duty. Whenever he perceived a problem at Goldcorp, he often just asked how, what, and why until he got an answer. Often it turned out that the problem didn't lie with the company itself, but with industry practices, which were rarely questioned.

"I just didn't see eye to eye with them," McEwen says of those he dealt with in the industry. "To them mining was drilling, blasting and mucking, which is the movement of the rock. I was continually told that's what mining is all about. But I said 'Those are just processes. What's the result you want to produce? Isn't it to produce gold at a profit?' But profit wasn't part of their daily conversation. They liked what they were doing and didn't think about profit."

The engineering-based disciplines at the root of mining are directed at performing tasks, not at creatively studying and organizing their outcomes. This is more properly the realm of corporate governance, and McEwen rightly discerned that the people who were charged with completing the job—the doers—were also in charge of analyzing and employing the outcomes of that job. To do this successfully, however, they had to have a broader view of areas such as marketing, finance and technology. This wider view was in short supply, and McEwen became convinced that the industry had hit a creative wall.

McEwen cites the case of a mine that Goldcorp owned in South Dakota. The company also had a large interest in a nearby ski hill. The mine had a severe problem with disposal of the water it used in its processes and had to build expensive earth containers to hold it. Next door, the ski hill was complaining that it couldn't find enough water for its snowmaking machines. Stated this way, the solution is obvious: the ski hill should use the mine's excess water. But his management couldn't make that creative leap and McEwen had to work hard to convince them.

Says McEwen: "At the mine site, I said we should borrow a snow gun or two and make snow to deal with this water problem, and they looked at me as if I'd come off another planet. But I kept badgering them and six months later they got around to using a snow gun. A year or two later we had 12 snow guns operating and the industry was coming to us to learn how we used this method to control water balances."

What McEwen had done was employ Edward de Bono's creative method—lateral thinking—in which logic is applied to an ancillary premise created from a different perspective, which leads to a creative solution. Lateral thinking is just one example of creativity paradigms that are increasingly being used to solve problems in many forward-thinking organizations. For the most part, these paradigms can be grouped into four large techniques: restating the problem, generating ideas, transferring knowledge from other fields, and identifying combinations.

In turn, these creativity techniques, formerly the realm of outside consultants brought in to generate ideas, are now commonly used every day within organizations of all sizes and types. According to creativity consultants Diane Ritter and Michael Brassard, organized creativity involves

- consistently producing many ideas;
- putting existing or new ideas together in different combinations;
- breaking an idea down to take a fresh look at its parts;
- making connections between the topics at hand and seemingly unrelated facts, events or observations.[2]

The most popular tool for this process is brainstorming, where ideas are generated from group members in rapid succession without any judgment of their value or appropriateness.

TURN ON THE LIGHT BULB

Creativity is an essential ingredient. Create this kind of dynamic culture by encouraging individualism in the organization and by not dismissing uncommon solutions at first instance. While it is prudent to ask why no one else does it that way, it is shortsighted to rule out novel suggestions simply because they sound unusual.

With the Goldcorp Challenge, Rob McEwen steadfastly employed this toolkit. His use of the Internet was a classic case of transferring knowledge from other fields, as was the creation of a contest framework, which he borrowed from the marketing world. Uploading Goldcorp data on its mines for the entire world to see involved a restatement of the problem as well as a combination of technology, mass

---

2   Diane Ritter & Michael Brassard, *The Creativity Tools Memory Jogger: A Pocket Guide For Creative Thinking*, GOAL/QPC, 1998.

communications and science. Most of all, however, inviting the world to study its data and arrive at solutions was pure brainstorming, but on a scale that was breathtaking in its scope.

With the Goldcorp Challenge, McEwen first set out his problem for those within his company to brainstorm—what's the best way to find the gold we know is there? Then McEwen came up with the real "ah-ha" moment: why not ask the world to brainstorm an answer?

Says McEwen: "We had made the mines profitable, so we had money to do exploration. This produced results that showed there was a lot of gold there that hadn't been identified before. So, I said 'Let's have a brainstorming session, bring in everyone and I want to hear all the ideas that have been shot down before.' After two days, we had lots of ideas, and I thought we should make this bigger. I was wondering how we could do that and was down at MIT for a course on information technology and the light bulb went on. I thought, 'There's the format—we'll use the web to disseminate our geological data, which at that point was considered proprietary. We'll ask the rest of the world where we can find the next six million ounces of gold.'"

The change process is commonly seen as having three basic stages, drawn from seminal social psychologist Kurt Lewin's concept of dynamic stability. These stages, known as unfreezing, changing and refreezing, allow a change agent to think in terms of an orderly sequence of change. However, while this sequence view may be orderly, it can also constrain change in that it does not account for more transformative or unstable situations. For that reason, change agents also use other processes, such as comfort zone remodelling (comfort zone to stretch zone to panic zone and then the reverse); the transition process model of resistance to change (ending, neutrality, beginning)[3]; or the SARA (Shock, Anger, Resistance and Acceptance) model of cyclical emotions associated with change. As well, most change managers use all or some of the following four basic strategies when implementing change:

- **Rational–Empirical.** People are rational and will follow their self-interest—once it is revealed to them. Change is based on the communication of information and the proffering of incentives.

---

3   William Bridges, *Managing Transitions: Making the most of change*, Addison-Wesley Publishing, 1999.

- **Normative–Re-educative.** People are social beings and will adhere to cultural norms and values. Change is based on redefining and reinterpreting existing norms and values, and developing commitments to new ones.

- **Power–Coercive.** People are basically compliant and will generally do what they are told, or can be made to do so. Change is based on the exercise of authority and the imposition of sanctions.[4]

- **Environmental—Adaptive.** People oppose loss and disruption but they adapt readily to new circumstances. Change is based on building a new organization and gradually transferring people from the old one to the new one.[5]

> **OFFER YOUR HAND**
>
> Change is threatening, and few people have the fortitude to embrace it. Resistance and criticism will be inevitable. Don't fight the pressure or become overly defensive; it will only mobilize your detractors. Instead, offer your hand to those who will take it, both friend and foe, to guide them through the process.

Because the Goldcorp Challenge was such a radical departure from the norm, McEwen had to adapt many of the methods listed above in a unique way. The stakes were high and the time frame was short— McEwen was trying to find out quickly how to access the millions of ounces of gold he believed existed within the Red Lake mine. He persisted in the face of resistance in his own company, because he clearly understood the objective he was pursuing.

Says McEwen: "The problem with the Challenge was that it pushed people into a real zone of discomfort. Right before we launched, the geological staff came to me and said, 'We have real concerns; you're going to ask the rest of the world to tell you where we're going to find gold in our mine, and we think they're going to think we're really dumb and that you don't have any confidence in us.' I had to explain that it was quite the contrary, that I hired them because of their expertise,

---

4   W.G. Bennis, K. D. Bennis, R. Chin, *The Planning of Change*, Bennis, Rinehardt & Winston (London), 1961.

5   Fred Nickols, *Change Management: A Primer*, International Society of Performance Improvement, 1997.

they had done this to the best of their ability, had followed industry standards, and that there was nothing to hide from, to be afraid of."

McEwen also ran into resistance from the industry as a whole. He knew the path he thought it should take—applying modern communications technology to a narrowly focused industry—but few wanted to listen. Because of its colourful history of claim jumping, corporate theft and competition, the industry had developed a tradition of holding exploration results very close to the vest. By exposing himself to the world, McEwen faced censure from industry peers livid that he had gone against accepted processes. Peer condemnation, especially in a close-knit group, can be hard on the ego, and debilitating. But again McEwen persisted because he understood that what he was trying to achieve would concretely solve a problem plaguing the company. He would have to guide his peers and others along the path he had laid before them.

Says McEwen: "You can't worry about [the condemnation]; it has to be like water off a duck's back. You have a purpose and you have to follow it. Analysts thought it was some kind of children's game and mining people couldn't understand the reasoning behind it. There were also doubts on the web about whether we'd pay the prize money, because there were all sorts of schemes on the web. It didn't appeal to everybody. But it did appeal to a small group of innovators around the world who saw it, and joined in."

McEwen also had another objective for the contest, which was simply to restore outside confidence in his own industry. Not long before the Goldcorp Challenge, the Bre-X mining scandal in 1997 had forced the world to question the Canadian mining industry's integrity and ability. The purported gold find in Indonesia by Bre-X had turned out to be a spectacular fraud that hurt thousands of investors. Everyone's suspicions about the gold mining industry appeared to have been confirmed, and no one wanted to believe a word that came out of its collective mouth. In response, the industry in Canada closed ranks, ducked for cover, and everyone in it was quietly maintaining a very low profile until the heat and anger dissipated. Everyone except McEwen.

Says McEwen: "We were at the extreme end of the scale from Bre-X in terms of the richness of the ore body. But this wasn't a comfortable place to be sitting, given that the rest of the world thought that every Canadian mining company was a crook and a liar. So, by putting our data on the Internet, it exposed us to the scrutiny of the world, which was what I wanted. There were doubts about our deposit because of Bre-X but when we put the information out there, when people saw it, they went wow, look at this! Exposing what most people never expose gave us strength."

By exposing his data, McEwen may have convinced the world of the Red Lake mine's potential, but he had yet to convince the mine's employees. They were still involved in the strike, which had now gone on so long the workers had almost become comfortable in their resistance to his change initiatives. Indeed, they had had the luxury of being able to stay on the outside of them. But not for long. McEwen needed to implement.

Throughout the strike, McEwen had kept in touch with the union's headquarters. But he would not be moved from his position that, if the mine was to thrive and achieve its potential, decades-old practices had to change. He wanted to operate the mine—which employed two shifts of miners and shut down on weekends—24/7. He wanted to bring in better technology that would increase productivity. As an example, McEwen eventually created a virtual mining laboratory at the mine site where geologists could test and prove or disprove theories.

PLAY A LITTLE HARDBALL AND A LITTLE SOFTBALL

You're the one with the vision, so play hardball when you have to. But also know when to back off and give people the opportunity to absorb the changes laid out before them. A mix of sensitivity, maturity and grace will earn you a lot of points.

Says McEwen, "The strike was hard. My employees didn't like it, my management didn't like it, my directors didn't like it and my shareholders didn't like it. The industry didn't like it. While we were on strike, we didn't produce one ounce of gold, but instead put all our money into exploration and development. We tore down the old mine in front of the strikers' eyes and built a new one. We said, 'When we go back into production we'll only need a third of you. Furthermore, that third is going to need more training. Here's the new contract.' Right on the front page was the statement: *The purpose of this mine is to make money.* We told them that in order to make money we have to introduce new technology, new training and a new attitude of mutual responsibility toward safety and a bunch of other issues. If we make money, we can share it. We'll give stock options and bonuses, none of which had ever been done before."

After 46 months, McEwen got his contract, but not without some difficulty. At one time, someone took shots at his house—he replaced all his windows with bulletproof glass—and he received a death threat. But he responded with firmness. In a newspaper ad, he put a bounty on the person who had made the threat and brought in an investigative team to find the culprit. Although he was never found, McEwen's combined responses cooled the climate considerably.

McEwen also had to convince his management staff to stand firm. At one time, they were brainstorming what technology to bring in and the management advised that there was no point because the union would never go for it. McEwen resolutely showed them that the union had nothing to say about the matter: new technology simply had to be brought in. Then a financing deal fell through because the bank was worried about the atmosphere created by the strike. A sympathetic McEwen allowed it to back out of the deal. Six months later, he went back and got the deal, and at better terms.

But it was not all hardball, all the time. McEwen understood the strikers' positions and their fears about change. He spoke often to the workers, their families and the union management, always trying to maintain a rapport and always hammering home one message: the situation that had almost killed the mine had to change. Once, after speaking to a group of miners' wives, he wandered down the road to the mine site and visited with his staff on the picket lines. It was midnight and they were huddled around a fire. "I thought I'd see what people were thinking. For two hours we talked about plans, swatted mosquitoes and drank pop," he says. "It put them off balance, because in the normal process, if you're on strike, you don't have the head of the company talking to you on the line. But I thought the downside risk was small and maybe I'd learn something. And I did. It gave me a better idea of their position so I could talk more directly to them the next day."

Not many managers would brave the emotions of strikers who had been out of work for almost four years, but Rob McEwen wasn't like most managers. Although he recognized the need for process, it didn't rule his life. Neither did convention, habit or the view of his peers in the mining world. McEwen was a manager who didn't just think outside the box, he acted as if the box did not exist in the first place.

This belief that everything should be seen from a different point of view continued long after the Goldcorp Challenge, after employees had returned to work, after new technologies from outside the industry were adapted for use inside it, and after the now-efficient and focused company began clawing its way up the ladder of mining companies. It continued until 2004 when McEwen decided it was time for him to step down and let someone else take over. There are now, however, new issues on the horizon. Changing currency rates are affecting production costs and the problem of an aging workforce, which is going to require compensation through intense and creative capitalization efforts, weighs heavy on the future of the industry.

Late in 2004, after Goldcorp had vaulted to the big leagues of the mining industry, Rob McEwen announced that he was going to step away from his position as CEO and take on the less intensive role of Chairman. However, he said he would help form a succession plan to find a replacement to continue the change process that was now a recognized staple in the industry. Typically, his style was creative and it shocked his peers. As his last hurrah, Goldcorp took over Vancouver-based Wheaton River Minerals to form a top-tier mining empire with a market capitalization of about $5 billion.

The new CEO of the new Goldcorp would be Ian Telfer, the Wheaton River CEO who had been rocking the industry quite regularly himself through a series of deft and bold acquisition moves. Telfer also believed in the value of change, and his succession signalled to the mining world that Goldcorp had not grown comfortable and complacent. The merger hit a snag when another company, Glamis Gold, moved to swallow Goldcorp first, but McEwen and Telfer beat back the challenge. And they sent a clear message. . . .

This was only the seventh inning stretch.

5 THINGS YOU NEED TO KNOW

To undertake real and lasting change, a manager must institute a clear process that involves several crucial moves. Each alone is necessary, but only together are they sufficient. These include:

1. Take a Good Look Around

You can't fix what you don't understand. Before taking a business through radical, disruptive change, you must first get under the hood and intimately feel for the environment in which it operates. This requires not only a thorough knowledge of the usual metrics and insider know-how of the day-to-day affairs, but a deep, schooled understanding of its processes, thinking, norms and culture. Without this, the business will fragment under the inevitable pressures created by the change process.

2. Then Take a Good Look In the Mirror

Familiarity encourages complacency, and complacency encourages blindness. To be effective, change agents must step outside conventional thinking and view their surroundings from a different perspective. Constantly examining industry norms from first principles—and asking how, what and why is it done that way—will help identify which should be cast aside as having lost their usefulness.

3. Turn On the Light Bulb

Creativity is an essential ingredient. Create this kind of dynamic culture by encouraging individualism in the organization and by not dismissing uncommon solutions at first instance. While it is prudent to ask why no one else does it that way, it is shortsighted to rule out novel suggestions simply because they sound unusual.

4. Offer Your Hand

Change is threatening, and few people have the fortitude to embrace it. Resistance and criticism will be inevitable. Don't fight the pressure or become overly defensive; it will only mobilize your detractors. Instead, offer your hand to those who will take it, both friend and foe, to guide them through the process.

5. Play a Little Hardball and a Little Softball

You're the one with the vision, so play hardball when you have to. But also know when to back off and give people the opportunity to absorb the changes laid out before them. A mix of sensitivity, maturity and grace will earn you a lot of points.

CHAPTER FOURTEEN

Speed Thrills

Growth from Zero to a Billion

FEATURING THE WISDOM OF CRAIG DOBBIN

Almost 20 years ago, self-educated Newfoundland entrepreneur Craig Dobbin stitched together CHC Corp. out of a handful of Canadian helicopter operations, including one he'd founded in the 1970s called Sealand Helicopters. Since taking CHC public in 1987, Dobbin has expanded with such velocity that he's now nearing the billion-dollar club. Built through acquisition and internal growth, CHC has emerged from a small regional player to the world leader in helicopter services for the offshore oil and gas industry.

Speed has defined the CHC story from day one—from the powerful helicopters that are the essence of the company to Dobbin himself, a colourful businessman whose speech is laced with simple axioms, including one that best captures his business approach: "Time is the enemy."

His track record reflects that. He has propelled CHC to $1.5 billion in assets, $734 million in sales, and profits of $64 million in 2004. Clients are world heavyweights: BP, Exxon Mobil and ConocoPhillips. CHC has 3,500 employees around the world and owns or controls 400 choppers operating in 30 countries. It trades on the TSE and became the first Atlantic Canadian firm to achieve a listing on the New York Stock Exchange.

It's been a wild race that has not been without missteps. But Dobbin has no intention of coming down for a landing anytime soon. In a radical move, he transferred his St. John's headquarters to expansive new digs in Vancouver, where most of his administrative staff are based, to better position the company. He wants to double CHC's asset size and aims to take the firm *in new directions at a pace "ten percent faster than the speed limit." If it can keep up its current trajectory, the company will soon surpass $1 billion in annual revenues. (Perhaps by the time you are reading this.)*

Is this entrepreneurial moxie or astute corporate maxim? Speed can thrill; but it can also be deadly. Too much done too fast can have devastating results. Consistently, however, this entrepreneur from the Rock has managed to keep CHC perched in the clouds.

—₥—

Update: We regret to announce that Craig Dobbin passed away in 2006 in Beachy Cove, Newfoundland, after a brief illness. Craig launched CHC in 1977 and helped transform the company into the largest helicopter service provider in the world.

The urge to grow a business is almost primitive in today's bigger-is-better economy. Grow or die is a mantra recited by managers at all levels of enterprise. Corporate habits are mimicking our dietary regimes—an obsessive culture of more.

Growth becomes a defence mechanism; many companies feel they have no choice. Survival in a global economy where large competitors often crush pint-sized players can require bulking up until you're in their weight class. Also, the lure of growth can be enticing—empire building can provide an ego rush (witness Donald Trump)—and the desire to see your name in headlines as the leader of a fast-growing business is hard to resist.

Typically, the urge to grow is purely financial. Ownership of growth stocks can seduce with promises of big gains. The value of an enterprise—and the net worth of its owners—can rocket up if expansion goes well. It's far more satisfying and lucrative in the long run to manage a billion-dollar company than a million-dollar one. (Many experienced entrepreneurs would say both require the same amount of effort.)

Usually those who are in expansion mode also want to do it quickly. Company lives are shortening in this hurry-up entrepreneurial world, and the traditional growth path—steadily increasing profit margins—has become only one of several paths to accession. Entrepreneurs now often name not just growth, but speed, as their number one mandate.

"Rapid growth is an attitude," explains author Michael McGrath. "[It is] an ambitious vision for growth that is transformed into a growth strategy. Rapid-growth companies make a commitment to grow and have a deliberate proactive process to make sure they do so. The primary [rationale] is that accelerating revenue growth is more important than increasing profit margins since the assumption is that eventually a larger company will generate more profit than a smaller one. A rapidly growing company will be able to take advantage of more opportunities in the new economy, making it stronger and better positioned for the future."[1]

But, as alluring as it seems, fast growth can be both a drug and an Achilles heel. Sure, it's intoxicating for owners and managers to boast regular increased revenues, rising profits, market domination and fawning media profiles about their success. However, expansion, improperly managed, can lead companies to suffer from what legendary management expert Peter Drucker calls a "massive growth hangover."

Drucker uses the term to describe historic periods in the corporate world—such as the 1950s and 1960s—when the common belief was that everything had to grow, and that there was no semblance of a satiation point. However, "nothing can grow forever, let alone at an exponential rate," he says.[2]

Because of that, management experts share a single overarching rule for a growth company that wants to proceed rapidly: the business must have a well-articulated strategy in place to achieve its goal. Companies can't just grow for the sake of growth and expect things to go smoothly.

As a company expands, hiring quickly dominates the operational landscape. If it grows too quickly, then it may face a significant human resource dilemma. As the U.S. government's Small Business Administration noted: "[Suddenly] you are understaffed and [must] hire in a hurry. You hire people who are not properly screened and trained. Or maybe the employees that you've had in the past just aren't cut out for the 'new' business, and they need to be replaced."[3] Either way, while a hasty pace is beneficial in some ways, it often begets an inheritance of problems.

Another strategy—growth by acquisition—presents its own unique challenges, among them the need for a clearly defined rationale. Many

---

1   Michael McGrath, *Product Strategy for High-Technology Companies*, McGraw-Hill, 2000.
2   Peter F. Drucker, *Managing in Turbulent Times*, Harper & Row, 1980.
3   Online Women's Business Center, U.S. Small Business Administration, www.onlinewbc.gov/.

growth-by-acquisition plans are really just versions of the traditional profit growth model, in that they are done merely to inflate revenues. A company with $50 million in revenues buys one with $10 million so it can boost its top line to $60 million. Acquisition, however, should be part of a leveraging strategy that adds rocket fuel to the tank.

"Many rapidly growing companies like Cisco Systems have followed the acquisition highway to growth," explains McGrath. "The acquisition itself is actually the trigger to pursue an opportunity. When an acquisition is used to grow revenue for both companies by expanding into a new or related market, it's more like adding five and one to get ten (instead of five and one to get six)! Driving the acquisition highway to growth can be powerful, but it must be a deliberate, integrated strategy, not just opportunistic. The strategic direction requires absolute commitment."[4]

Also, integration issues can sometimes create cultural gulfs separating the acquirer from the entity being purchased. In that case, "the organization must … proactively address the cultural issues that might impede the challenges that are necessary to nurture strong growth," says business writer Joanne Sammer.[5]

Experts also point out that zooming along with growth ambitions too quickly can raise problems of undercapitalization. A company on the fast track can suddenly be deluged with customer orders—products to ship, services to provide—and it may not have the capacity to fulfill its own prophecy. The fallout can be chilling. Advisors suggest that unmanaged or mismanaged growth can lead to customer dissatisfaction, unfulfilled projects that produce no revenue, and expenses that exceed cash flows or available financing. Unmanaged growth can be as quick a path to bankruptcy as operational failure from the outset.

Many companies that began as small entrepreneurial operations face another challenge when they decide to go public to finance further expansion. This can be an enormous transition, especially for a one-man show that started off with no knowledge about securities regulations, shareholder meetings or public financial reporting. A listed company is suddenly no longer the entrepreneur's personal fief, or that of his family and friends. The founder must now play by someone else's rules (those of the regulators), do so in the harsh light of the public eye, and face many new layers of accountability: to shareholders, analysts, stock

---

4   Michael McGrath, *Product Strategy for High-Technology Companies*, McGraw-Hill, 2000.
5   Joanne Sammer, More, Please!, *Business Finance*, July, 2000.

exchanges and the media. The pressure to adjust can be tremendous. In fact, being a reporting issuer doubles the burden on the entrepreneur, as he or she is now effectively running two businesses: the actual operations, and the business of running a public company.

Newfoundland entrepreneur Craig Laurence Dobbin faced many of these issues as he undertook a rocket ride of growth that now has him operating the world's largest helicopter provider to the offshore energy business. Started as a side business to his other entrepreneurial pursuits in the early 1980s, Dobbin's CHC Helicopters now has assets of $1.5 billion, generated sales of $734 million in fiscal 2004, and showed a profit of $64 million. CHC's main business is providing helicopter transport for the offshore oil and gas industry, although it also does air ambulance, search and rescue and repair work. The company now operates in 30 countries and has 3,400 employees.

Not bad for the son of a truck driver with a very large family to feed. Dobbin, one of 11 children, grew up in rural Newfoundland, where he finished high school but never went to university. His entrepreneurial personality initially was manifested in real estate projects in Eastern Canada. Before getting into the helicopter business, he had a short stint working at his father's lumber company, followed by some time in the trucking business and in underwater salvage operations. Subsequently, he set up Omega Investments to hold commercial real estate properties, which it still does today.

Dobbin admits his humble roots left him with a certain insecurity and hunger to leave an impression. "[It] contributed to the point where you have to make a mark," he says. "You've really got to want, not in a thin or fragile way. You've got to want with your guts."

This yearning to leave a legacy is a classic entrepreneurial characteristic that, when combined with other native traits, often ignites their drive. According to researchers, most successful entrepreneurs show five psychological factors to varying degrees:

- *Independence.* Successful entrepreneurs have a strong internal need to be self-reliant. This is often driven by a low tolerance for rules, established social norms and predefined structure.

- *Risk tolerance.* An entrepreneur must also have a strong ability to tolerate risk. This is manifested by an individual's comfort, or discomfort, with taking the initiative, by his or her ability to overcome setbacks and by challenging or changing a predefined structure.

- *Achievement.* A strong need to achieve lies in an individual's subconscious desire to excel by individual actions. Entrepreneurs with large doses of this trait set challenging goals for themselves and take personal responsibility for accomplishing them.

- *A need for social power (also called power motivation).* This is a subconscious concern for acquiring status and having an impact on others. It is necessary because it pushes entrepreneurs to engage in socially influential behaviour, which is mandatory for effective leadership.

- *A need for moral authority.* The high need for moral authority is the moderating characteristic that channels the high need for social influence in a positive direction. The result is leaders who are altruistic, group-focused and ethical, and behaviour that promotes employee trust, respect and commitment to the leader's vision. [6]

Company builders also exhibit specific leadership styles, according to Ivey Business School professor John Eggars. "What growth-oriented entrepreneurs do and how they act is also important," he says. "Essentially, they upset the status quo, disrupt the accepted ways of doing things and alter traditional patterns. As they exert social influence, they also display a series of leadership skills that enhance their own chance of success. Those skills include creating and managing change, building effective organizations, serving as resource architects, and marketing and selling like entrepreneurs. Furthermore, the skills are found in a cluster of leadership types variously referred to as: charismatic, transformational or visionary."[7]

Dobbin is all three. He's a born storyteller who favours the use of plain metaphors to illustrate complex business principles. He's decisive. He's confident. For example, he doesn't believe in chance (paradoxical, considering one widely accepted definition of an entrepreneur: a lightning rod for risks).

"There is no risk," he insists. "If you're an entrepreneur, you believe you're infallible. You really believe in what you're doing. If

---

6   John H. Eggars, Developing Entrepreneurial Growth, *Ivey Business Journal,* 5/1/1999.
7   Ibid.

you have failures, you put them behind you. You clean up as quickly as possible and get on with it."

Over more than 20 years, Dobbin has grown CHC Helicopters primarily through acquisition, continually snapping up companies around the world and far from CHC's original Newfoundland home base. He bet on the offshore oil and gas industry as it boomed around the world. CHC's growth trajectory has been a heady ride that soared and swooped as much as some of Dobbin's choppers.

Unlike most successful entrepreneurs, however, Dobbin did not have a master plan all along. But his expressed dislike of "dawdling" indicates he did have goals and a direction. It wasn't until later in CHC's life that it became clear Dobbin was on a high-speed growth path. At first, however, his rise began in the usual way—organically.

"I never planned to own a helicopter, let alone establish the world's biggest helicopter company," he admitted in his 2000 convocation address to Newfoundland's Memorial University graduating class. Instead, Dobbin got into the business almost by accident. Flush with a little money from his real estate holdings, all he wanted to do was enjoy himself. Like many Newfoundlanders, he liked to go fly fishing once in a while. And he liked to do it in Labrador. So he took $85,000 in extra money from his real estate company and bought himself a used helicopter in 1977 to get himself to prime fly fishing country more quickly.

But the chopper cost almost as much to maintain and operate annually as it cost in the first place, so Dobbin did what would later become a signature of his business style: he turned an expense into an opportunity. First he chartered out his "expensive toy" to cover some of his costs. Then he bought a handful of other helicopters, financing them with real estate projects he was involved in, and with the extra inventory, launched a company called Sealand Helicopters.

Cannily, he figured out how to make the new acquisitions pay off—to turn what was essentially a consumption item into an investment—by creating an asset that could work for him. He used his fleet of light helicopters for firefighting, ferrying around VIPs, and the like. Then it struck him: the same skill sets his pilots needed to fly small helicopters could be used to fly medium and large ones. But the bigger machines would generate far more revenue—up to $6 million a year, compared to $100,000 annually he was earning from the small ones.

Dobbin's bright idea is an example of the genesis of many entre-preneurial ventures. The entrepreneur invariably gets a spark and evaluates it to see if it presents a business opportunity. Not all ideas do, but that's all right because most entrepreneurs have plenty more where that came from. What they don't always have, at that particular moment, is the right opportunity to allow their current ideas to take root and thrive. That's why entrepreneurs are constantly looking for and evaluating opportunities: it's part of their mental makeup.

When he moved into helicopters, Dobbin began down a path that is also common among nimble opportunity-seekers—the passion quickly turns into a significant going concern. What started as a side business set up to pay for a toy within a few years became his central focus. By 1981, Sealand was operating throughout Eastern Canada. Then, dur-ing the rest of the 1980s, Dobbin began his expansion through acquisi-tion: he bought up competitors and their contracts, including Toronto and Okanagan Helicopters.

SHOP SO YOU DON'T DROP

If you want to dominate a sector, you'd better make acquisitions a key part of your strategy. Do your strategic spending, not in the boom times, but when the chips are down. It sounds counter-intuitive, but making a purchase when you're struggling is one way to dilute the original problem.

The Okanagan purchase was an illustration of another Dobbin belief: When times get tough, the tough go shopping. At the time of purchase in 1986, both Sealand and Okanagan were struggling be-cause they were competing head to head to supply helicopter services in Canada and had begun to engage in a price war, undercutting each other on bids.

In an industry where there is no dominant player, this is usually a race to the bottom which none of the participants can win because it often results in costs surpassing margins—a battle that only a company with deep pockets can survive. And neither Sealand nor Dobbin had deep pockets. Most companies would retreat before they were fatally wounded, but Dobbin activated this cardinal rule instead: when your company is struggling, you "go out and buy something and dilute the problem."

While this might imply that Dobbin shops as some kind of short-term therapy, it's really more strategic than that. In the case of Okanagan, he gobbled up a competitor and stopped the bidding war that was cutting into his own bottom line. In addition, he added Okanagan's revenue to his own top line. Furthermore, he believes, by buying something when you're in a weakened position, you shore up your expansion strategy instead of retreating from it. "You're looking out, rather than in," is the way he describes it. At first, it seems to be a counterintuitive strategy. But it really speaks to the essence of entrepreneurship—an almost blind belief that you will succeed.

Also, in the fragmented helicopter services industry of several decades ago, consolidation made sense. By snapping up Okanagan Helicopters, Toronto Helicopters, and later, British International Helicopters, Dobbin mushroomed his company from a bit player to one of the world's three largest firms.

It was an acquisition strategy that was top of mind for CHC for more than a decade. In 1987, Dobbin bought out his last major Canadian rival, Quebec-based Viking Helicopters, and CHC was born. The next watershed year was 1999, when CHC purchased control of Helicopter Services Group ASA of Norway and tripled in size. Then in February 2004, CHC acquired Dutch-based Schreiner Aviation Group, securing its status as the largest provider of helicopter transport services on the planet.

This shop-till-you-drop management principle isn't for everyone, especially those who can't keep a careful eye on their debt ratios. Some companies that rely on M&A strategies when they're not in a financial position to do so suffer the consequences. Witness Campeau Corp., a Canadian company that, in 1988, used a $6.2-billion leveraged buyout (LBO) to swallow up American retail jewel Federated Department Stores (owner of Bloomingdale's, Filene's and others). Two years after the feast, Federated filed for bankruptcy protection. Other companies in the heady LBO era of the 1980s, when companies financed huge acquisitions with debt, also ended up spinning off parts of newly purchased companies to pay down the debt they acquired to do so. Among them was Quebec grocery icon Steinberg Inc.

GROW WITH WHAT YOU KNOW

Too many companies think successful growth entails veering off from the original flight path—that if they can manage one sector, they can manage anything. Some succeed, but many learn that they should stick with what they know. If you're a helicopter expert who wants to expand, buy more choppers. Don't open a chain of grocery stores.

Diversification, once the trendiest of business concepts, has not been a mantra at CHC. Dobbin ensures the company does not veer off into different directions when it looks at potential targets. It buys helicopter companies and, in doing so, creates efficiencies. It can buy around the world and still land a local contract, because it has expertise on the ground in a particular market. Its local experts know and understand the local business culture. "Because it's such a small [sector], I can get decent people who are steeped in this industry," explains Dobbin.

After he consolidated the Canadian helicopter industry, it was time for his biggest transition—the one that would position CHC for global growth. CHC went public in 1987 for $10 a share and raised $47 million. Dobbin says the IPO began a process that has helped his company avoid the undercapitalization problem that plagues growth companies, and he has been conscious of avoiding that scenario ever since. Continually, he has skirted capital issues by using the public markets instead of piling on excess debt. Several years ago, for instance, he took his North American helicopter maintenance organization public to raise cash, when most companies would have gone to the debt markets for the money.

Of course, capitalization through the public markets can also have a serious downside—you're dependent on investors to keep your stock liquid and its price high so you can replenish your cash resources as needed, at non-dilutive valuations. Maintaining investor interest is one reason many growth companies continually expand their markets between acquisitions. Not only do they have to feed the hungry investor, they have to continue feeding their own hungry monster—the need to expand. If there isn't any other company to feed on, the food supply has to come from market expansion.

"A stronger competitive position can sometimes be a highway to growth," explains McGrath. "In a rapidly growing market, a winning and sustainable vector of differentiation will provide [this] highway."[8] But market expansion doesn't mean veering off into new directions completely. It may make far more sense to grab market share in an environment you already know than to try to gain access to foreign territory.

Dobbin was able to avoid this often frantic and destructive hunt for new markets because his own native market was proliferating. With new enabling technology, offshore oil expansion boomed—particularly through the Hibernia project off the Newfoundland coast, and in the North Sea off Britain—so CHC's share of the business expanded considerably along with it.

Of course, Dobbin's building process was not without its failures. Like any entrepreneur, he has had his share of fiascos and disappointments. But an important factor in his success has been his tolerance for them. Failures didn't fell him; they made him more resolute. For example, when the Canadian government announced the Hibernia oil project, Dobbin jumped on the news and invested heavily in anticipation of it. He assembled an expensive fleet of helicopters, supply boats and some 20 engineers. But the project was delayed because of political wrangling. So, true to form, Dobbin followed his own advice and looked forward, not back. If Hibernia wasn't going to work for him he'd look elsewhere. He turned his business sights to the North Sea oil fields where he could serve the offshore oilrigs that were sprouting off the coast of Scotland.

The decision was a major factor in CHC's expansion into a world leader in servicing the oil industry. It allowed CHC to continue its growth trajectory—but in this case, through traditional methods. It grew with what it knew. This is a common, and prudent, tactic with growth companies that can't be buying all the time, argue many experts. In fact, it is not unusual for rapidly growing companies to employ both acquisition and expansion strategies in tandem.

It is also common for them to recognize that sometimes you just have to sit back and let all your food digest. As Drucker said, nothing grows continually and the prudent company every so often has to stop and look around itself. This is especially true for entrepreneurial firms

---

8   Michael McGrath, Product Strategy for High-Technology Companies, McGraw-Hill, 2000.

that have reached a significant size and market presence. Among other things, such a company needs to monitor finances to ensure it's not spinning out of control into the hands of creditors; it might have to make strategic changes based on its new, broader scope.

RELAX, DIGEST AND ENJOY THE MEAL

Don't grow wildly just to inflate your top line. Stop every so often; assess where growth has taken the company, and where it's headed. Enjoy the ride. This is especially necessary for entrepreneurial firms that have reached a significant size and market presence. Reflection is a lost art among many executives today—the gear is always in overdrive. Take time to experience neutral and park.

By the turn of the century, CHC, vast in size and geographic scope, dominating its market and many times its original size, had to stop and do a rethink. In particular, it needed to examine its management practices. After his last acquisition, Dobbin consciously put a halt to further purchases until he properly integrated the European concern into CHC. Also, he paused to take the financial pulse of his new company. To that end, Dobbin has ensured processes are in place that allow for daily monitoring of key financial indicators such as debt to cash flow ratios.

Taking stock also means adapting to the day's business currents, especially if you're publicly listed. Dobbin, however, has had experience with this and knows how to tackle it head on. Several years ago, when horror stories of corporate corruption made headlines, the Toronto Stock Exchange began introducing new corporate governance rules. The topic became a big part of CHC's 2002 annual meeting, complete with questions regarding a stock options plan shareholders felt was overly generous. (The plan passed but Dobbin refrained from exercising his 62-percent vote.)

In response to the corporate governance issue, Dobbin made moves to open up the cozy club that was his board of directors. He got rid of five directors who were friends and replaced them with eminent Canadian businesspeople such as former Canadian Pacific CEO William Stinson; C.D. Howe President Jack Mintz; American businessman George Gillett, who owns the Montreal Canadiens hockey club; former American Airlines CEO Don Carty; and Quebec businesswoman and corporate governance specialist Guylaine Saucier. One son, Mark, left the board, while another son, Craig Jr., remains a director. These changes reflected Dobbin's willingness to adapt.

> **WATCH YOUR WEIGHT**
>
> Even as it grows far beyond the scope of the individual who created it, a small company that could once nimbly expand must not become overly bureaucratic and bloated. It must keep its entrepreneurial culture or risk becoming so burdened in red tape—including further expansion—nothing gets done. Evolution in physical size does not require the numbing of the entrepreneurial spirit that built the company in the first place.

Assessment also means recognizing that after years of expansion, a company is no longer the entrepreneurial adolescent it once was. It has become transformed by expansion into a large global entity. While some companies get into trouble by thinking they can grow forever, others merely sputter out into time-consuming bureaucracy and operational wrangling. Often with these companies, many of the acquired assets are eventually sold off. But unlike with other businesses that have developed so much they need to divest themselves of assets, Dobbin rarely lets go of anything he's accumulated. It's part of the entrepreneurial mindset, he explains, and that never leaves him, even though he's now distanced himself somewhat from the business to scout out deals.

"I'm very reluctant to sell anything," he says, perhaps harkening back to his impoverished boyhood. "There's some kind of security that's innate [in owning something]."

Despite CHC's large size, Dobbin vows to keep it unencumbered by excess managerial bloat. He dislikes flabbiness, needless lines of authority and excessive structure. His decision to move CHC's headquarters to Vancouver in 2004 was precipitated by this desire to keep the operation trim. The radical move from the company's home on the Rock was designed to reduce costs and centralize functions such as marketing. "There's not a lot of bureaucracy [at CHC]," Dobbin explains. "The strategies that we employ come out pretty fast. They don't filter down to the third and second floor trying to make its way to the lobby. When I ask for something, anything, I get it immediately."

BE THE LOWEST COMMON DENOMINATOR

You won't be the centre of the company's universe forever. As your company grows, you'll have to hire outside management. They will likely know a lot more than you in their specialized areas, such as human resources, marketing and finance. Ensuring executive hires are the best in their fields will help take the company to new heights. Always retain people that are smarter than you. Don't let ego get in the way of having yourself surrounded by the best.

But even an entrepreneur like Dobbin recognizes that CHC is not the entrepreneurial company it once was and is now more of an operating entity. So, after he realized CHC had pole position in the market, Dobbin made a major strategic change. He transferred the day-to-day operations to expert managers, eventually replacing himself as CEO. In late 2004 Sylvain Allard, a former helicopter pilot and MBA who has been with Dobbin for 22 years (including the past several years as president), was named to the top post. Dobbin continues as Executive Chairman.

Hiring the best and giving them their space are two business principles Dobbin believes in passionately. He knows that while entrepreneurs are very good at some things, they're not good at everything. And so he looks for in others what he knows isn't in his fabric. For example, he's almost proud he's a dealmaker instead of a details-oriented manager. As he told a group of students, "I never had a desk in 25 years; I never opened my mail or wrote a cheque."

This self-recognition allows Dobbin to acknowledge that others are better suited than he is to running a billion-dollar global entity. "Mercifully, I haven't got the ability to run a company operationally," he says, only perhaps jokingly. Success, he adds, comes from having "good people around me to operate these companies that sometimes I get my stupid nose into."

Dobbin has stepped so far back from operations he now refers to himself as an "employee" rather than an owner (although an employee with a healthy net worth, several houses across North America and friends such as the first President Bush).

"I'm not an expert in anything," he once said. "I subscribe to one business belief—whatever the job, whatever the challenge, somebody out there can do it better than I can. I don't get threatened by people who are better. True entrepreneurs surround themselves with professional managers that share their vision and put form around it. Not only can you not do it all by yourself, but it's not necessary and it doesn't make sense. I believe in being a good casting director of people who work together and share together."

Sometimes it can be exceedingly difficult for someone who gave birth to a business—and who projects an image of running it in a back-of-the-napkin fashion—to cede a measure of decision making to outsiders. But not for Dobbin. As fits a company of its magnitude, CHC is full of highly competent management that were sourced from around the globe. Dobbin says hiving off managerial duties to others allows him to concentrate on his true love, deal making, which, after so many years of building CHC, has helped him maintain his entrepreneurial zeal. Now, as he approaches age 70, Dobbin still has entrepreneurial ambitions befitting a younger man.

He wants to grow CHC's asset size to about $3 billion. He plans to continue to expand the company internally and through acquisitions, the latter in the repair and overhaul sector. He'll integrate operations at his new Vancouver headquarters, a process he hopes will save the company millions of dollars. He'll seize opportunities in search and rescue, because much of the world's military is abandoning those functions.

"We just hit our first $1-billion market capitalization, and I want to make it a $2-billion, $3-billion and a $4-billion company," he enthused in an interview in late 2004.[9]

This kind of moxie embodies Craig Dobbin who, more than 30 years ago, while doing some commercial diving in St. John's Harbour ("tantamount to being in a cesspool," he recalls) had his gear malfunction. He was dragged out of the muck, blue from lack of oxygen and so weak that helpers had to cut off his wetsuit.

Dobbin stared death down at the bottom of the harbour's filthy, cold water. While he was down there, he thought about his choices. He could perish, or he could rise quickly to the top.

He chose the latter, pushed his way to the surface, went to church, had a few beers with his buddies . . . and went back to work the next morning.

---

9   Gordon Pitts, "Onwards and Upwards," *Globe and Mail*, 12/24/2004.

5 THINGS YOU NEED TO KNOW

Craig Dobbin believes there are several ways to expand a business while avoiding the potential crash and burn:

1. Shop So You Don't Drop

If you want to dominate a sector, you'd better make acquisitions a key part of your strategy. Make your strategic spends not in the boom times, but when the chips are down. It sounds counterintuitive, but making a purchase when you're struggling is one way to dilute the original problem.

2. Grow with What You Know

Too many companies think successful growth entails veering off from the original flight path—that if they can manage one sector, they can manage anything. Some succeed, but many learn that they should stick with what they know. If you're a helicopter expert who wants to expand, buy more choppers. Don't open a chain of grocery stores.

3. Relax, Digest and Enjoy the Meal

Don't grow wildly just to inflate your top line. Stop every so often; assess where growth has taken the company, and where it's headed. Enjoy the ride. This is especially necessary for entrepreneurial firms that have reached a significant size and market presence. Reflection is a lost art among many executives today—the gear is always in overdrive. Take time to experience neutral and park.

4. Watch Your Weight

Even as it grows far beyond the scope of the individual who created it, a small company that could once nimbly expand must not become overly bureaucratic and bloated. It must keep its entrepreneurial culture or risk becoming so burdened in red tape—including further expansion—nothing gets done. Evolution in physical size does not require the numbing of the entrepreneurial spirit that built the company in the first place.

5. Be the Lowest Common Denominator

You won't be the centre of the company's universe forever. As your company grows, you'll have to hire outside management. They will likely know a lot more than you in their specialized areas, such as human resources, marketing and finance. Ensuring executive hires are the best in their fields will help take the company to new heights. Always retain people that are smarter than you. Don't let ego get in the way of having yourself surrounded by the best.

CHAPTER FIFTEEN

How to Sell Your Company Without Really Trying

And Do It in One Week

FEATURING THE WISDOM OF LESLIE DAN

Leslie Dan, a Holocaust survivor and post-war immigrant to Canada from Hungary, worked as a logger, tobacco picker and cocktail waiter to pay his way through school. A true entrepreneur, while interning at a pharmacy in Toronto he started the first of what would become a series of solid companies. Ten years later, in 1965, he founded Novopharm Ltd. Its first product was a generic version of the antibiotic drug tetracycline. The company had first-year sales of Cdn$165,000 and by 1999, it had become a generic-drug powerhouse with revenues of US$383 million and 3,000 employees worldwide.

In 2000, Dan sold Novopharm to the world's largest producer of generic drugs, Teva Pharmaceuticals of Israel, for US$262 million in stock. Dan, now 74, continues to be a director of Teva, as well as serving on the boards of Draxis Pharma and Viventia Biotech Inc.

Dan did not initially build his company with a view toward an exit. It was built with an old-fashioned purpose—to earn a living. However, from the very beginning, he shrewdly laid the foundations for a lucrative sale that both met his personal goals and provided for the orderly succession of his business.

—⁂—

Update: The Leslie L. Dan Pharmacy Building at the University of Toronto, designed by Sir Norman Foster, was completed in 2006. Dan continues his philanthropic works, most recently co-sponsoring the building of a three-storey museum with actors Kirk and Michael Douglas. The museum, located opposite the Western Wall in Jerusalem, will focus on celebrating the history and accomplishments of the Jewish people.

In the path of every entrepreneur who has ever built a business, a decision inevitably comes. While the legal definition of a corporation is that it is a unique person in its own right, that is clearly a misnomer. A corporation may be a separate living thing in law, but the blood that keeps it alive is the people that run it. Eventually, a decision must be made as to how that legacy continues. Management must seriously examine how to pass on the torch to another generation.

Today, this very issue is facing thousands of business owners as the North American population rapidly ages. Since 55 has become the *de facto* age when most people begin to think of pulling back, some 80 million North Americans are nearing the traditional end of their working lives. As many of those who belong to this generational bracket are also entrepreneurs or small-business people, the orderly transfer of control is becoming as common an issue as the day-to-day running of a business itself. Business succession, a subject that until recently was of most concern to accountants, financial planners and merger and acquisition specialists, is increasingly becoming a top-of-mind issue for most executives.

If this is the case, trouble looms for many of these entrepreneurs. Too often businesses fail to plan for succession and, as a result, either don't survive the loss of a founder or fail to provide him/her full value for a life's work. Succession issues have an enormous impact on a business owner who has spent years, likely decades, building a venture. Many years of coddling create intense emotional bonds between the entrepreneur, the company and the various members of his or her family. Perhaps that is why many surveys report that most owner-operated firms are woefully unprepared for life events such as death, disability or retirement that may require the individual to divest quickly from his/her company.

This lack of preparation, or a corporate "will," is not simply an oversight on the part of the owner-operator. It is often an expression of fear—of loss of control, the inevitability of time, the loss of emotional involvement, or the extinguishing of a life's purpose. A business can be very much like a child to the founder who launched, nurtured and struggled with it during the difficult years and watched it grow to maturity. The prospect of that child fleeing the nest is often unbearable.

For those executives nearing retirement age, this lack of planning can also be an expression of defiance against the inevitability of aging, of the need to be replaced. It can be very hard on someone who has headed a company for many years, and provided a living for his or her family and the families of employees, to be forced to face the fact that soon he/she may no longer have the right stuff. Whether the owner has family to pass the business on to or not, the usual response to this feeling is evasion, a hope that it will all just go away. It doesn't, you will either be ready or you won't.

Business owners pondering how to transfer themselves out of their companies have several options. Each angle has its pros and cons and must be examined for probability and achievability (How likely is it that it can be implemented?); appropriateness to the company (Will the company survive the switch?); and for the entrepreneur's personal objectives (Does he/she want to cash out completely, decrease involvement gradually or accept liquidation of his investment over time?). The spectrum of alternatives is typically:

1. Transferring control of the business to one or more of their children, or

2. Transferring day-to-day control to the existing management team, or

3. Bringing in new management to help run the operations while the owner pulls back and takes on more of an oversight role (a temporary solution that does not deal with the ultimate succession issue), or

4. Selling the company and cashing in on the equity built up in the business.

Increasing numbers of individuals, faced with a lack of family interest, are choosing the last of the four options—an outright sale. A survey of 300 large U.S. businesses that had been sold or transferred showed that, among the respondents, the average owner had held the business for 22 years, and the average length of time for a sale process was 11.4 months.[1]

This is the classic small to mid-size company scenario, in which the company's owner probably bought or started the business during late youth and grew it during his or her adult years. At this stage, the owner has usually reaped many of the financial and other rewards and is ready to either slow down, or, as is happening more often, exit the company completely. But if he/she chooses this last option, a process begins that is far more complicated and difficult than that of the other three options. The successful sale of a company usually involves an extremely intricate—and often prolonged—mating dance between buyer and seller.

Someone who has seen this courtship from both sides of the ballroom is Leslie Dan, a post-war refugee from Hungary who survived the Holocaust as a child and spent 35 years building his generic drug manufacturing company, Novopharm, before he sold it in 2000 to the world's largest producer of generic drugs, Teva Pharmaceuticals of Israel, for US$262 million in stock. While such sales can often take six months to a year from initial discussion to closing, Dan wrapped up the sale of Novopharm in a week. While he never planned to sell when he started out, he always operated his company as if that were an eventuality. When the dance started, he was ready.

Clever, painfully shy, and schooled by his experiences during the war, Dan arrived in Canada in 1947 as a 17-year-old. He quickly learned English, completed high school in Toronto, and then worked as a logger, a tobacco farm worker and a cocktail waiter to put himself through pharmacy school. An entrepreneur to the core, Dan wanted to start a pharmacy manufacturing business when he graduated in 1954, but had saved only $500. So he went to work as a pharmacy intern during the day, while attending Masters of Business Administration classes at night.

The next year, he opened International Pharmacy, a company that arranged for the translation and shipment of foreign prescriptions. A true "garage startup," operating in the back room of a drug store, the company was soon filling 20,000 prescriptions a year and continued to serve Canadians for more than 16 years. Five years later, in 1960, Dan established Interpharm Ltd. to introduce Calmex

---

1. Survey of Business Owners Sheds Light on Succession Challenges, PricewaterhouseCoopers, *Business Wire*, 1999.

as a replacement for the tranquillizer meprobamate, which had been changed from an over-the-counter product to one requiring a prescription. In 1965, recognizing that the industry was changing and the need for affordable pharmaceuticals was on the rise, Dan rented a small warehouse and formed Novopharm to produce generic drugs to cater to the demand.

From its beginnings, when first year sales were roughly $165,000, Novopharm continually grew and expanded. By 1979, it had grown to 230 employees and included a new manufacturing facility and a nearby penicillin plant. In the 1980s, it expanded into the Canadian hospital and U.S. pharmaceutical markets. In 1985, Dan created CAN-MAP, an organization that donated Novopharm drugs to Third World countries. Dan considers CAN-MAP, which to date has donated almost $30 million in pharmaceuticals, to be one of his greatest life achievements.

On its twenty-fifth anniversary in 1990, Novopharm began a repositioning as global demand for affordable pharmaceuticals increased. During the 1990s, the company embarked on a rapid and bold acquisition strategy, which, in addition to sculpting the company, educated Dan by providing knowledge that would be used in his own exit strategy years later. By 1999, Dan, then 69, realized he had to pull back from daily business life. None of his three children was as interested in operating Novopharm as he had been, and he deduced that, while they were all capable, they would not be the right candidates to manage a company of Novopharm's size. Reluctantly at first, but then decisively once he recognized the situation, Dan began to look for an alternative. Like many other business owners in that position, the alternative he chose was to sell his company.

FREQUENT THE DANCE CARDS OF POTENTIAL SUITORS

Spend a considerable amount of face time with colleagues and competitors, even if the sale of the company is not in your plan at all. When an exit is an option, familiarity and relationships with the matrix of potential buyers will allow for unprecedented expediency through the courtship stage, which is often the lengthiest in the process. Merger & Acquisition preparation starts on day one of the life cycle of a corporation, not at its end point.

Although Leslie Dan never imagined selling Novopharm, throughout the years he was developing the company he instinctively acted as if he might at any time. He tried to ensure that the company was always viable, always growing, displayed solid leadership in its field, and, above all, maintained a steady flow of business intelligence about its industry and the players within it.

Most important, Dan continuously developed strong touchpoints with the universe of potential buyers for Novopharm. He was continually in touch with the people in the industry who could influence and direct a sale—including the eventual purchaser. When the time came and he had decided selling Novopharm was his preferred option, Dan was able to move very quickly. He proceeded coolly, and unemotionally, and spent less than a week finding a buyer for the company and engaging them in the process that would conclude the deal.

Says Dan: "You have to know the market—who are the players, what are the financials that mark their positions, their ability, the competence of management, all these things. We were in a particular business where I did know the market and when it came time I looked for an organization with a good reputation [as business people], capable management and sound earnings growth. I made a few phone calls, and we soon had three companies trying to buy Novopharm."

By laying the foundation in advance, all it took to trigger the starter pistol was Dan picking up the phone. That fated call went to the CEO of Teva Pharmaceuticals, whom Dan knew very well. Teva didn't offer the highest price, although it had stock that was growing in value, but it had more distinct, ephemeral appeal to Dan. It had a strategic plan—to establish a beachhead in North America—which would make integration easier; its operations were compatible with Novopharm's; it was on a growth trajectory; management was solid, in Dan's view; and, most important, a sale to Teva would provide for the continuity of his life's work.

"The activity of both parties has to be congruent," he explains. "Both parties have to win and operations must fit. You shouldn't just go for the money. The art of the deal doesn't entirely involve wringing the most out of the other guy. It also involves other issues."

Part of this foundation is a prior personal relationship. Novopharm and Teva had done business together before and therefore shared a history. "It's advisable to have an existing relationship that evolves over time, so that you don't have to improvise at the last minute," says Dan. "I was able to make a phone call and set up the sale because we had previous business dealings with this firm. We purchased raw materials from Teva and we had visited each other many times, so we each knew the central characters involved."

ACCEPT THAT EMOTIONS ARE A PART OF IT AND PLAN ACCORDINGLY

Pay attention to what makes people tick, including yourself. The entire succession process is about people and people will always have emotions when things you do affect their livelihood. With a founder-run company, like it or not, it is always personal in every sense of the term. By accepting that these emotions exist, you can prevent them from becoming an impediment.

In his reference to relationship and company fit, Dan is touching on something that many business operators often find uncomfortable—emotional connection. Schooled in modern business strategy and management, most business operators possess some form of a warrior mentality or a "doer" temperament—they plan, make decisions and act. What they don't do much of is examine emotions, their own and those of others around them. When companies begin preparing to merge, when the mating dance begins, it's not all about examining financials and operations, although that is what most merger and acquisition advisors emphasize. As with any courtship, a merger of two companies can be an extremely intense relationship-building process, and emotions are part of the blueprint.

For the seller, who has spent years building a company, the auctioning off of that enterprise creates feelings that must be accepted so they do not derail the process. If not properly managed, failure is almost a certainty. The problem is that in a business culture that doesn't like to recognize emotions, they are usually suppressed and as a result can run riot.

In business, and especially at critical life points such as retirement, the entrepreneur has to first acknowledge that his/her emotions exist and then master the art of controlling them. Emotional storms get in the way of accurate decision-making and bleed energy from productive human interaction, the basis of all transactions. Because of this, organizational behaviour sections of most business schools are now putting a new emphasis on the management of emotions and their role in enterprise, a discipline that is often termed Emotional Intelligence, or EI.

An important aspect of emotional intelligence is the recognition of the power of emotions and the discipline it takes to control them. Leslie Dan understood both. In a modern world governed by technological advance, a preoccupation with being "victims" and the de-humanization of the workplace, self-discipline—the patient focusing of attention on a final goal and a corresponding procedure to advance one to that goal— is a concept that is often considered anachronistic, old-fashioned or unscientific. Yet it is the basis of success for most spiritual, athletic, social, military and business leaders. It is the secret that marks the fine line between failure and flawless execution.

In North American business circles, self-discipline is often lauded, but rarely practised. Some say the instantaneous nature of North American culture—with its day traders, its emphasis on short-term trends, and business strategies that lurch from quarter to quarter earnings reports—erodes the usefulness of self-discipline. It can be difficult to keep your mind on a goal when instant gratification rules, "news" is a distracting stimulant, market chatter is at a constant crescendo, and everyone is always talking about right now, yesterday, last quarter or ten minutes ago. Self-discipline is the fine art of cutting through the noise and being laser-focused on the purpose. It is an emotional regimen that Leslie Dan charged himself with learning quite early, and which he continued to develop and practice as he grew his business. It certainly came into play during the emotional whirl that emerged when he began the process of exiting the company he had operated for more than 30 years.

"You have to train yourself to be disciplined," Dan says. "You do this through many small experiences. Every business has its challenges, its times of bad luck and good luck, and you have to learn how to deal with them unemotionally, while also recognizing the emotional implications. That way you will be able to deal with the big challenges when they come."

This maxim strongly came into play once when Dan faced the prospect of losing $80 million on a botched business deal. He had paid the sum for the rights to a drug patent, only to see it then turned over through various legal manipulations to another company. Instead of lamenting the loss of his $80 million, he coolly assessed the situation, found a legal precedent that allowed him to retain the rights and subsequently sold them to another company. By keeping his head, he turned an $80-million loss into a profit that grew to be several times larger. This, all at the hand of a little old-fashioned discipline.

"It was just bad luck and turning it into an opportunity was just good luck," he says of that difficult period. "But like many things it was a case of being aware of your emotions—I was very upset when I thought I was losing $80 million—and putting them aside while you plan carefully. You have to understand emotions and how they affect people. But you also have to be able to put them to the side and plan."

As Dan suggests, planning is the oil that smooths a successful company transition to new ownership, whether that is by another family member, a new management team or another parent altogether. Because the succession process is difficult for any company's owners and employees, good planning can lessen some of the friction that inevitably arises. An essential component of any plan is clear visibility into the end game. Therefore, most advisors who deal regularly with succession scenarios suggest that owners forming plans begin by goal visioning: what do they want to accomplish by transferring control of their organizations?

Each business has its own personality, so the ideal succession plan varies depending on the size, type, makeup and characteristics of the enterprise in question. Most surveys show that when setting goals for the liquidation of their companies, owner-operators are concerned, in descending order of importance, with maximizing financial return, minimizing tax liability, protecting the future viability of the business, minimizing risk to the selling owners and protecting employee jobs.[2]

Like most business owners, Leslie Dan was concerned first with the financial aspects, such as the value of his company and the tax implications of selling. However, he did not have to worry about maximizing the value of his company because, while he was building Novopharm into a generic drug-manufacturing powerhouse, he had already taken care of many of the financial aspects. Novopharm was built from day

---

2 Survey of Business Owners Sheds Light on Succession Challenges, PricewaterhouseCoopers, *Business Wire*, 1999.

one as a "feed" company—to be profitable and to provide a livelihood, not just for the founder and his family, but also for his many employees, who numbered some 3,000 at the time of the sale. It was built to put bread on the table.

WHAT IS THE END GAME?

Think carefully about the reasons behind the desire for an exit—succession of the business, continued employment for your employees, ability to stay on to oversee the transition, and especially the valuation of the company. Go into negotiations knowing exactly the result you are looking for. Be prepared to defend your positions vehemently, which is difficult to do unless you are constantly doing your homework. A profitable exit satisfies all of the needs of the seller, not just the predominant but obvious few.

When it came time to find a buyer, Dan worried more about a "softer" aspect of ownership transfer—the effect it would have on his company's culture. A man who throughout his life considered the feelings of others as his paramount concern, he sought to preserve the jobs of his employees and continue the Novopharm culture that had developed over three decades. A company's culture, he says, is built on integrity and honesty when dealing with employees, competitors and allies. By the time the sale process began, Novopharm was not only Canada's largest generic drug maker; it had also established strong personal and emotional connections with employees, researchers, suppliers, financiers and, particularly, customers. Therefore, the continuance of the company's culture became extremely important when Dan began looking for a suitor.

Company culture—the way a company governs the interactions between its human capital—is much more difficult to measure than financial matters, but it is as important when considering a sale. If a company's culture is created by a philosophy of business conduct that grows from the mentality of management, the temperament of owners and the treatment of employees, a sale to someone who does not share this philosophy—assuming it's a positive one, which is not always the case—can result in rapid disintegration of the company.

It is important, therefore, as a seller, that the buying company shares your attitudes toward just about everything. When there is a difference in approach, integrating the two cultures is a burden often too heavy to bear. Although this cultural fit may be more difficult to measure than dollars and cents, it is ultimately more important to the continued viability of both companies. The business landscape is littered with failed acquisitions in which companies ignored this ephemeral but important factor and were never able to fully merge into one— so they died as two.

Says Dan: "In every company there are two or three people who call the shots, so to speak. The personality of these people puts a stamp on the company. There are several ways of management: one is where you have a family type of spirit, regardless of size, and we had that at Novopharm; then with another you have the autocratic type where people have to do what they are told, and there is not much dialogue. I believe the culture of a company is very important and I wanted it to continue after the sale. Teva had a cultural fit with us. It's important that a buyer can work with you and your people."

When Leslie Dan decided to sell his company, he was able to move at lightning pace, as he was intimately familiar with the process. During his 35 years at the helm of Novopharm, he had purchased several companies and was therefore quite cognizant of the acquisition game. When he was selling his company, this familiarity provided him with the ability to see it from both sides. Too often, the process places companies into camps—a transaction riddled with "us versus them." Dan knew not to get caught in that trap. He looked for the same things in a buyer that he would if he was acquiring the company for Novopharm.

LOOK FOR THE SAME THINGS IN A BUYER THAT YOU WOULD IF YOU WERE THE BUYER

Too often, people forget that the most important factor when seeking a buyer is a shared worldview. Anything less diminishes the value of the equity in the new merged enterprise. Understand what you are looking for in the sale and align those requirements with companies that are shopping for what your total package offers. This will require addressing more than just valuation issues— it can involve compatibility in operations, culture and other intangibles. Think as if the tables were turned and the buyer was the takeover target.

"When you're selling," he explains, "you look for exactly the same thing you would look for if you were buying a company. If you want to buy a business, you don't buy without doing your due diligence. If you're selling, you do the same kind of due diligence."

Much of this due diligence involves aligning the goals of both the buy and sell sides of the equation. Commonly, buyers of a business have the following concerns: valuation, or the purchase price to the buyer; financing, or how the buyer will pay; the investment potential created by the acquisition; image, or feeling about the sale; and integration, or how quickly the new company can be used to its potential in the new parent.

The seller, on the other hand, approaches the acquisition process with an array of different questions that depend upon what motivated them to proceed to an exit. Essentially, the seller is concerned with valuation; emotions surrounding the process; tax and other financial implications; potential disruption of his or her operation; and risks that may exist after the deal is concluded. These concerns can often be summed up in the following five questions:

1. Does a sale make sense?

2. What will be the results of a sale?

3. Who is the best buyer?

4. What is the best way to protect the business and ensure continuity?

5. What is the best way to minimize post-deal risks?

Throughout Novopharm's growth period, when Dan was buying businesses, he always ensured that the price was right by maintaining a continual flow of business intelligence. In essence, because he regularly paid attention to what was happening in his industry, including mergers and acquisitions, he always knew what other players in his industry, large and small, were worth. Therefore, when it came time to sell his own company, he was not only well versed in the value of Novopharm, but also knew how that value aligned with the desires of potential buyers and similarly situated deals.

Dan could also answer all the usual seller's questions very quickly and with little need for extensive research. Thorough knowledge of his industry and his own financials allowed him to put a price on Novopharm that would match valuations buyers might determine.

Because he knew the financial conditions of the buyers he had targeted, he knew how they would pay the purchase price and he also understood and could articulate to a buyer Novopharm's investment potential. By delineating a goal to see the continuance of the Novopharm culture, he had taken care of potential buyers' feelings about the deal. Lastly, because he intimately understood his suitors' own styles of operation, he knew how quickly his company could be integrated with them. Therefore, when it came time, he could rapidly negotiate a final price, with credibility and with confidence.

FAMILY MATTERS

Whether they are actively involved in your business or not, they will be affected by your actions and thus you will be affected by their reactions. Family can also be an effective sounding board in the decision-making process. Inform them before you act and bring them into the process.

This confidence also allowed Dan to keep his family apprised of the situation. Novopharm was not a family business in the sense that members of his family were actively involved—certainly he, his wife and their three children didn't sit around the dinner table discussing the business landscape in depth. But, as with most companies, Novopharm was intertwined with the family's very being, because with all its demands and requirements for investment of time, energy and, often, funds, work is ever-present in the family dynamic. In this sense, almost all businesses are family businesses—whether they involve active participation by actual members or not. For this reason, every succession plan must take into account another part of the emotional equation—the views and concerns of the entrepreneur's family.

When they begin to think about stepping back from day-to-day operations, all business owners think first of their children as possible successors. It is a natural human characteristic and was the most common method of business transferral until recently. However, social changes—many of today's independent-minded young men and women prefer to strike out on their own rather than follow in someone else's footsteps or work in an industry that does not interest them—mean business operators must now consider alternatives to passing on the business to the most appropriate child.

Like most business owners, Leslie Dan consulted with his children before choosing the option to sell. It was a natural result of the business being a part of the family for most of their lives. "We never really talked business very much at home, but I always tried to let them know what was happening," he says. "We would have periodic discussions about larger issues. I did bring up the concept of family business succession and we discussed it. But my children and I recognized that they were not capable of running a big operation, although they were certainly competent in other ways. So, when it came time to find a successor, I had to find a buyer."

This is not an uncommon situation today. The selection of the right successor in a business is mission critical, as a poor decision could mean the demise of the company. The most suitable candidate to succeed to management of the company must have leadership potential and be willing and capable to not just pick up the ball, but to run with it. Despite a business owner's wishes, not all children have these qualities or wish to learn them. Instead, many have their own alternative career dreams and a wise parent lets them pursue them, since pushing a child into a role as operator of a company can lead to resentment later, and often, the slow death of the company. Perhaps that is why only a third of family businesses survive in the second generation.[3]

Therefore, Dan suggests that all business owners treat their families as another shareholder when deciding on succession issues. Because they have been so intimately involved through most of their lives, the business is, in a sense, theirs as well. They will care what happens to it. "If you sell your business, your family will be affected, so you better talk to them about it," he says. "You don't want them finding out in the newspapers. If you don't inform them, there might be a family feud."

If a company can also be said to be a family of sorts, Leslie Dan completed the business owner's primary task regarding succession. After years of careful business building that resulted in the successful sale of Novopharm to Teva, Dan ensured that his company would survive after his departure. The child had grown up and moved out—so to speak. But that did not mean he departed the industry completely.

Like any parent whose children strike out on their own in life, Dan still stays involved by acting as a guide, not only for his former

---

3   *Family Business Succession: Fourth Generation*, Succession Planning, Business Development Bank of Canada, July 2003.

company, but also for several others. He currently serves as a director on the board of Teva Pharmaceuticals and remains as chairman of the board of (and a large investor in) Viventia Biotech, a former subsidiary of Novopharm, which is developing a portfolio of potential cancer-fighting biopharmaceuticals and is publicly listed on the Toronto Stock Exchange.

After three decades in the generic drug manufacturing industry, Dan is now focusing his attention on the research and development of targeted biotherapeutics, an interest he has harboured for many years. While biotechnology can be said to be a different game than drug manufacturing, in that purposes differ and the time in the lab is longer, Viventia allows him to be a player in a game he enjoys and feels he was born for.

"Viventia will go very far," enthuses Dan, his entrepreneurial juices flowing again. "I am not involved in day-to-day operations, but act more as a guide and, in some respects, an angel investor. It's a second-nature venture. When Novopharm was sold, I just made room for the next one."

And so, the life cycle is repeated.

5 THINGS YOU NEED TO KNOW

Leslie Dan's top five considerations when selling a company that has been founder-owned and operated the majority of its lifecycle:

1. Frequent the Dance Cards of Potential Suitors

Spend a considerable amount of face time with colleagues and competitors, even if the sale of the company is not in your plan at all. When an exit is an option, familiarity and relationships with the matrix of potential buyers will allow for unprecedented expediency through the courtship stage, which is often the lengthiest in the process. M&A preparation starts on day one of the life cycle of a corporation, not at its end point.

2. Accept that Emotions Are a Part of It and Plan Accordingly

Pay attention to what makes people tick, including yourself. The entire succession process is about people and people will always have emotions when things you do affect their livelihood. With a founder-run company, like it or not, it is always personal in every sense of the term. By accepting that these emotions exist, you can prevent them from becoming an impediment.

3. What Is the End Game?

Think carefully about the reasons behind the desire for an exit—succession of the business, continued employment for your employees, ability to stay on to oversee the transition, and especially the valuation of the company. Go into negotiations knowing exactly the result you are looking for. Be prepared to defend your positions vehemently, which is difficult to do unless you are constantly doing your homework. A profitable exit satisfies all of the needs of the seller, not just the predominant but obvious few.

4. Look For the Same Things in a Buyer What You Would if You Were the Buyer

Too often, people forget that the most important factor when seeking a buyer is a shared worldview. Anything less diminishes the value of the equity in the new merged enterprise. Understand what you are looking for in the sale and align those requirements with companies that are shopping for what your total package offers. This will require addressing more than just valuation issues—it can involve compatibility in operations, culture and other intangibles. Think as if the tables were turned and the buyer was the takeover target.

5. Family Matters

Whether they are actively involved in your business or not, they will be affected by your actions and thus you will be affected by their reactions. Family can also be an effective sounding board in the decision-making process. Inform them before you act and bring them into the process.

CHAPTER SIXTEEN

Technology Revolution

How the Net Generation Is Changing the World, and Why Businesses Need to Pay Attention

FEATURING THE WISDOM OF DON TAPSCOTT

Don Tapscott has always been fascinated by technology's impact on business and society. A visionary thinker, he has been lauded as an international authority on the strategic value of information technology. Washington Technology Report *referred to him as "... the most influential Canadian media authority since Marshal McLuhan."*

The Toronto-born entrepreneur has built several successful businesses and co-authored 13 books on technology and business. His penultimate book, Wikinomics: How Mass Collaboration Changes Everything, *investigated the untapped potential of emerging collaborative technologies. The book explored how businesses can leverage self-organizing and mass participatory communities to harness the powers of innovation. It was listed on the* New York Times *and* Business Week *business bestseller lists, and* Amazon *sales numbers list it as the top-selling management book in the United States in 2007. It is probably the bestselling management book by a Canadian ever.*

Tapscott's love of research, coupled with an insatiable desire to understand the "why's" behind the numbers and cases, fuelled his success as a researcher, entrepreneur, author, speaker and thought leader. He has shared the stage with the likes of Colin Powell, Al Gore and Michael Dell and advises CEOs and heads of state in many countries.

Tapscott is an Adjunct Professor of Management at the Joseph L. Rotman School of Management at the University of Toronto, and holds two honourary Doctor of Law degrees, from the University of Alberta and Trent

University. His Toronto-based think tank, New Paradigm (now rebranded as the nGenera Innovation Network), was acquired in 2008 by BSG Alliance for a estimated eight-figure sum.

In his latest book, Grown Up Digital: How the Net Generation Will Change the World, *Tapscott explores how the first generation to grow up "bathed in bits" will redefine the workplace, marketplace, education system and government. Based on the findings of a $4 million research project, the book carries forward the groundbreaking ideas first expressed in* Growing Up Digital, *the bestseller he had written nearly a decade earlier.*

Tapscott predicts a period of extreme transition and upheaval for companies who must not only keep up with fast-paced technological advancement, but also have to grapple with recruiting and retaining today's young workforce as an imminent talent crisis looms on the horizon.

In April 1965, three years before he would co-found Intel Corporation, Gordon Moore published an article in *Electronics* magazine titled "Cramming More Components onto Integrated Circuits." Elaborating on an internal paper he had published as the Research and Development Director of Fairchild Semiconductors, Moore described a trend he had observed in computer hardware. Using existing data, he extrapolated that the number of transistors (small components that amplify or switch electronic signals) found per computer chip was growing exponentially, and doubling every two years since the invention of the integrated circuit. Dubbed "Moore's Law," the theory would grow to encompass the high-speed rate of improvements in nearly all digital electronic devices.

We have all experienced this in our daily lives. A top-of-the-line laptop computer or digital camera purchased one year is dwarfed the next year by an exponentially improved newly released version. Electronics are getting better, smaller and cheaper as consumers and businesses struggle to keep up.

There are those who say that Moore's Law set in motion a self-fulfilling prophecy within the semiconductor industry, as companies raced to produce the necessary increase in processing power before their competitors. As faster and more powerful computers began to appear in the marketplace, their impacts on the workplace were still relatively unknown. However, organizations were eager to learn more about the methods by which these technologies could improve their business.

In 1978, Don Tapscott joined the "Office of the Future Group" at Bell Northern Research (BNR). The division's mandate was to explore office communication systems at a time when managers would write out reports and memos by hand and send them to the "word-processing" department. In Tapscott's case, the department was a room located in the basement of the building where the staff would rush to type up the document in order to return it to its owner within twenty-four hours.

For Tapscott, who held a Bachelor of Science in Psychology and Statistics as well as a Master's degree in Education, studying the link between technology and human behaviour was fascinating. He gained a reputation for accurately predicting upcoming trends and quickly rose through the ranks of the organization. "I was having a lot of fun and within two years, was one of the senior executives running this whole department," he says.

In 1981, he published a body of work around technology and workplace efficiency. Despite his innovative and forward-thinking perspective, the book did not perform as well as he had hoped. "Thankfully, my mother bought many copies," he joked. Reflecting back, Tapscott believes that while the topic was relevant, the timing was off. "It was probably 15 years too early for that book," he says.

Still, one of Tapscott's colleagues, Del Langdon, saw tremendous value in his instincts and knew that he had hit on something big. She suggested that they leave BNR to start their own consulting practice. "I wasn't sure," he says of his initial reaction. "I had a corner office and nice perks. Why would I leave?" Langdon proved to be quite persuasive, and Tapscott, who had no prior entrepreneurial aspirations, took the leap into self-employment. Several BNR employees came with them. Trigon Systems Group, named for the trifecta of computing, communications and content, was formed in 1982.

From its initial six employees to 140, the consultancy grew rapidly. As producers of cutting-edge research, their studies about the impacts of technology on the efficiency and cohesion of a department would eventually lay the groundwork for multifunction work systems and thus for software suites like Microsoft Office.

Trigon Systems was acquired by DMR, an international information services company, in 1986. Tapscott continued fuelling his passion for research, and became DMR's Vice-President. However, a couple of years later, conflicts between investors and management flared, and Tapscott found himself disillusioned with the idea of working for someone else. Once again, Del Langdon suggested they venture back out into entrepreneurialism, and Tapscott left another well-paying job for the thrill of the unknown and the opportunity to control his destiny. He founded New Paradigm, a Toronto-based think tank specializing in research on information technology and competitive advantage, and set out to convince corporations of technology's benefits.

As a futurist, Tapscott wanted to prepare companies for an increasingly technological future. He knew it would be a difficult task and soon grew accustomed to the rampant skepticism he faced when describing how technology would alter a company's decision-making processes. "The biggest argument I had against me was that people said that managers would never learn to type," he says ruefully of the early challenges he encountered. "All these great things about the computer revolution supporting knowledge workers was reduced to the stupid issue of could you learn to type or not." Tapscott resigned himself to manoeuvring around this barrier by delivering encouraging messages to mid-level managers ensuring them that "Really, you can learn to type!" Once again, he was too far ahead of the curve. This time he knew he would have to wait until the market was ready to listen.

That time would come in 1992, when Tapscott would publish a book that would compellingly capture the "big idea" at the exact time when the public needed to hear it. Comprised of the findings of a New Paradigm large-scale research project, *Paradigm Shift* was the first book to describe in detail the implications of information technology on the corporation and suggest actionable and practical advice on the subject. It was an instant bestseller, and elevated Tapscott to international acclaim. He soon began sharing his vision of the future with audiences worldwide.

Grown Up Digital cemented Tapscott's credibility as an expert futurist in the field of information technology. Over the next decade Tapscott would publish several more ground-breaking books, including *Digital Economy: Paradise and Peril in the Age of a Networked World*, *The Naked Corporation: How the Age of Transparency Will Revolutionize*

Business, and *Wikinomics: How Mass Collaboration Changes Everything*. The *Financial Post* named him Canada's leading tech guru in 2008.

Tapscott noticed another interesting trend in the marketplace. Corporations that had taken too long to adapt to changing technologies were struggling, plagued by outdated work processes and a lack of understanding of the youth entering the workforce. They were ready to learn and the timing had never been more critical. Technology's unforgiving pace mixed with the maturation of the largest demographic created a volatile environment that was effortlessly disrupting longstanding management theories.

He saw how YouTube, the video sharing site acquired by Google that was created by two members of the Net Generation, could completely disrupt the distribution platforms of major broadcasting networks. Suddenly viewers no longer needed their television to watch and share content.

Intrigued, he once again turned to his research for the answers. In a $4 million dollar research project, the largest of its kind, Tapscott launched an in-depth investigation to see how the generation he had written about in 1998 was turning out. The results were summarized in his latest book, *Grown Up Digital: How the Net Generation Will Change the World*. It's a particularly special venture for Tapscott, as it carries forward the ideas he had presented nearly a decade earlier.

The findings in his latest investigation were clear. Companies needed to be faster, better and smarter in order to survive this period of transition. Whether it's strategy, sales or information technology, the rules of the game have changed, and those who aren't ready to play will be left in the dust.

The Bridge from Strategy to Execution Is Value

For many entrepreneurs, there are no shortages of "Big Ideas" that come to mind when contemplating the future potential of their businesses. Rather, it's the space between imagination and execution that seems to be so difficult to navigate.

For Tapscott, strategy is essential. Business owners need to know where they are going as well as how they plan to get there. As an idea man, Tapscott understands this well. "There is a fine line between vision and hallucination," he says. "A vision needs to be translatable into a strategy that can be executed."

Many businesses are bogged down in complex strategy-generating exercises and quickly lose focus. "Strategy is not a complicated thing," Tapscott explains. "It's about where to play and how to win. That's it." Ultimately, he insists that business owners must ask themselves two fundamental questions. "What value will I create for which customers? How will that value be different from my competitors'?" Tapscott understood early that his ability to forecast trends coupled with the right timing would be invaluable to organizations who were overwhelmed at the pace of change in the new marketplace and remained chained to antiquated legacy systems.

Tapscott disagrees with those who claim success comes from operational efficiencies or customer focus. Those things are irrelevant without understanding the big picture of an organization's goals and what it hopes to one day accomplish. "If you don't have a strategy, you're not going to be successful," he argues. He focused his efforts on providing research that would answer essential questions needed for his clients to manage their business.

By concentrating on value-adding services, Tapscott avoided another common entrepreneurial pitfall: being motivated solely by numbers. He created New Paradigm to make positive and meaningful contributions to society. "I wanted to be a thought leader from day one, and it hasn't been about making money," he says of his career choices. "The business successes have been a by-product of bringing about the types of changes that I thought would improve innovation and business."

THE BRIDGE FROM STRATEGY TO EXECUTION IS VALUE

The space between vision and execution is difficult for entrepreneurs to navigate, and it's becoming even more so as technology accelerates the rate of change. Don't get bogged down in overly complex strategic frameworks that can complicate this process. Businesses should focus on who their customers are and how they can provide a value-adding service or product that is differentiated. Emphasis should be creating value, not reaping profit.

You are Only as Good as Your Weakest Salesperson

Once the strategy is set, it is essential to find the best people to execute your vision. Often, entrepreneurs will overlook the importance of salespeople. These are the essential players who can convincingly communicate the value of your product or service to customers. A product or service is only as good as its worst salesperson. Tapscott learned this lesson early on, especially when proposing ideas that countered the norm.

"It's always a challenge to be ahead of the market. My business life has been one of trying to win people over to some new way of thinking," he said. "The people who really create value are the people who can sell your stuff." Ideas alone are not enough, and even all the great consultants in your organization will be no matches for a weak sales team. His early experiences with disbelieving corporations have trained him in the art of "the sell." Through repeatedly having to prove his views against every possible objection, he learned the intricacies of building client relationships, establishing rapport and delivering on a client need.

"I'm a sales guy," he says of his own role within his corporation. "I'm selling ideas and business. It's unglamorous but that's how you build a company."

Peter Drucker, considered by many to have fathered "modern management," was once quoted as saying "the purpose of a business is to create customers." For Tapscott, this meant creating buy-in from clients and convincing them of the value-add of his research and consulting expertise. Even though Ngenera boasts its own sales force, Tapscott still enjoys accompanying sales staff on a few client pitches. The experience helps him gauge his clients' state of mind while ensuring the company is not overlooking any latent needs.

YOU ARE ONLY AS GOOD AS YOUR WEAKEST SALESPERSON

Invest in a strong sales and marketing team, since it is their job to convince consumers to buy your brand. A product is only as good as its weakest salesperson, and this is especially true when selling new technologies or ways of doing business. Sales teams often have a bigger challenge today than just selling a product or service; they may also have to sell a vision of the future.

Living Amidst Generation Net

The Net generation comprises 81 million youth, born between 1977 and 1997. (They are also called Generation Y or Millennials.) They are the biggest demographic since the Baby Boomers and are unique in that they are the first generation to have grown up with the Internet.

They are the world's first global generation. From talking and playing to interacting and working, they are doing everything differently. Their attitudes, expectations and outlooks are going to turn industries on their heads. According to Tapscott, smart companies will sit up and take notice. "This is an unprecedented force of change in every aspect of how companies operate."

Tapscott's instinct for spotting trends kicked into full gear in the early nineties when he observed his daughter Niki, then 7, discuss how she planned to keep in touch with a friend she had met during a family vacation to St. Lucia in the early nineties. Since they both had computers, maybe the two machines could speak to each other? "They were describing electronic mail, even though neither had ever used it," he recalled. "I knew there was something going on here. With these kids, it's not technology to them; it's like the air." These insights were examined in *Growing Up Digital*.

"I originally thought my kids were prodigies," he says, laughing. "And then I noticed that all their friends were just like them." For the first time ever, Tapscott saw an interesting development at the intersection of kids and technologies. "Young people were using a new medium of communication, and they knew more about it than old people did, and this is a formula for fear, or worse—mockery and hostility."

In the later book, *Grown Up Digital*, Tapscott argued that disruptive technological innovation would only be half the battle. Companies would also need to manage the entry of the world's first Internet generation into the workforce, an endeavour that would require a tremendous amount of change.

Tapscott's research into the characteristics of this demographic yielded eight "generational norms" that represent unique clusters of behaviours and attitude that are profoundly different than those of their parents:

- *Freedom* – Accustomed to the endless choices available to them, this generation thrives on choices. They are used to sifting through online clutter in order to find the information that they need. Tapscott writes that this generation "uses technology to escape traditional office constraints and integrate their work lives with their home lives and social lives. Net Geners seek the freedom to change jobs, freedom to take their own path, and to express themselves."

- *Customization* – The Net Generation is accustomed to personalizing everything they own, from a desktop to an iPod. No longer satisfied with passively browsing the web, Net Geners will create the content they want to see online. Tapscott foresees this need evolving from the digital world into their offline lives. From job descriptions to university curricula, this generation refuses to buy into a one-size-fits-all policy.

- *Scrutiny* – Bombarded by never-ending advertisements and corporate messaging, youth today have developed an increasing skill in scrutinizing the activities of corporations online. They demand transparency and honesty, and companies who refuse to comply with these new standards will feel the wrath of this powerful purchasing demographic.

- *Integrity* – Their expectations of corporate authenticity will naturally extend into their relationship with employers. Corporations that wish to recruit the brightest talent will need to ensure internal culture aligns with the Net Generation's outlook.

- *Entertainment* – With childhoods full of interactive experiences such as video games, this generation brings a playful mindset to everything they do, including work. They are not satisfied with boring routines and insist on using their outside-the-box thinking to problem-solve and collaborate.

- *Collaboration* – Tapscott cites the creation of social networks such as Facebook and MySpace with providing new platforms to build relationships. This is a generation that is used to being in touch with their network of friends all the time, through email, text, or instant messaging. They influence each other and will openly discuss products, brands and organizations online.

- *Speed* – Instant messaging and push email have made real-time communication a norm for the Net Generation. Tapscott warns organizations that their customers and young employees will expect instant responses to their communication.

- *Innovation* – The Net Generation has used the Internet to create an unprecedented volume of information. From blogs and websites to photos and videos, youth today are constantly seeking new ways to engage with the world.

"They are going to change companies because they are bringing a whole new mode of operation into the corporation," Tapscott says. "They have huge power; they are natural collaborators, which is paradoxical to the traditional power structure. They work differently, they are very social, and of course they exist through social networks." He already foresees corporate issues. "We have a generational firewall that exists, because instead of understanding, we ban their tools." He refers to the emergence of new technological policies within corporations that ban the use of Facebook and MySpace from the office.

LIVING AMIDST GENERATION NET

The largest demographic since the Baby Boomers, the Net Generation is poised to enter the workforce. As the first generation to be raised with the Internet, they are collaborative, tech-savvy and have high expectations of the organizations that want to hire them. They will profoundly affect all industries from business to education to government. You must make every effort to not only understand them, but learn from them.

The Endangered Species of Management

Whether you're an entrepreneur or a manager, decisions like the one described above are creating a ripple across all workplaces. Entrepreneurialism is on the rise, especially among young knowledge workers who are frustrated with the current state of affairs within traditional corporations. Tapscott's research explains the psychology behind this occurrence and the role technology plays in the marketplace.

Opportunities are bigger than ever. With collaborative technologies on the rise, Tapscott says entrepreneurs can "behave like a big company without being one." In essence, small groups of networked free agents can enjoy many of the benefits of being a large company without the liability or bureaucracy.

This results in the rise of loosely formed alliances between individuals, what author Dan Pink referred to as the "Hollywood Model" in his book *Free Agent Nation*.

"A group of talented people come together for one particular project," wrote Pink. "Why they complete the project, they disband, each participant having learned new skills, forged new connections, deepened existing relationships, enhanced their reputations within the industry and earned a credit they can add to their resume." This model now extends into several industries. Alliances of free agents empowered by the availability of collaborative technologies are able to create, organize and execute client projects faster than their larger counterparts. "Instead of laboring in loneliness," Pink continues, "independent workers are inventing an array of small groups."

The Net Generation has grown up collaborating as opposed to being passive recipients of broadcast, and are naturally more entrepreneurial. "Most of them are going to go work for someone and aren't going to like what they see. That doesn't mean they've been coddled or don't know how to manage expectations," Tapscott explains. "I think they just have a different view, where they don't want to be put in a cubicle and told what to do for the rest of their lives."

This stems from watching their Boomer parents toil at corporate jobs for long hours only to be rewarded by higher-paying jobs that demanded even longer hours. This generation wants something different; they want more work/life balance. Tapscott's research revealed that one of every two Net Geners valued family time more than work, compared to only 41 percent of Baby Boomers.

Tapscott foresees what he describes as a "major collision between freewheeling Net Generation and Baby Boomer employers." The conflict stems from two divergent ideologies about work. As the eight norms previously described, these new employees want a fun, free, flexible job that allows them to interact, have fun and collaborate — all at a fast pace. Is it any wonder that they are clashing with older managers? Many young people are turning to entrepreneurialism, willing to face ambiguity instead of clearly outlined job descriptions.

Unless companies are willing to transform into more attractive work environments, they will become training grounds for young employees to foster the skills eventually needed to strike out on their own.

This development will have strong implications for businesses that are already struggling to fill open positions.

As the Baby Boomers reach retirement, they will leave behind a vast number of open positions ready for the next generation. There is only one problem: the next generation doesn't seem to want them. This is quite the reversal for companies who only a few decades ago had an overflow of CVs from eager young Boomers. Managers could choose from a wealth of the country's brightest candidates. Tapscott recalls a time where Boomers were happy just to have a job and even more eager to keep it. They would have never considered proposing drastic changes to the workplace.

Today, the power rests in the hands of the employee. Tapscott's research paints a disturbing picture:

In the U.S. alone there will be a shortfall of 10 million workers by the year 2010.

Despite a forecast of 23 million college grads over the next 10 years, labour analysts say there will be a demand for 30 million college-educated workers.

In the next few years, some of America's biggest organizations will lose half of their senior management team to retirement.

The Net Generation spends an average term of about two years at a corporation before searching for the next big challenge. Job-hopping is considered normal and being a "lifer" at a corporation has become an antiquated concept. Corporations will face fierce competition to both win and keep young talent. According to Tapscott this will translate into "unprecedented power for the highly capable knowledge worker."

Companies are starting to feel the effects of this crisis already. A recent Deloitte survey of HR professionals in the U.S. found that 70 percent of respondents considered the difficulty in finding enough staff to fill open job positions to be the greatest threat to business performance.

THE ENDANGERED SPECIES OF MANAGEMENT

With the Baby Boomers' retirement over the next several years, and entrepreneurialism on the rise among young people, companies are facing an extreme talent shortage. Corporate culture, job descriptions and the very ideology of work will have to be examined in an effort to evolve into a next-generation workplace.

The Networked Corporation

If they want to retain this young and technologically savvy workforce, companies will need to redefine how to differentiate their organizations.

After all, according to Randall Hansen, founder of the popular career development site Quintessential Careers, the Net Generation "is the foundation for the next three decades of employment and leadership."

At the very least, a corporate culture that embodies some of the Net Generation's values is a good place to start. "You're going to need to create an attractive corporate culture, but even that's not going to win it," Tapscott warns. "You're going to have to have a network model of a corporation that's going to militate even further towards the concept of a business web, where talent is not just inside your walls, but outside it as well."

In a connected and global economy, work becomes dependent on technology and not geography. Smart corporations will leverage this trend and utilize teams of employees that are located worldwide to collaborate and innovate remotely as well as tap into the collective knowledge of communities that exist outside of their corporations.

Get Comfortable Being a Digital Immigrant

The maturation of the Net Generation combined with the rapid pace of technological innovation will force managers and "digital immigrants," those who have not grown up with digital technology, to adapt their behaviour to master these new and emerging forms of communication.

This particular communication revolution is unique. "The printing press, radio, television, they were all centralized," says Tapscott. "They were one-directional, they were immutable and they were controlled by owners or by advertisers." The Internet changed all of that. "What we have now is the antithesis of all of that. It's a multi-directional form of communication that cherishes a new neutrality." Youth are no longer content to sit complacently while being lectured to. Older generations must start to do the same.

Tapscott gives the following advice to those who are interested in embracing this technological age:

- *You have to walk the walk.* Personal use is a pre-condition for any comprehension. "You cannot fully understand a new technology without actually using it," Tapscott says. "Sign up and experiment with social networks, blogs and web 2.0 tools." Despite busy schedules it is important to devote a few hours each month to simply exploring some of the fascinating new sites that are emerging online.

- *Get new teachers.* Engage young people in both personal and professional settings to demonstrate how these tools can be applied. Several organizations have capitalized on this trend by creating reverse-mentoring programs that pair young workers with older managers in an exchange of technological tutoring and career mentoring.

- *Be curious.* Especially when faced with a new technology that appears to be completely unnecessary, confusing or even plain absurd. Tapscott recommends suspending initial disbelief in favour of asking, "What does this mean? Where could this go and what are the implications?"

It is often difficult to envision a new technology's full potential when it is first released. Approaching a new innovation with an open mind and the willingness to consider the possibilities will help organizations embrace this new age of change.

GET COMFORTABLE BEING A DIGITAL IMMIGRANT

Business people need to develop the skills to help them adapt to the constant onslaught of new technologies. Digital Immigrants, or those who have grown up without digital technology and must now learn it, will need to suspend hard-wired responses and be open to accepting guidance from experts who are younger then they are.

Conclusion

For Tapscott, companies that quickly adapt in this space will enjoy increased competitive advantage as well as the talents of the best and brightest this generation has to offer. He remains fascinated by his studies on the impacts of technology, and his curiosity shows no signs of abating. "I've always been a research guy," he said. "I just love knowing what's behind all the numbers." He likens the process to facing an intricate and complex puzzle that he feels compelled to solve.

As a forward thinker, he has often grappled with finding the right timing for sharing his ideas. Knowing the right timing is a skill that mixes trial and error, luck, and an instinct for spotting the interesting story buried within piles of data. "The first ten years for me was realizing that while it was cool to be way ahead of the market, you're probably not going to build a strong business like that," he laughs. "I've always wanted to change the course of things through building a successful business. And for me, the big idea ultimately served me well because ultimately I was able to nail the timing."

Today, he feels as though he has hit his stride and is once again enjoying the rewards of expressing an idea at the exact time when it needs to be heard the most. He is already working on his next book, and says he has many more left to write.

During his presentations he'll often quote Victor Hugo, who famously said "There's nothing so powerful as an idea whose time has come." Tapscott firmly believes that there is a technological revolution afoot that will affect every business. The question is no longer whether or not the revolution is here, but whether or not organizations will be ready.

5 THINGS YOU NEED TO KNOW

1. The Bridge from Strategy to Execution Is Value

The space between vision and execution is difficult for entrepreneurs to navigate, and it's becoming even more so as technology accelerates the rate of change. Don't get bogged down in overly complex strategic frameworks that can complicate this process. Businesses should focus on who their customers are and how they can provide a value-adding service or product that is differentiated. Emphasis should be creating value, not reaping profit.

2. You Are Only As Good As Your Weakest Salesperson

Invest in a strong sales and marketing team, since it is their job to convince consumers to buy your brand. A product is only as good as its weakest salesperson, and this is especially true when selling new technologies or ways of doing business. Sales teams often have a bigger challenge today than just selling a product or service; they may also have to sell a vision of the future.

3. Living Amidst Generation Net

The largest demographic since the Baby Boomers, the Net Generation is poised to enter the workforce. As the first generation to be raised with the Internet, they are collaborative, tech-savvy and have high expectations of the organizations that want to hire them. They will profoundly affect all industries from business to education to government. You must make every effort to not only understand them, but learn from them.

4. The Endangered Species of Management

With the Baby Boomers' retirement over the next several years, and entrepreneurialism on the rise among young people, companies are facing an extreme talent shortage. Corporate culture, job descriptions and the very ideology of work will have to be examined in an effort to evolve into a next-generation workplace.

5. Get Comfortable Being a Digital Immigrant

Business people will need to develop the skills to help them adapt to the constant onslaught of new technologies. Digital Immigrants, or those who have grown up without digital technology and must now learn it, will need to suspend hard-wired responses and be open to accepting guidance from experts who are younger then they are.

CHAPTER SEVENTEEN

What's Next:
Change and Growth

FEATURING THE WISDOM OF GARRETT CAMP, FOUNDER, STUMBLEUPON

STUMBLING UPON AGILITY

In 2007, online auction giant eBay paid $75 million for a social bookmarking site called StumbleUpon, a property that helps users discover new and interesting content based on their shared preferences. Today, StumbleUpon has over five million registered users and made *Time* magazine's "50 Best Websites for 2007" list.

While starting his postgraduate degree at the University of Calgary, Garrett Camp, then 23, recognized the challenge of finding high-quality relevant content among the billions of pages available online. In 2001, Camp, along with Geoff Smith and Justin LaFrance, came up with a simple idea: build a web application that helps people discover great websites without spending hours searching for them.

By the time Camp graduated in 2005, StumbleUpon was 600,000 registered users strong and growing. After the site caught the attention of prominent Silicon Valley investor Brad O'Neill, Camp relocated to San Francisco to focus on the business full time.

StumbleUpon's tools were specifically designed to address the problems of dealing with the barrage of information available online, taking into account the unpredictability of the online marketplace and the fact that consumers' preferences and surfing habits keep changing. Camp recognized this need and built a business around it. True entrepreneurialism at work—identify a big pain point and solve it.

LEVERAGE YOUR NETWORK'S COLLECTIVE KNOWLEDGE

Businesses, in particular, need to manage an information flow that is constantly changing. Information overload is an epidemic, especially for executives. If you exclude technology diehards who live and die on the web, many people admit that the Internet can hurt their productivity and can often be a bigger drain on time and resources than a savings. Information overload can swamp businesses that monitor the activities of their consumers, their competitors and their industry.

For Camp, gathering relevant information is a responsibility he shares with his network. He does this in different ways. First, he has identified a handful of leading bloggers in his industry and has subscribed to their RSS feeds, ensuring he remains connected to important information.

Second, Camp relies on his extensive lists of online contacts to send him news of interest, especially about competitors. "I know a few people who have a deep knowledge in certain areas. These people are my filters, because they send me the things they think I need to know."

Camp increases his productivity and efficiency by leveraging the skills and knowledge of those who spend more time online or who focus on a particular topic.

MAKE IT EASY FOR PEOPLE
TO USE YOUR PLATFORM TO COMMUNICATE

In addition to information about a company's industry and competitors, companies today have access to their customers in a way that was unheard of a few years ago. This is an incredible opportunity to open a dialogue with the people who matter most to your business—your customers. In an age when consumers can effortlessly change brand allegiances, developing a relationship based on trust and communication can make an enormous difference.

"You have to encourage continual feedback on content," says Camp. "We took a look at our customer feedback and tried almost daily to release new versions of code. We created forums where customers could share their thoughts and ask for more stuff." StumbleUpon programmers were able to understand what was lacking in the current user experience, and they prioritized the release of new features accordingly.

Camp insists that any attempt to solicit feedback must be "easy and intuitive." Understanding the way consumers interact with your organization's website is key. "People want to get in contact with anyone, at any time, about anything," he adds. "So the easier you make it for them, the more they will do it."

The Internet has put the power back into the hands of consumers, who now have the ability to communicate what they are looking for easily. Companies that do not meet their needs will quickly find themselves replaced.

DOES THE YEARLY PLAN BECOME THE WEEKLY PLAN?

This shift means that companies have to be able to respond to consumer needs in order to retain the agility that will keep them competitive. Plans that are set in stone risk being derailed by changing market conditions.

As for planning, Camp admits he doesn't put a lot of stock in year-long plans anymore. There is simply too much change. Instead, long-term goals are considered loose guidance—an affirmation of the direction he wants to go instead of a set destination. "I plan a fairly high level of precision a week out, and a month out, the plan is still hazy," he explains.

He does check in periodically, either quarterly or at the project mid-point to make sure that "what you thought was a good idea is still a good idea." The ideal time period is one week, especially with his team of developers. "I focus on what we're trying to accomplish by this week. If something takes longer than a week then we break it down into weekly installments." This allows his team the flexibility to quickly shift priorities if something urgent comes up. "If you had a set two-month plan and something comes up, you might not be able to act on it for six or seven weeks." In Camp's industry, that might be too late.

Constant change has also forced him to re-evaluate his concept of product readiness. "I don't believe in spending a long time with your head down trying to improve something until it's perfect," he says. "It's better to get the first draft out, get feedback, and continually course-correct and remain agile."

For now, Camp is happy to continue to explore the potential of StumbleUpon, and is open to new, interesting opportunities. "Maybe StumbleUpon is a reflection of my own personality," he says, laughing. "I like to explore a lot of things in a lot of different ways. I plan things out but leave a lot of room for experimentation."

PART FOUR

---------------------------------- 🍁 ----------------------------------

Overtime

Values, Culture and What You Stand For

CHAPTER EIGHTEEN

Do'h!

Five Lessons Homer Simpson Taught Me about Teamwork

FEATURING THE WISDOM OF JOEL COHEN

The Simpsons, *the longest-running comedy on television, features America's favourite suburban father, Homer, a fat, bald bonehead obsessed with doughnuts and beer. He loves to spit out twisted homilies but can never seem to get anything right. The Simpsons is a sly satire on North American values, good and bad. Over 16 seasons, Homer Simpson has been issuing warped guidance on life, politics, social issues, and, yes, even business, to all who cross his path.*

One of the creators behind this advice is Joel Cohen, from Calgary, Alberta, who joined the writing team at The Simpsons *more than five years ago. The animated situation comedy, now in its seventeenth year, has earned a Peabody Award, 18 Emmys and a star on the Hollywood Walk of Fame.* Time *magazine named it the best TV show of the twentieth century. It has also generated millions of dollars for its broadcaster, the Fox Network.*

Now Co-Executive Producer of the show, Cohen has learned many lessons about morality (and a lot about the collaboration process) from Homer Simpson. In fact, The Simpsons' *production process is a model for team development everywhere.*

—⁂—

Update: *Joel continues to work on* The Simpsons *and was awarded an Emmy in 2006 for his contribution to the series. He was also nominated for several other awards, including a Golden Globe and a Writers Guild Award. In 2007, he joined the writing team of the highly successful* Simpsons *movie, which grossed $526 million worldwide. Joel is also a renowned speaker who shares his insights about innovation and creativity with corporations such as IBM, Merrill Lynch & AOL.*

Homer Simpson is not alone in his quest for independence from the drudgery of the rat race. In a way, millions of North Americans are daring to act on the same thoughts. Although they are not entertaining Homer's fantasy literally, they are doing so figuratively by chucking their jobs and electing for free agency at an unprecedented pace. Surveys in schools have shown that entrepreneurship is becoming the career choice among youth, and graduate business schools are increasingly introducing entrepreneurship streams into their curricula to meet demand. Similarly, older workers are taking up the entrepreneurial torch. Small businesses, often owner-operated, now account for more than 75 percent of businesses in North America; micro-businesses—those with fewer than 10 employees—account for the majority of that number.[1]

This growing entrepreneurial movement has several implications for managers. The term *entrepreneurship* is often referred to in popular discourse when anyone starts a business of any kind. In fact, it is a distinct discipline with its own requirements and methods. Entrepreneurship is not simply hanging out a shingle and selling a service or product; it is the genesis of a business around a concept, followed by its relentless pursuit. The idea may involve the development of a disruptive product or service, or a new way of producing or delivering that product or service. The Harvard Business School defines entrepreneurship as "a way of managing opportunities over time—an approach to management that entails the continuous identification and pursuit of opportunity, the marshalling and organization of resources to address evolving opportunities, and the ongoing reassessment of needs as the context changes over time."[2]

Research at the Stanford Graduate School of Business shows that in the rush to romanticize successful entrepreneurs as tough individualists (and to attack them viciously when they fail) there is one side of the entrepreneur that is often forgotten—the social being who revels in the people process. "Building a company entails hiring, organizing

---

1   US Census Bureau, Statistics Canada.
2   http://www.hbs.edu/units/em/about.html.

and inspiring a collection of people who typically need to get startup funds from others, to buy things from other people, and, ultimately, to flourish or fail together as a result of the ability to sell things to yet another group of people. The emphasis on rugged individualism is so prevalent in western culture that many of the lists of characteristics of successful entrepreneurs barely reflect that launching a startup entails constant interaction with others. It is a social activity."[3]

This fact has repercussions for anyone who starts a business, belongs to a team of any kind, or follows the entrepreneurial path. Business is a constant collaboration—with partners, employees and customers. Because it always involves working with others, commerce is a community activity. In an early-stage or start-up company, the process of building the company is a very creative one, much like the creative process that goes into producing music, a film or a TV show.

Teams are the skeletons of all ventures. Typically, teams are created to accomplish a specific task—to produce a technology product, for example. If it is a new business, partners and early employees come together to plan the business's direction. Even if a business has only one employee, he or she will be regularly collaborating with outside sources. In fact, single-employee, or soloist, businesses are constantly involved in team development as they link with others to complete a particular project. In all cases, the dynamics of team development come into play.

Quality and timely input are essential elements of the collaborative process, which is, in turn, a prerequisite for success in the early stages of business building. All corporate environments, whether partnerships, sole operations or interdepartmental teams developing a product or service, require continual collaboration among various stakeholders as the business tries to focus on development of its product, its market niche, and the values that go into the company's culture.

If you're ever in the middle of a really big meeting and have something important to say, well, that's why you should always keep an air horn in your briefcase.—Joel Cohen

Invariably, teams go through a process of development in which

---

3   Tom Byers, Heleen Kist, Stanford University, and Robert I. Sutton, Haas School of Business, *Characteristics of the Entrepreneur: Social Creatures, Not Solo Heroes*, 1997.

members hope to achieve a collaborative state. This process is described in the well-known Bruce Tuckman model[4] as "forming" (introducing team members to each other), "storming" (jockeying for position and roles—the conflict stage), "norming" (working together), and "performing" (accomplishing tasks required to reach the objective). Most teams perform best when individual team members exhibit strong self-interest and strong interest in the others—they recognize they are part of the team and put aside their individual agendas to make the team function effectively. The result is usually compromise and an orderly drive to the goal, or, better yet, true collaboration, which often results in breakthrough achievements. True collaboration is rare, because personal agendas and insecurities obscure honest, collaborative input.

Andy Dickson, a consultant with the Buckinghamshire School Improvement Service in the U.K., suggests that teamwork is more than just the sum of the abilities of individual team members. He says high-performing teams usually display an extra value that comes from a combination of skills, experience and creative thought. These teams function well at all three levels of team activity, which Dickson labels purpose, strategy and implementation.

Says Dickson: "A high-performing team must know why it exists and what its purpose is. A high-performing team demands answers and is clear about its mission. A well-defined mission includes a well-defined statement of intent, which is understood by all team members. The team mission or task should also be in line with the organization's mission and should be accompanied by clear team targets, goals or objectives. A clear objective should be stated as 'to achieve such and such an aim by such and such a date.'

Don't buy life insurance from a company with a hand-written sign—no matter how endearing the spelling mistakes are.—Joel Cohen

Furthermore, each objective must have clear success criteria that are clearly measurable as being achieved or not achieved by some indicator or behaviour at some time in the future. If there is any doubt, the team objectives must be clarified so that team members understand what they are trying to achieve, how they will know they have achieved it and by when.

"The strategy level falls into two broad areas. On the one hand it's all about the selection of people, skills and structure and on the other

4   *Team Development*, Virginia Commonwealth University, www.people.vcu.edu/~rsleeth/TeamDevelopmentSheet.html.

hand it's about values, strategy, attitude and commitment ... After the strategy level comes implementation. By this stage it is a case of carrying out the plan, operating to the refined working practice and behaving in line with the agreed values. What are we actually going to do? How will we measure and evaluate? When and where will we do it?"[5]

Joel Cohen, 37, is a writer and Co-Executive Producer of the Fox Network's animated television comedy show, *The Simpsons*, currently in its seventeenth year and the longest-running comedy in American television history. Cohen grew up in Calgary, attended the University of Alberta in Edmonton and then received his MBA at the Shulich School of Business at York University in Toronto.

He learned early that while collaborating is necessary in life in general, it is particularly important when writing a television show. After graduate school, Cohen, a fast man with a fast quip, decided he wanted to be a comedy writer and moved to Los Angeles to try his luck. He landed a job as a junior writer with the show *Suddenly Susan*, which only lasted for a year, and then was invited to join *The Simpsons* writing team.

> *Greed is good. So is camembert—really, all the French cheeses.*
> *—Joel Cohen*

The new job was as shocking as a cold bath. As *The Simpsons* evolved from a series of shorts in another show to the comic juggernaut it is today, it developed a collaborative production process that is considered among the best in the business. Unlike some other shows that spring from the agile mind of one writer, or the usual sitcom group of about eight, *The Simpsons* is a well-oiled idea machine that has as many as 20 writers producing scripts over a nine-month writing cycle. It is a continual process of brainstorming, refining, rewriting and ultimately breakthrough collaboration. Known simply as "being in the room," after the real room where writers, chowing on sugary, high-octane foods, thrash out their ideas, this collaboration is not easy. Writers rapidly toss out ideas in quick succession, and each is weighed and judged by the others. A writer may pitch 200 jokes and see only 10 considered for a script; even those 10 will be massaged and handled by other writers until the team judges that they work perfectly. Sometimes, if a writer pitches an entire script, only a bare hint of it will remain in the final draft. For writers, who operate in the realm of ideas

---

5. *High Performance, Management Skills and Development* magazine, www.managementskills.co.uk/articles/May 1998.

and struggle continually, often in isolation, to dream up material, this can be unnerving—and confidence-shattering. Cohen realized quickly that television writing is the ultimate form of teamwork and that it must be treated that way.

"Sometimes, writing is like killing your babies because you have to get rid of things," he muses. "At first I found this hard, but after a while, with the thunderstorm of rejection, I learned that you don't attach yourself personally to it. You try to make it as good as you can, put it in the lab, and once you get feedback, adapt and incorporate the feedback. You don't tie your ego to it. The idea is to bring the best product to market. You trust and believe that you're all working toward the same goal."

"BART, YOU'RE SAYING BUTT KISSER LIKE IT'S A BAD THING!"

Create an atmosphere of frankness and openness. When a team needs to generate creative ideas on a regular basis, participants have to be comfortable working closely together in intense situations. That requires checking egos at the door and being open to all participants' thoughts—and criticism. The art of the leader is to ensure that everyone is treated fairly and respectfully, while mercilessly killing bad ideas.

This is really the same process any company or organization must go through. The team must be able to "kill the baby" and move on if it is not working. In Cohen's case, the time to chew on an idea is very short. In day-to-day business reality, time is important for another reason: the evolving competitive landscape. To keep ahead, you must quickly kill bad ideas and move on. And, of course, many companies have limited financial resources; funds cannot be wasted on the wrong idea.

If you're thinking about setting up a multinational conglomerate based on revenues from siphoning and then reselling gas, then fair warning, you're gonna have ME as a competitor.
—Joel Cohen

In "Mr. Plow," a *Simpsons* episode famous for a sarcastic take on North American business practices, Homer Simpson decides to be his own boss by starting a snow plowing business. Under the company name Mr. Plow—"My prices are so low, you'll think I've suffered brain damage," he asserts in a late-night

TV ad—he becomes a success and a celebrity and is handed the keys to the city of Springfield.

But soon this success draws competition from his belching, beer-chugging bar pal Barney Gumble, who sets up a rival business—Plow King. The competition between the two of them is so destructive it almost ruins their friendship, along with both their businesses. Eventually, Homer rescues his pal from an avalanche and they vow to stop the competition. As always in *The Simpsons*, Homer returns to his regular job at the Springield nuclear plant, none the wiser for his experience.

The Mr. Plow episode holds a lesson (as usual, somewhat twisted) for all teams: nothing will be accomplished if everyone is always trying to win. "Winning" is not judged on the small yards made by individual running backs. Instead, it's the entire team's moving of the ball that results in a touchdown that counts.

Alternatively, projects will fail if team members try to avoid any conflict by deferring to each other. Human beings have been naturally forming teams since they first formed packs in order to hunt more effectively. When people join together to perform a task, an interesting psychological dynamic takes place. They usually approach the situation from a natural personal temperament, but find they must put that temperament aside, or at least leverage its strengths, in order to function effectively on the team.

"I WAS VOTED MOST LIKELY TO BE A MENTAL PATIENT OR A HILLBILLY OR A CHIMPANZEE."

Put together the right mix of people with the right assets. A team that has members with ancillary, and sometimes opposing, skills can create great results. A group of like-minded people may fall prey to groupthink, killing the creative process. However, radically opposite views do have the potential to foster competition and undermine or even destroy the collaborative process. The secret is in the balance.

Team functioning is a constant collaborative process, and Joel Cohen is involved in it almost daily. He has come to know it well, referring to it as "controlled anarchy," essential to enhancing creativity. "When you do an episode, you pitch an idea and everyone in the writers' room looks at it," he explains. "There are seven to 15 writers in The Room and they go over it for three or four days, trying to find the jokes and the story. Then you outline it for a week, ship it to the upper echelon of writers and it comes back with notes; the group in the writers' room picks it over again and improves it. Then it's sent to the animators for a rough 'animatic,' or drawing, which you study for holes, and then you go back and rewrite again. The Room is usually controlled chaos with everyone throwing in ideas, but under a kind of martial law as the group takes the nugget

> *Mr. Scorpio says productivity is up two percent, and it's all because of my motivational techniques, like doughnuts and the possibility of more doughnuts to come.—Homer Simpson*

and develops it. Everyone is enthusiastic, but someone has to be the arbiter, so high-level writers are usually given the sceptre and run the room." This is the fine balance of leadership that needs to be shown in a corporation—control anarchy without stifling the creativity that comes with it.

Leadership in an entrepreneurial or creative situation where development is still taking place looks different from the way it does in more mature business settings. Leaders in entrepreneurial circumstances tend to possess certain characteristics that have been measured and catalogued by researchers. Numerous studies have shown that, generally, entrepreneurial leaders show most of the following characteristics: commitment and determination; opportunity obsession; tolerance of risk, ambiguity and uncertainty; creativity, self-reliance and ability to adapt; and motivation to excel.

In sports parlance, players are said to be "good in the room" if their leadership or teamwork skills are superior to their athletic abilities. Such players keep sports teams cohesive and focused, without imposing a rigid structure on them. Being good in the room is all about leadership and is a prime requisite for success in any team setting, sports or elsewhere. It is especially important for any early-stage venture with a more free-flowing view of what it wants to achieve and how it will achieve it.

Although Homer Simpson may have a twisted sense of what constitutes motivation—doughnuts alone won't cut it—he does recognize the need for it. Any team that is working on a project, whether developing a product or a business, requires a motivator, a vision of

If you choose a job you're passionate about, it will feel like you've never worked a day in your life. Another way to get that feeling is to go on welfare.—Joel Cohen

what it wants to achieve. Generally, the team (or business) leader creates this, although it may be manifested in several ways—through top-down command-and-control management (although this is rare), through inspiration, and especially through participative management. Each may be used at different times, depending on the situation.

Effective leaders, including team leaders, according to Wharton Business School professor Steward D. Friedman, exhibit these typical characteristics: authenticity (or being real); integrity (or being whole); and creativity (or being innovative).[6]

Team leaders, like all leaders, must keep the team focused on the vision, or the objective. Having the team compose a purpose statement as the basis for the group's work is a useful team leadership exercise. This is not to be confused with the hackneyed mission statement, often the object of ridicule. Instead, it energizes the team by answering the question "Why are we doing this?"

"IF ADULTS DON'T LIKE THEIR JOBS, THEY DON'T GO ON STRIKE. THEY JUST GO IN EVERY DAY AND DO IT REALLY HALF-ASSED."

Rigid structures and procedures will hold back the team-based development process and can result in "phoned-in" thinking. One of the tricks of leadership in any business is to unchain the creative process without letting it become unfocused.

Teamwork, says Cohen, involves putting aside your inhibitions and joining a process for a greater purpose. This is often done at the instigation of others. "It's really continual brainstorming," he says, "and someone once called brainstorming like a conga line at a party. You wouldn't get up and dance by yourself, but if you see a conga line, you might get up and join it and do something crazy because it comes out of a group. When you enter The Room, you realize the way to be successful is to be unrestrained."

"When I first started working with other writers on *The Simpsons*, I was hesitant," Cohen says. "I was worried about rejection. But I

---

6   Steward D. Friedman, *Cultivating Total Leadership with Authenticity, Integrity and Creativity*, Wharton Business School, knowledge@Wharton, 2002.

learned that if you fully commit to something, have a passion for it, and people respond to it, even on the small level of a joke, they find value in it. I often see this in other people. If you have the nugget of something and you throw passion at it and commit to it, you can elevate it to the really great."

Similarly, businesses require stakeholder participation and vocal encouragement, not just to generate good ideas, but also to ensure potential mistakes are caught. It is useless for the CEO to hear, six months after some catastrophic failure in the company, one of the team members say, "I had a concern about that when we did it but...." A large business might survive such an event. In a small business or a startup, these breakdowns in communication and truth can destroy the business.

Passion is the blood that runs through the veins of any successful group or team. It keeps the team focused and makes every member feel like a contributor to the ultimate objective. San Diego consultants Drs. Kevin and Jackie Freiberg have studied passion and suggest how crucial it is to an organization's performance:

- *Passion intensifies focus.* It's the magnetic force that keeps people working on things that make the business more competitive.

- *Passion helps innovation and creativity* by injecting fresh new perspectives that activate minds, expand awareness and challenge people to think.

- *Passion protects and promotes the values driving the business.* It often requires passion to stand upon convictions.

- *Passionate people raise the standards of performance.* They have a tendency to hold others accountable and demand commitment of everyone around them. This commitment to a higher standard becomes contagious.

- *Passionate people create an electric, exciting work environment* that energizes others. They contribute to building the kind of culture that attracts world-class people.

- *Passion creates a sense of urgency* that is required of every organization going through change in today's highly competitive world. Passion is the enemy of apathy, complacency and procrastination.

- *Passion helps people deal with fear.* Change is scary—for anybody! But when passions are bigger than fears, people develop the courage to take risks.[7]

However, this passionate state, in which team members freely trade opinions, is not easily reached. The stumbling block: the human personality. Whenever human beings get together in groups, the strong-willed and driven invariably attempt to control the group, a process called "persuading," whether by bullying, or by more subtle methods (praise; opinion trading). Meanwhile, others may seek to avoid all conflict and strife by quietly acquiescing to group decisions even if they don't believe in them.

All teams feature versions of these two larger divisions. Some persuaders may also be inspirers; some of those who acquiesce may mask this by being very good organizers. Teams whose members cannot put aside or leverage these natural personality traits reach only moderate performance levels. At best they reach Tuckman's "norming," a condition of suspended animation in which tasks are grudgingly accomplished. To perform well, all teams must reach a state where members are interested not only in themselves, but also in the ultimate performance of the team.

"IF SOMETHING IS HARD TO DO THEN IT'S NOT WORTH DOING."

Despite Homer's cynicism, teamwork can be challenging, but is well worth the time and effort. On a well-functioning team, members join a process for a greater purpose than their own agendas. They should defend their views passionately, but also be flexible when others object. If everyone refuses to budge, nothing will get done.

Athletes and sports psychologists often talk about operating in the zone, an almost hypnotic state in which all of a person's being is focused on one task, whether that is playing music, writing, designing, planning or running a marathon. It is peak athletic and mental performance. Finding the zone is therefore extremely important to any new business or organization trying to determine what it is, what it is going to do and

---

7 Drs. Kevin and Jackie Freiberg, *Passion: Finding it in your life, building it in your business,* Speakers Platform, www.speaking.com/.

why it is going to do it. The zone, sometimes called "flow," is also an optimal state of teamwork, akin to the Tuckman state of "performing." All members of the team are working at a high level.

Teams operating in the zone do not have time for emotional storms, intra-team competition, criticism from outsiders, time-consuming suggestions from higher-ups, or other distractions. One aspect of operating in the zone, or focusing, is an ability to ignore the noise around you.

Freedom from outside forces allows team members to concentrate fully on the tasks at hand and to work together smoothly to accomplish those tasks. According to Aynsley Smith (PhD), a sports psychology consultant at the Mayo Clinic Sports Medicine Center in Rochester, Minnesota, training your mind is an important step toward getting in the zone. Aspects of such training include increasing concentration and focus, controlling emotions, trying to feel relaxed but energized, being calm and positive, and aiming to feel challenged and confident.

"THE THREE LITTLE SENTENCES THAT WILL GET YOU THROUGH LIFE: 1. COVER FOR ME 2. OH, GOOD IDEA, BOSS! 3. IT WAS LIKE THAT WHEN I GOT HERE."

To be effective, a team must be able to operate free from outside control, from intensive input from superiors, or from the general noise of society. Keep control over the process—don't let boards, investors or outside managers meddle in operations they don't understand as well as the team does. Respect their need to know, but don't let them get too close.

Mental conditioning is different for everyone, Smith says, and an individual may have to modify conditioning techniques to suit his or her own situations. But there are core techniques that are useful for everyone and can help maintain levels of excitement or relaxation that work best. These include:

- *Relaxation.* Relaxation can help relieve anxiety and tension and improve your concentration and focus. Smile when your nerves start to fray. Enjoy yourself. Remember your love of the game. Stay calm. Rushing things generally results in bad moves. Focus on the present rather than the possible upsets that could happen.

- *Imagery.* Imagery can help you reduce anxiety, increase your concentration and confidence and serve as mental practice or rehearsal. Imagery works well with relaxation techniques because the relaxation can help you better imagine yourself performing the skill required. It's impossible to feel anxiety and relaxation at the same time. Try picturing yourself doing your sport or activity. Imagine yourself dressed as you would be, hearing what you might hear and smelling what you might smell—feeling your muscles and your emotions. Then envision yourself practicing your skills, running your race—whatever it might be. Imagine yourself doing things correctly, successfully, with confidence and skill, and feeling energetic but relaxed.

- *Goal setting.* Setting goals can increase your motivation, provide you with a sense of challenge and help you determine what you can and can't control, leading to greater confidence. Set some long-term goals but also set some short-term goals. Goals should be challenging but manageable and measurable. Include performance, outcome and process goals. Performance goals pertain to your personal best, regardless of how well the competition does. Outcome goals pertain to whether you win or lose. Process goals pertain to the actions you must take to accomplish your objectives. Set strategies to meet your goals and measure your progress.

- *Positive thinking.* Negative thoughts can get in the way of concentration and confidence. Telling yourself, "Don't miss the shot" or "Don't strike out" can cause you to do the exact thing you were trying to avoid. Instead of dwelling on a poor performance, remind yourself that you can do it. Rather than blaming factors you can't control, focus on changes you can make to improve your performance. Positive thinking can lead to confidence, focus and inner calm—qualities that help move you into the zone.[8]

Mental conditioning is just as important to a young business's team members as it is in a sports team. Anything that helps deal with the stress involved in corporate life can make a difference to the bottom

8 Aynsley Smith, *In the zone: Training your mind as well as your body*, Mayo Foundation for Education and Research (MFMER),www.mayoclinic.com, April 30, 2004.

line by helping members stay relaxed and focused on the task and to deal diplomatically with outside noise and interference. For example, to be effective, all companies need to ensure that outside investors and board members do not tread too closely on the creative process. Outsiders, especially if they are financially involved, often display a natural tendency to try to inject their ideas and thoughts into the process. This can be a delicate situation, but, while their needs must be respected, it is vital that the team be able to manage this interference and keep control of the process. In the early stage, it is imperative that those living and breathing the creation of the company continue to do so without too much outside interference.

Joel Cohen credits much of the success of *The Simpsons* team writing or product development process to this kind of freedom from interference. *The Simpsons* is a television show that generates millions of dollars for its network, a situation almost guaranteed to draw interference from outsiders in the organization who would like to manage the process more closely. But the show's producer, James L. Brooks, guards his team closely to keep outside interference at bay. Certainly, the comedy will occasionally work in other televised events, such as the Super Bowl, but, for the most part, a hands-off policy reigns.

"Jim Brooks is a famous director and producer," Cohen says. "And one of his rules to Fox was, 'Don't give us any notes.' With most shows, you have people in the network or studio who are sending notes, telling you 'I don't like this, this actor shouldn't do that, the story should be about this.' And as a writer you have to incorporate that. But because it was Jim Brooks, and he said don't give us notes, we don't have that. No external group is allowed to get their mitts on it. I don't know if that's a product of the success, or a cause of it, but it provides a lot of freedom."

It has been said that inside the mind of every person who launches a venture, whether a new business or just a project, lies a vision of a future state that is preferable to the present state. But not all achieve that vision. In fact, the rate of new business failure over five years is thought to be in the neighbourhood of 80 percent. Product development boasts a lower rate of failure but it is still very high, as much as 50 percent. Does that mean all those

Kids, you tried your best and you failed miserably. The lesson is, never try.
—*Homer Simpson*

thousands who start businesses every year, or decide to launch new products or services, return, as Homer advises, to their old jobs, licking their wounds and being bitter?

Of course not. All successful entrepreneurs have made mistakes and experienced failure. But they invariably pick themselves up and try it again from a different angle. True entrepreneurs do try again, and again. They just don't go about it blindly. They learn lessons from their mistakes and approach new ventures with renewed fervour. Within Homer's cynical advice is a nugget of a lesson: recognize when you're failing, and retreat. Then, when you have learned what went wrong, try it again, but on a new trajectory.

Similarly, failures or mistakes occur regularly when any venture is in the start-up phase. Every day is a day of exploration. The players—usually a very small core of people—often find themselves on dead-end paths or at odds with each other over how to get where they want to go. This usually passes if everyone recognizes the goal and agrees to work together to achieve it. If the unencumbered exchange of thoughts and ideas is the fuel that gets you there, teamwork alone is the vehicle.

You can't depend on me all your life. You have to learn
there's a little Homer Simpson in all of us.
—Homer Simpson

5 THINGS YOU NEED TO KNOW

How *The Simpsons* creative team operates—with a few quotes from Homer thrown in—is truly a guide for any organization, large or small:

1. "Bart, you're saying Butt Kisser like it's a bad thing!"

Create an atmosphere of frankness and openness. When a team needs to generate creative ideas on a regular basis, participants have to be comfortable working closely together in intense situations. That requires checking egos at the door and being open to all participants' thoughts—and criticism. The art of the leader is to ensure that everyone is treated fairly and respectfully, while mercilessly killing bad ideas.

2. "I was voted most likely to be a mental patient or a hillbilly or a chimpanzee."

Put together the right mix of people with the right assets. A team that has members with ancillary, and sometimes opposing, skills can create great results. A group of like-minded people may fall prey to groupthink, killing the creative process. However, radically opposite views do have the potential to foster competition and undermine or even destroy the collaborative process. The secret is in the balance.

3. "If adults don't like their jobs, they don't go on strike. They just go in every day and do it really half-assed."

Rigid structures and procedures will hold back the team-based development process and can result in "phoned-in" thinking. One of the tricks of leadership in any business is to unchain the creative process without letting it become unfocused.

4. "If something is hard to do then it's not worth doing."

Despite Homer's cynicism, teamwork can be challenging, but is well worth the time and effort.On a well-functioning team, members join a process for a greater purpose than their own agendas. They should defend their views passionately, but also be flexible when others object. If everyone refuses to budge, nothing will get done.

5. "The three little sentences that will get you through life: 1.Cover for me 2. Oh, good idea, Boss! 3. It was like that when I got here."

To be effective, a team must be able to operate free from outside control, from intensive input from superiors, or from the general noise of society. Keep control over the process—don't let boards, investors or outside managers meddle in operations they don't understand as well as the team does. Respect their need to know, but don't let them get too close.

CHAPTER NINETEEN

Managing the Perfect Storm
Leadership when the Chips are Down

FEATURING THE WISDOM OF PAUL TELLIER

In January 2003, Paul Tellier was named CEO of Montreal-based transportation giant Bombardier Inc., the legendary company founded by Joseph-Armand Bombardier 60 years ago to produce his invention, the Ski-Doo. Bombardier has grown into a global giant, listed on the Toronto, Brussels and Frankfurt stock exchanges with revenues of US$15 billion in fiscal 2004. Its rail transport equipment and regional and business aircraft are used by millions of people daily.

Tellier, one of a very few non-family CEOs to head up Bombardier, was appointed during one of the company's darkest periods. In the post September 11 era, demand for its aircraft had tumbled precipitously. After heady growth in the 1990s, its profits and stock price plunged amid lost contracts and sluggish sales. Bombardier's legacy of government financial support also led some to question its real value. And there was a family that, through multiple voting shares, controlled almost 60 percent of the company.

Unforeseen turbulence rocked Bombardier during Tellier's tenure in the form of a rapid spike in the Canadian dollar—anathema to export companies—combined with a steep rise in fuel prices. Eventually, Tellier himself fell victim to the turbulence. Late last year, he abruptly departed after what insiders say was a standoff at the board level with the founding family members.

Challenge is nothing new to Tellier, whose career has been marked by strong leadership during extraordinarily difficult times. He steered Canadian

National Railways from a stodgy government-owned operation to a lean, private-sector railway. Previously, he was Clerk of the Privy Council—Canada's top mandarin—where he put out fires on a regular basis. Even earlier, he worked for federal and provincial cabinet ministers, helping handle some of the country's major upheavals.

In both government and the private sector, Tellier consistently delivers a signature no-nonsense, decisive style of leadership that has earned him a reputation as one of North America's leading CEOs—as his lengthy list of leadership awards would attest. A hallmark of his style is his comportment in crisis—when, due to inside and outside forces, he is pushed to manage a perfect storm.

—⁂—

Update: *In October of 2007, Paul Tellier was appointed by Prime Minister Stephen Harper to a panel responsible for reviewing Canada's mission in Afghanistan.*

The best pilots in the world are the ones who know how to handle their aircraft when conditions are choppy. Experienced airlines and fliers know that and seek them out. Shareholders, customers, board members and employees are no different. High-stakes business requires strong leadership at the helm.

There is, however, a big difference between managing and leading. Managers control or guide a process by virtue of the authority they have over subordinates. Leaders inspire, motivate and influence an organization, coaxing the best performance from their staff, often by personal example. If management is supervising people within an organization, leadership is influencing people within that same environment. Moreover, it is about getting them to want to achieve goals, rather than having to be told to do so. It has been said that "managers are people who do things right, while leaders are people who do the right thing."[1] The former requires an understanding of how to use management tools and can be taught, while the latter requires more innate personal abilities such as decisiveness, communicative aptitude and, usually, experience.

This distinction does not mean managers cannot be leaders. However, there is usually a process in which they *become* leaders instead of managers, and it is not simply because they are appointed to the job or that they have taken a few courses on the subject. Bernard Bass, an

---

1   Warren Bennis, *On Becoming a Leader*, Addison-Wesley, 1994.

organizational behaviour professor at Binghamton University in New York, believes there are three theories to explain how people become leaders:

- *Trait Theory* believes some personality traits may lead people naturally into leadership roles. In other words, they are born leaders.

- *Great Events Theory* suggests that a crisis or important event may bring out extraordinary leadership qualities in an ordinary person. For example, mothers whose children had been killed by drunk drivers then formed Mothers Against Drunk Driving (MADD). Instead of being devastated into inaction, their losses motivated them to take charge and create a campaign of awareness around the problem.

- *Transformational Leadership Theory* postulates that people can choose to become leaders and is, traditionally, the most widely accepted theory of leadership.[2]

If transformational leadership is the most common form, it stands to reason that high-performing leaders grow through a combination of both events and learning. They likely choose to take the leadership track at some point and then train rigorously for it. This training is not only required for the day-to-day operations of a company; it is also an essential when that company is undergoing massive change, as so many are today. Globalization, sudden market shifts, financial chaos and other factors can cause upheaval in the operations of any organization. Often, several of these environmental factors occur within striking distance of each other, creating a "perfect storm" of events. It is in these times when leadership is truly under the spotlight and called into action.

Paul Tellier has captained many a ship through the very eye of the storm. In January 2003, he was named CEO of Montreal-based Bombardier after spending a decade as CEO of Canadian National Railways. There, he converted an inefficient, complacent, Canadian government-owned operation into a lean, private sector entity that is today the most efficient railroad in North America. Previous to that,

---

2   Bernard M. Bass, *Bass and Stogdill's Handbook of Leadership*, Free Press, 1990.

he had been the Canadian government's top civil servant, Clerk of the Privy Council, a crisis-containment job of immense proportions. Earlier in his career he had been an advisor to federal and provincial governments during some of Canada's worst upheavals, such as the rise of the separatist Parti Québécois in the province of Quebec and the 1970 October Crisis, which involved the kidnapping of a British Consul and the murder of a Quebec cabinet minister.

Battle-scarred, and schooled in the brimstone of several cataclysmic events, Tellier arrived at Bombardier amid profound crisis. The company, which in the 1990s had shown robust earnings, strong growth and high stock prices, was spiralling downward. After September 11, 2001, most recreational travellers elected to stay at home, causing demand for Bombardier's airplanes, particularly its line of small regional jets, to recede. Meanwhile, the economic downturn was putting pressure on sales of its business jets: companies just weren't paying for those big-ticket luxury toys anymore. The terrorist aftermath hit its biggest airline clients like a tsunami. One of them, U.S. Airways, was in bankruptcy protection in late 2004.

If the crisis in the airline industry was not enough, what really added insult to injury was an unforeseen set of problems in 2004 that were well beyond the company's control—a spike in the Canadian dollar coupled with a dramatic rise in fuel prices. For an export firm like Bombardier, a strong Canadian dollar had a devastating impact on revenues and ultimately the bottom line. Similarly, rising fuel prices stifled demand for fuel price-sensitive aircraft. This double whammy sent Bombardier's already sinking stock price lower. The one-time stock-market darling hovered in humiliating penny-stock territory.

DEVELOP AN APPETITE FOR THE HARD STUFF

Seek out tough situations and embrace them. While others naturally gravitate to the low-risk roles, seek out the arduous ones and take them head on. Make your career your own personal boot camp. Don't be afraid of change, conflict or the insurmountable challenge. Embrace them and accept the bumps ahead.

Tellier, a veteran crisis manager, faced these upheavals stalwartly, knowing that for a company with so many units, staff, plants and the like, turmoil came with the territory. Bombardier required strong, logical stewardship of the sort Tellier was renowned for delivering. He's not one to slip quietly into the executive suite and hide behind the brass plate on the door. If obstacles appear, he deals with them head on and is fearless about executing his plan.

Bombardier is a case in point. When Tellier arrived, he quickly set out to transform the company, which, in addition to its other woes, also suffered from lacklustre corporate governance. Tellier unveiled a detailed three-year restructuring plan. And in his two years in office he truly moved mountains: a new stock offering, asset sales, an overhaul of the railcar business and thousands of layoffs. As many industry watchers noted, the once Byzantine financial statements became more informative and the company's poor corporate governance radically improved.

His leadership impressed many financial analysts. New York money manager Robert Callander said, "Paul Tellier is trying to fix what became a mess. Tellier is a strong leader and he appears to know what needs to be done."[3] Had he always been like this? More to the point, are strong leaders born or created? Tellier says his own leadership gift is more a process of acquiring the necessary traits than something he innately carried. However, he admits nature may have blessed him with the right foundations. "You can train somebody to become a leader from scratch and I am a strong believer in mentoring, coaching and training," he points out. "But . . . a person has to have the basics first. Otherwise, there are a great many managers but very few leaders."

From an early age, it was clear Tellier owned a strong will and was unafraid to speak his mind—traits that would prove useful later in his career. Born in Joliette, Quebec, northeast of Montreal, in May 1939, he was not exactly a compliant youth. As a teen, he ran away from boarding school and later left a Jesuit college to become a ski bum. "I was known for having views," he recalls. "I was very visible." He made the transition from outspoken youth to blunt, no-nonsense leader in two ways—by consciously seeking out the messy, tough jobs he believed he could really learn from, and by associating with the brightest and the best mentors—experts at defusing hot situations. From each person and experience, his confidence grew stronger, his repertoire of skills amid critical situations more impressive.

3 *Bloomberg News*, November, 2004.

"I was extremely fortunate to be associated with outstanding people who could teach me a lot," he says of his youth. These included professors who later became judges, cabinet ministers and two former Prime Ministers—Pierre Trudeau and Brian Mulroney. At university, he underwent rigorous intellectual training and then continued his apprenticeship on the job in various government roles where he was able to observe the best in the business.

One-time Trudeau cabinet minister Jean-Luc Pepin, who hired Tellier as his executive assistant, defined the notion of "work ethic" for his charge. He told Tellier that even if he had a 102-degree fever, he still had to go to work, reasoning, "You'll still have the fever at home, so you may as well go to work with it." And Tellier lived by that creed. Illness doesn't keep him off the job. He also abhors wasting time and to that end will fill every spare moment, while taking a cab to the airport, for instance, with work.

"This is the kind of guy who lays out his clothes in the morning while the shower's getting warm so that he doesn't waste any time," observed Michael Sabia, CEO of BCE Inc., who worked with Tellier at the Privy Council and CN.[4]

Through mentorship, experience and traits such as self-discipline, Tellier developed his own definition of leadership. It is, he says, both about vision and management, "about getting on with things and focusing not on the past, but on the present—and the future." It is also about "getting an optimal performance from the people that you are with. How do you achieve this? You've got to set the objectives and you've got to do this collectively."

This kind of leadership is important in everyday affairs, and especially when the landscape turns rocky. Management guru Peter Drucker argues in his seminal 1980 book, *Managing in Turbulent Times*, that successful managers must always look after both today— the fundamentals—and tomorrow. In turbulent times, leaders cannot assume tomorrow will be an extension of today. "Unique events cannot be planned," he notes. "They can, however, be foreseen, or rather, one can prepare to take advantage of them. One can have strategies for tomorrow that anticipate the areas in which the greatest challenges are likely to occur, strategies that enable a business or public service institution to take advantage of the unforeseen and unforeseeable."

4   *Globe and Mail*, Dec. 14, 2004.

Tellier lived by that philosophy at Bombardier. The company is part of a highly volatile industry in which economic, political and unexpected geopolitical forces are at play. It competes against airlines whose governments support them, such as Brazil-based Embraer, but gets criticized at home for approaching the government for financial assistance. Throw in founding family members as the controlling shareholders—with clear ideas about what should be done at "their" company—the leader has a deeper layer of complexity to sort through.

Tellier needed a strategy in place for the everyday things Drucker mentions, yet had to be flexible enough to drop it at a moment's notice in favour of tactics that would address an urgent problem. His decision to personally visit his European bankers after a series of bad Bombardier earnings reports and debt downgrades in late 2004 is an example. With the financiers, he focused on the unexpected—the downgrades—yet also addressed the topic of a next series of larger commercial aircraft Bombardier was contemplating. His message to these key stakeholders was that the company was staying the course amid tough times. "Don't be distracted because the company received three negative analyst reports," he advised.

Tellier is adamant about having full managerial authority. He discussed his expectations for more than 13 hours with Laurent Beaudoin, son-in-law of the company founder, before taking on the top job. "It was clear that if I came, there could be only one CEO and I would have 100 percent of the job," he told author Peter Hadekel. "Also, I didn't have a good fix on the degree of involvement . . . of the family. Again, I had to make myself clear on that."[5]

There were times during his tenure at Bombardier when this complete authority was granted. For example, one of Tellier's first moves to get the company back into shape involved selling its recreational products division—the original business of the company. Understandably, he faced intense resistance from founding family members: this business had been Bombardier's heart and soul. The trademark Ski-Doo (motorized snowmobile) had laid the foundation for the global giant the company had become. Both it and the Sea-Doo, or personal watercraft vehicles, were household names.

As an outsider and a naturally logical thinker, Tellier brought a more detached business view of the division to the table. Tellier did

---

5. Peter Hadekel, *Silent Partners*, Key Porters Books, 2004.

not think the turnaround he had promised Bombardier shareholders lay in the recreational products division. Its profitability was waning, a result of a weakening economy and consequent lessening of consumer demand. And the unit represented only 10 percent of Bombardier's total revenues. It also represented a potential source of cash, which he needed to reduce high debt levels.

However, the family was so attached to this division that one family member, Pierre Beaudoin, grandson of J. Armand Bombardier and head of Bombardier's aerospace division, decided to quit and head a family bid to buy back the division. "He was deadly opposed to the sale . . . He was very angry," Tellier says. But Tellier acted as a strong leader throughout, sticking with his vision in the face of serious opposition from no less a force than the founding family. His decision was no surprise; he'd warned Bombardier its sale was a possibility. "I had told (chairman Laurent) Beaudoin that, you know, there was no sacred cow, that everything was on the table." Finally the family came around and bought the division with other investors. To this day, Tellier characterizes the sale as the best business decision of his career.

However, even after this success, he ultimately received neither full managerial control nor authority over the family, and his tenure with Bombardier ended. Tellier's comportment during the sale of the family firm's signature business was classic leadership methodology of the type that can't easily be taught. He was focused and fearless despite the family histrionics.

START BY DRAWING YOUR LINE IN THE SAND

Ensure your leadership features a clear line of authority. When outsiders control the company, as in Bombardier's case, the task is especially crucial. Get clear and binding agreement with the stakeholders on the scope of your mandate. You cannot lead effectively without clear marching orders. Don't wait for an issue to arise to confidently mark your territory. Do it on day one.

He maintained this focused leadership style even more during what appeared to be a boardroom struggle that led to his eventual departure from Bombardier. It will likely never be fully understood, at least publicly, what went on in the boardroom in the days leading up to Tellier's exit. But the abrupt, and extremely rare, resignation of two board members after Tellier's departure, combined with a subsequent steep drop in the company's stock price, indicated to many observers that a boardroom battle was going on over his leadership. Did the controlling family panic as stormy forces intensified around the company? It is difficult to tell, but the question has intrigued analysts and other business writers since the event. Someday, perhaps, the question will be firmly answered. In the meantime, however, indications are that after Tellier drew his line in the sand, some board members decided to cross it—and the results were as he predicted.

It is in these tumultuous times that true leaders block out the panic and resolutely adhere to their vision. Episodes of extreme pressure and turmoil, conflict and feverish emotions—particularly if they're demonstrated by controlling shareholders—can cripple a company. One way to prevent this organizational breakdown is to constantly and clearly communicate goals so that everyone in the organization relates to them each day when they arrive at work.

DON'T BE A GHOST

Communicate regularly with everyone in your organization, in both good and bad times. Ensure employees, board members and, most important, major stakeholders (such as bankers and investors) all know your game plan. Don't leave them in an information vacuum, especially during crisis periods when their likely source of news will be from third parties. Treat the situation like your own family; you wouldn't want your children getting their family knowledge from the street either.

Tellier is a consummate communicator. He is straightforward, blunt and fearless when it comes to transmitting the tough messages. And when he sets out to spread his truths he includes everyone—no easy feat for a company like Bombardier, with some 60,000 employees and plants in North and South America, Asia, Oceania and Europe.

"The welder in the shop in Germany has to be able to relate to not only the broad objectives but what he's got to do better that will contribute to the overall strategy," Tellier explains. By providing the German welder with the message that he is as important to the company as the aerospace worker in Belfast, the leader ties the disparate units of the company together—and toward a common goal. In short, he inspires them.

Talking to everyone from his suited executive colleagues to those on the shop floor is typical of the Tellier leadership style. He is not afraid to be honest—and, most important, visible—even when the message he's serving up is far from appetizing. During the CN privatization, he had to lop thousands of jobs from the payroll. He travelled the country, meeting railway employees face to face to explain why his actions were necessary. He would talk to employees on their turf—in the cafeteria of their shops. He'd speak for 10 minutes then answer questions for an hour. As for Bombardier employees, when the quarterly results come out, he'd reach 800 staff members around the globe via a conference call. Twice a year he assembled the top 200 managers to review the company's outlook. In a time when CEOs are scrambling to keep just their investors informed on a timely basis, Tellier's efforts sent a very clear message to the team: You matter.

Sometimes, however, leadership involves communicating in a way that pushes the troops beyond the problem. Tellier needed that skill during his tenure at CN. In 1999, he'd struck a $28-billion deal to buy Burlington Northern Santa Fe Corp. The transaction would have made CN the largest—and in Tellier's mind, the best—railway in North America.

But the merger was not to be. The U.S. railways that weren't involved, fearing for their own future if the deal went through, lobbied Washington hard to make their interests heard. The result was that the Surface Transportation Board, which controls U.S. rail activity, declared a moratorium on railway transactions until it could develop rules to deal with the four big remaining Class 1 U.S. rail lines. The tactics were effective and the deal was called off. Once the moratorium was lifted, the board said it planned to make it more difficult for the few remaining North American railroads to merge.

"We would have had to wait another 15 months as a result of the moratorium," says Tellier, explaining why the deal died. This is a hard message to hear when you have been working for some time toward an objective you believe in. Tellier's team was devastated. But when it came time to break the news that the corporate marriage was off, Tellier did not publicly express bitterness or anger. Instead, he summoned his team to an 8 a.m. meeting shortly after the decision and walked them crisply through the process of the failed deal. He concluded by saying, simply,

"Listen, this is over. Let's turn the page. And let's show the world we can become the world's best railway without anybody."

As a result, he nullified any temptation for those who had worked long and hard on the deal to feel anger or defeat—counterproductive, self-pitying emotions, in his mind, that could have stalled employees from staying the course and making CN a better company. "If I had reacted differently . . . everybody would have been downbeat for six months," he says. "We didn't miss a beat because I didn't make any fuss about this." Privately, he advised that it was very tough to maintain this exterior in light of his own personal disappointment in the failure of the deal.

Tellier is not afraid to admit that his honest communication style can sometimes backfire. He readily admits that the biggest mistake he made in his entire career was laying out in lavish detail his turnaround plan for Bombardier and promising it would be done in just three years. While this fast-paced leader did succeed in achieving a number of things he'd set out in his plan, unforeseen events conspired to delay the time-table. Therefore, by December 2004 when Tellier released the company's third-quarter 2004 results showing a 93 percent drop in profits, it became painfully apparent that shareholders—especially the majority shareholders in the family who relied on their shares for their income—were not going to see the fruits of his labours anytime soon. No doubt, this shocking news had something to do with his leaving the company shortly thereafter.

Still, good leaders have to hold a wider scope. At Bombardier, once the double whammy of the high dollar and oil prices hit and things were not looking good for the company, Tellier initiated an extensive trip to Europe, and then North America, to communicate to his vast network of financiers an upbeat, yet realistic, message about where the company stood. He didn't want them getting jittery by reading too many negative headlines. The meetings with his New York bankers were the last Tellier would hold as Bombardier's CEO. They wrapped up on a Friday and the following Monday at 8 a.m. he was gone from the company, as were two other independent directors who resigned. The bankers may have been soothed, but the family that controlled the board apparently decided it no longer had faith in the captain of their listed ship.

SEEK COMPANY

Global firms will typically have a strong board of directors. Use your board to mentor your leadership. Yes, you are ultimately accountable to these people, but when tough decisions are required, directors can be great sources of support. Also, make sure to sit on other boards for perspective. This will allow you to learn from the leadership techniques of other CEOs. Find some strong mentors and use them. Being a CEO is often said to be the loneliest job. Change that.

Despite this setback, Paul Tellier has always viewed a board of directors as central to his job as leader. It may be ironic that in this case it was a standoff with the board that resulted in his departure from the company, but Tellier has made it a rule throughout his career to rely on directors and his earlier mentors for support and help. A CEO can easily feel isolated, especially in times when tough decision-making is required. Tellier has always been aware that a CEO cannot operate in a bubble and believes in using the board and his mentors to his, and the company's, advantage.

"I don't know to what extent I am typical, but I use the board a lot in sharing my frustrations and challenges," he explains. As a result, he ensures his boards are stocked with the best possible experts in their fields. He doesn't like to waste the opportunity to use a top director's brainpower. "With Andre Desmarais (son of Power Corp. founder Paul Desmarais) on my board, for a CEO not to pick his brain would be silly."

For a leader, professional development must be lifelong, but it can be difficult to achieve with the realities of the post. It's not as if the CEO can just drop down on a whim to the local business school for an executive education refresher on some aspect of leadership. Therefore, presence on your company's and other boards of directors can provide valuable business intelligence. Tellier believes that if a CEO sits on outside boards, he or she can see how other CEOs perform and can consequently learn from their mistakes and victories. To that end, he is a director of Alcan Aluminium, BCE Inc., CN and several other companies. Prior to his becoming CEO of Bombardier, he sat on that board too.

TOUGHEN UP FOR THE GAME BETWEEN PERIODS

The days of one-dimensional workaholic CEOs are over. Find ways to reduce stress and increase mental and physical toughness by working out, eating well and finding spiritual escapes from the day-to-day reality of the job. This is especially important when running a global operation requiring constant travel and time change challenges. It is even more important when the business requires you to constantly be putting out fires.

Perspective can come from other sources. The demands of leadership can be all consuming and it can be easy to forget where to put the emphasis—while examining the problems on one tree, you can forget about the entire forest. For that reason, Tellier has learned to lean on his private life to help him find balance. Often, after a particularly difficult day, he takes his wife out for dinner. She helps him arrange his priorities, he says. "I remember one day was tough because I had to lay off 250 people. I was whining, and after half an hour, my wife said, 'You once laid off 11,000 people.' We switched to another topic."

Such realizations—that your decisions can affect so many people, and have so much impact—are part of the rigours of leadership, but they can take their toll, physically and mentally. Therefore, the position demands physical and mental fitness to cope with constant attendant stresses. To that end, Tellier says he eats properly and works out every day to stay energized, as his lean frame attests. He also fits in time for fun. To release steam, he cranks up the speed on his beloved motorcycles. He also limits his work hours—to 11-hour days—when he's not travelling. And he doesn't work Friday nights or Saturdays.

This kind of discipline also provides Tellier with the humility to understand that for a leader of his stature, a fall can be inevitable. In the corporate world, everyone is expendable, and a leader is often the first one to take the brunt when things don't go right. When you're running the ship in a storm, and that storm is too powerful, you'll be the one who goes down first: it's part of the territory. Paul Tellier no longer leads Bombardier, but, for a leader of his reputation, that is probably just fine. His credo, learned the hard way in the management trenches of his career, has been to stay flexible—and humble.

During the height of the Bombardier crisis, Tellier gave a hint that he knew the impossibility of achieving perfection when a reporter told him that a new website had been created in which the public could pick the next Canadian CEO destined to receive a pink slip—and he was one of the top choices. Tellier responded with his trademark bluntness, but also with the recognition that some forces just can't be managed. "If anyone thinks he can do a better job than me, he's welcome," he said.

Tellier also knows that flexibility is a handmaiden to humility. Throughout his career, he has moved from one crisis management scenario to the next. There were storms in government, at CN, and at Bombardier. There will be storms somewhere else, and, as with all the turbulence he has weathered before, he will walk in, assess the situation, and do what he thinks has to be done to ride it out. If someone in power doesn't agree, he will undoubtedly move on.

True leaders are remarkable and often display traits and confidence that appear to transcend the day-to-day lives of most. They are, however, in the end merely human beings. They are flexible and humble enough to know they can't fix everything and that all they can do is try. If they're very good at execution, as Paul Tellier is, they will always be welcome in the corporate world. There will always be a need for pilots like him.

5 THINGS YOU NEED TO KNOW

To guide an organization to success through turbulence, great leaders should heed the following:

1. Develop an Appetite for the Hard Stuff

Seek out tough situations and embrace them. While others naturally gravitate to the low-risk roles, seek out the arduous ones and take them head on. Make your career your own personal boot camp. Don't be afraid of change, conflict or the insurmountable challenge. Embrace them and accept the bumps ahead.

2. Start by Drawing Your Line in the Sand

Ensure your leadership features a clear line of authority. When outsiders control the company, as in Bombardier's case, the task is especially crucial. Get clear and binding agreement with the stakeholders on the scope of your mandate. You cannot lead effectively without clear marching orders. Don't wait for an issue to arise to confidently mark your territory. Do it on day one.

3. Don't Be a Ghost

Communicate regularly with everyone in your organization, in both good and bad times. Ensure employees, board members and, most important, major stakeholders (such as bankers and investors) all know your game plan. Don't leave them in an information vacuum, especially during crisis periods when their likely source of news will be from third parties. Treat the situation like your own family; you wouldn't want your children getting their family knowledge from the street either.

4. Seek Company

Global firms will typically have a strong board of directors. Use your board to mentor your leadership. Yes, you are ultimately accountable to these people, but when tough decisions are required, directors can be great sources of support. Also, make sure to sit on other boards for perspective. This will allow you to learn from the leadership techniques of other CEOs. Find some strong mentors and use them. Being a CEO is often said to be the loneliest job. Change that.

5. Toughen up for the Game Between Periods

The days of one-dimensional workaholic CEOs are over. Find ways to reduce stress and increase mental and physical toughness by working out, eating well and finding spiritual escapes from the day-to-day reality of the job. This is especially important when running a global operation requiring constant travel and time change challenges. It is even more important when the business requires you to constantly be putting out fires.

CHAPTER TWENTY

The Grandeur of Simplicity

Have Fun, Make Money and Grow

FEATURING THE WISDOM OF JIM PATTISON

Forty-five years ago a 31-year-old car salesman and entrepreneur mortgaged his house, borrowed $40,000 and opened his own car dealership. Today, at 76, that entrepreneur, Jim Pattison, is CEO of the Jim Pattison Group, a $5.5-billion empire that has headquarters in Vancouver; employs 26,000 people; includes radio and TV stations, car dealerships, and service business-es in food, entertainment, packaging and finance. The Jim Pattison Group differs from most large business consortiums in at least one fundamental way: no army of executives micromanages the operation. Instead, a core of eight key people make up the lean executive team that leads the entire conglomerate.

A consummate dealmaker, Jim Pattison would be the first to say he is an old-fashioned entrepreneur, just like proprietors of many smaller businesses who inspire, but do not overmanage, performance. Pattison believes a huge organization should be run on basic business principles (including the old favourite, "Keep It Simple, Stupid").

—⁓—

Update: *Pattison is currently involved with the committee for the 2010 Van-couver Winter Olympics. In 2008, his company announced the purchase of GWR, the company that owns the Guinness World Record Franchise. He con-tinues his philanthropic efforts and has donated millions of dollars to causes he supports. Forbes recently placed him as No. 178 on their 2008 list of the world's richest people.*

At the most basic level, organizations are networks of individuals drawn together to accomplish a task. Of course, that description masks a host of questions that are routinely asked and answered by organizational theorists. How are these networks formed? How are those individuals drawn together, and what keeps them together? Why do they work together to achieve a common goal, and why do they just as often fail to work together?

The most prominent theory of the past decade that answers these questions points to leadership as the force that forms, holds and inspires an organization. This is undoubtedly a result of the culture of entrepreneurship that has formed over the past 25 years in North America, a culture that provides top billing—and sometimes celebrity—to entrepreneurs, the driven leaders who by executing on their ideas seize opportunities and build organizations to support themselves in their quests.

For almost half a century, researchers and management gurus have been dissecting organizations to discover what makes them tick, and what pushes them to perform. For years, the military-style organizational structure—usually known as "command and control"—was considered optimal. In the middle of the twentieth century, with the Second World War still fresh in memory, command and control proved to work. This was the era of the company man, the man in the grey flannel suit, and other stereotypes of the extremely linear and heavily managed organizations that dominated the business scene.

However, as the business climate grew more turbulent and competitive, the concept of nimble, opportunistic entrepreneurship began to filter into the collective consciousness. Organizational revolutionaries started to rise to the fore. Tom Peters became a guru with the publication of his and Robert Waterman's bestseller *In Search of Excellence* in 1982. Peters advocated flattening the organization. A business that is top-heavy with management and clogged by systems, he suggested, is at a disadvantage in a dynamic environment in which companies must often change direction swiftly.

Despite the debates over which organizational structure is "correct," researchers now realize that no structure is ultimately right for every organization. In some cases, according to organizational contingency theory, it depends on the fit between two or more factors. In others, it depends on where the organization is in its lifecycle. The organizational lifecycle model assumes there is a regular pattern of development stages in organizations and that the sequence of these stages can be predicted. Different lifecycle theorists claim a differing number of stages of this lifecycle, but almost all, according to a paper written by David C.W. Chin of the Stillman School of Business, say generally that an organization proceeds in the following sequence—inception, growth, maturity, and decline or redevelopment:

- "During inception and early growth, the organization is characterized by a 'one man show,' with the founder bearing the responsibility of managing all aspects of the company. The way to achieve long-term stability in the inception stage is through the use of long working hours, informal communication and structure, centralization and personal leadership.

- "During the growth stage, rapid expansion takes place. The need for planning is elevated as a result of the increased size and complexity of running the operation. More emphasis is placed upon establishing rules and procedures and maintaining stability of the organizational structure. At this point, it is imperative for the founder to be able to delegate responsibilities in order for the company to survive. In this stage, the organization is distinguished by a more formalized structure, focus on task performance, functional specialization and departmentalization."[1]

Both these stages can be called "entrepreneurial," since they exhibit the classic signs of that type of business—rapid growth, inspired leadership, simple management systems. However, most large businesses, or institutions, have grown beyond the entrepreneurial stages and exhibit more corporate tendencies instead. Unfortunately, bureaucracy inevitably reigns in the process. This maturation of businesses, says Chin, often leads to rigid structures that inhibit an organization's adaptability to changes in the market environment.

This bureaucratic rigidity engulfed Tenneco Inc., a U.S. manufacturing consortium that ended the 1980s bleeding red ink and showing almost zero growth prospects. By 1991, the company was losing

---

1   David C.S. Chin, "Organizational life cycle: a review and proposed directions for research," Seton Hall University, *Mid-Atlantic Journal of Business*, 12/1/1994.

US$2 billion annually from its large assortment of mostly unprofitable businesses, was $11 billion in debt against $13 billion in revenue, and desperately needed a turnaround plan. It trimmed its portfolio of money-losing operations, focused its outlook, and, most important, completely altered its structure into a flatter, more responsive operation. It replaced a large managerial bureaucracy with a small corporate office of about 70 people, many times smaller than the original management group. Six years later Tenneco boasted a 50-percent debt-to-capital ratio, a market cap that had risen by more than 100 percent, and a return on assets above 15 percent.

Clearly, conversion of a company's entrepreneurial mindset to corporate thinking, while often demanded as the business becomes more complex, can often also lead to bureaucratization, stagnation, and, in the best cases, a requirement for a complete and radical restructuring. Can the simplicity of the entrepreneurial model be maintained instead, as the organization grows? Jim Pattison has shown that it can; businesses do not have to become more bureaucratic as they grow. Pattison runs a $5.5-billion revenue, 26,000-employee organization on a model that features separate operating divisions and a simple organizational structure. His model demonstrates that if organizations retain an entrepreneurial spirit and remain attuned to basic principles, they can function quite efficiently.

There is no doubt that Pattison, proprietor of an international business empire with assets of Cdn$3.4 billion, still possesses an unbridled entrepreneurial fervour. In April of 2004, Pattison received the Horatio Alger Association of Distinguished Americans Inc.'s rare international award. Although the awards are usually given to Americans, an international award has been awarded twice in the association's 57-year-history, once to hockey great Wayne Gretzky, and now to Pattison. The association gathers every year to honour the spirit of Horatio Alger, a discredited Massachusetts minister who wrote a series of novels in the late 1800s that helped define the American entrepreneurial attitude. Alger's stories were virtually always the same: a destitute but plucky lad cleverly and honestly pulls himself up by the bootstraps, overcomes various obstacles and eventually makes a success of himself. Although they now seem simplistic and clichéd, Alger's tales had an immense effect in the early part of the twentieth century, providing an entrepreneurial life-map for millions of Americans and admirers around the world. Horatio Alger was the direct ancestor of the American Dream.

At a State Department awards ceremony in Washington, attended by business leaders and politicians such as Colin Powell, Jim Pattison was acclaimed as embodying the Horatio Alger ideal. The folksy Pattison, who still favours the checked jackets of his car salesman days, won over the crowd by bringing on stage 90-year-old Harold Nelson, a Vancouver banker who went to bat for him in 1960 when Pattison was seeking a startup loan to open his first car dealership. Pattison couldn't meet the bank's lending criteria, but Nelson reworked the numbers three times. Eventually, Nelson convinced the central loan manager to talk to Pattison directly to truly understand the entrepreneurial spirit he displayed. He did, and Pattison got the loan.

Without Nelson, he wouldn't be there, Pattison told the crowd. The moment was vintage Jimmy ("Just call me Jimmy; everyone does") Pattison, in that it displayed characteristics he has shown throughout his life—the flair for the dramatic that had made him a great salesman, a basic belief about what is important in business, and an elephant-like memory of those who help him. It was also classic entrepreneurial management thinking. Pattison, 76, drew the interest of this iconic American organization because, despite heading an organization with eight divisions and 57 different businesses, he remains an entrepreneur in both form and in substance.

Pattison came by this entrepreneurial attitude early. An only child, he was born in Saskatchewan in 1936 into Depression-era poverty. After his family moved to Vancouver he worked with his father during the day fixing pianos and was home-schooled by his mother at night. The family moved every six months, and Pattison often sold garden seeds and magazine subscriptions door-to-door to help out. He worked his way through college, but left school nine units short of graduation to manage a used car lot. In 1961, Pattison launched his first business, another car lot, with the $40,000 loan facilitated by Nelson. Today, the Jim Pattison Group includes 21 radio stations, three TV stations, 14 car dealerships, and services in food, entertainment, advertising, packaging and financial services. The mythic Horatio Alger award may have been validating, but Pattison didn't need it to confirm that he is an entrepreneur. He knows it in his soul. "I'm just a salesman,"

Pattison likes to say. "A salesman who grew into operating a big holding company."

In truth, of course, Jimmy Pattison, Chairman, CEO and sole proprietor of the Jim Pattison Group, is far more than just a salesman. He is one of a very small group of entrepreneurs in the world who have built huge private consortiums of diversified companies. In a relentless pattern of growth, these typically founder-run operations continually add (or subtract) companies to their stables, commonly picking up businesses in industries they know well to help them launch into other, ancillary, fields. For the most part, these consortium builders ignore popular trends, except perhaps to dabble, because they have invariably built their businesses by supplying basic goods or services. They have also habitually presided over their empires through strong personal leadership and by keeping an unflinching eye on the bottom line. More common in Asia than North America, such a consortium builder would include Hong Kong's richest man, Li Ka-Shing, who controls three very large public companies through his 40-per-cent ownership of Cheung Kong, a property developer. Another example of such an organization is Samsung, the Korean family-owned business conglomerate that is still operated by descendants of late founder Lee Byung Chull.

Jim Pattison's consortium is described by financial analysts as a diversified organization with consumer-oriented lines of businesses that include food, broadcasting, automotive, news distribution, advertising, packaging and financial services. What is rarely discussed is his organizational methodology. Pattison did not build his organization and personal wealth by complicated financial maneuvers, elaborate takeover plans, invention of breakthrough innovations, total conquest of single markets, top-down management, or any of the other strategies studied in business schools.

Instead, he did it the old-fashioned way, employing a time-honoured business technique that doesn't get much attention today—he kept it simple and straightforward. Starting small, he learned a business—the car business—and then branched out one by one into ancillary areas that showed profit potential. In each case he studied the new businesses carefully, moved in when the time was right, then made sure he and his team understood the business inside and out.

Then he repeated the process.

"We've stuck with things that we understood," Pattison explains. "For instance, we didn't get into high tech; we certainly use it, but we never moved into it, because as a general proposition, we like things that are basic.

"Here's the process. I'm a car dealer, right? And from cars I went into radio. It wasn't much of a jump; I used to be a big advertiser when I was in the car business, so I understood advertising. I also understood selling and that's what radio is. What I didn't understand was programming, so we had to learn programming. Then we went into electrical signs through a public company we took over. We understood selling, that's what they do, sell signs, and we understood leasing because we'd been in the car leasing business. But we had to learn manufacturing. And so on. They were very basic businesses that weren't that hard to figure out. Look at our entertainment and attraction business, which is growing because we have a rough idea how it works. Of course we've had to learn something there as well. We have to learn every time."

This continual but strategic learning is a common trait of entrepreneurship. In fact, Karim Messeghem, Associate Professor at the Université de Franche-Comte (France), has postulated that entrepreneurial activity is itself an organizational technique. "Launching a new activity within an existing firm is an entrepreneurial attitude in so far as it involves innovation, proactiveness and risk-taking," he said. "These three dimensions allow one to assess a firm's entrepreneurial orientation (Miller, 1983). Stevenson and Jarillo (1990) … define entrepreneurship as: 'the process by which individuals—either on their own or inside organizations—pursue opportunities without regards to the resources they currently control.' Such a conception is interesting in that it allows one to assess a firm's entrepreneurial orientation notwithstanding its organizational context. We believe that firms characterized by a strong entrepreneurial orientation tend to react more immediately to new industrial conditions. We (also) believe that a firm can adopt an entrepreneurial orientation within a managerial framework."[2]

Underneath it all, Pattison is a dealmaker. He is fundamentally a small businessman who owns a widely diversified array of "smaller" (i.e., generally not industry-leading) businesses; together, they form a very large business. In conversation, Pattison makes it all seem quite simple.

---

2. Strategic Entrepreneurship and Managerial Activities in SMEs, *International Small Business Journal*, 5/1/2003.

- Stay with businesses you know something about.
- Do your due diligence.
- Know the financial situation of every company.
- Constantly ensure that every business is profitable; if it isn't,

either get rid of the management, or get rid of the business, if there is a problem in the sector.

AVOID "GOLD WATCH SYNDROME"

Big businesses often destroy the entrepreneurial spirit that started them. Entrepreneurs understand their objective, focus tightly on achieving their goals and react quickly to opportunities and challenges. Don't let growth hinder this mindset. Avoid the sluggishness tied to the mentality of organizations that operate on cruise control for 30 years until the gold watches are handed out.

Throughout more than 40 years in business, Jim Pattison has insistently maintained in his organization the entrepreneurial mindset he had when he began. By constant evangelism of an entrepreneurial growth ethos, he has enabled a now widespread—geographically and operationally—organization to expand continually. And by astute opportunity analysis, in itself another entrepreneurial trait, he has facilitated that growth. In a sense, Pattison uses a version of an organizational model called the matrix organization, which is sometimes used by companies as they extend their reach globally. With a true matrix model, large companies create small entrepreneurial entities capable of rapid, localized response in distant places to foster the growth of the entire business's product line. In Pattison's version, eight business divisions act as separate entrepreneurial entities rapidly responding to conditions in their industry. Within these divisions other businesses act with the same philosophy. Together they ensure that the entire organization continually enlarges.

Such entrepreneurial thinking is also a hallmark of leadership. According to Paul J. Meyer, an entrepreneur and author of more than 20 personal and professional improvement programs, "Although no two leaders possess exactly the same personality or management style, effective leaders exhibit a contagious enthusiasm for life, genuine concern for others, firm commitment to worthwhile values and goals, and clarity of purpose. As the strength of the foundation determines the height of the building, so a leader determines the future of the organization." [3]

CLARITY IS THE BEST MEMO

Be straightforward about the organization's objectives and communicate them clearly and frequently. A muddy message confuses employees and gets in the way of achieving the desired result.

Often, the primary tool used by these inspirers of entrepreneurship is a simple and clear definition of purpose and success. Unambiguous communication of purpose is a must in any enterprise, but it is more important in an environment that can feature continually evolving conditions. In volatile times, managers need a frame of reference in order to make quick decisions, and a clearly defined purpose can act as such a framework.

As the operator of a holding company overseeing many diverse businesses in different regions, Jim Pattison provides this simple frame by continually and clearly communicating his basic goals. Pattison does not believe in micromanaging or interfering in day-to-day operations. Neither does he believe in commissioning inch-thick strategy statements outlining elaborate implementation plans that his managers must follow to the letter. Instead, his approach is, as usual, more of the nuts-and-bolts variety. He picks managers appropriate to each business and industry, educates them in his general principles, tells them what he wants from them and then leaves them alone to do their work. "Here's what I tell our people," he says. "One is to have fun, two is to make money and three is to grow the business." If they do the job, and constantly remember the objective, they are well rewarded; if they don't, they are quickly replaced. Unlike a bureaucracy, an entrepreneurial business has no time for patience.

PREPARE TO SHIFT THE BOAT SLIGHTLY

A business must continually grow or it stagnates. Have a clear growth plan for the future, follow it religiously and adjust it when necessary, even if you make a mistake; complacency is a killer. Don't let ego get in the way of what the market is trying to tell you.

---

3   Paul J. Meyer, Expand your managerial skills, *New Straits Times*, 2/3/1998.

All of Pattison's divisions and businesses have one overarching imperative: to constantly grow. However, that growth must not be uncontrolled, or random, or cannibalistic—one division stealing from the other, common in bureaucracies. In fact it is much more outward looking. Pattison's business continually expands, partly because Pattison and his key leaders are tireless hunters, persistently searching out well-run businesses that fit his overall company dynamics. As an acquisitor with a fervent desire to continually add to his holdings, Pattison inculcates that passion in his managers and employees so that it becomes part of the culture.

But these acquisitions must also help to balance other aspects of the business; diversification is very important. Although he admires some companies that are focused on one activity, he sees them as vulnerable if that sector should experience a downturn. Pattison does not like to be vulnerable—he's been there (one time nearing bankruptcy because he bet almost everything on one business) and he didn't like it. So now he believes fervently in portfolio diversification (also known as not putting all your eggs in one basket).

"The stock market likes what they call 'pure play,'" he says. "I understand that. If I'm going to buy a coal company, I don't want to find out there's a sheep farm in New Zealand involved and I'm somehow in the loom business. But everybody's different. A lot of companies tend to their knitting and do a good job. I've got a different way, so if something goes in the ditch, we're protected. I look at it as diversification. If an industry deteriorates, or we get into a problem, we've got other divisions that can help us."

The recognition that a company is the sum of its parts and that a strategy of diversification can be used to mitigate risk for the whole entity is much easier for a privately held company. The venture capital world, which often deals with privately held companies, knows that the financial boost gained from taking a company public can also create market noise that may distract a business operator from the main objective—growing the business.

Some academics have pointed out that the operator of a closely held company is more able to take a long-term view instead of worrying about quarterly reports, daily trading patterns and all the other "instant" information that surrounds public companies. Too often, companies stumble when they focus too exclusively on the short term.

As the sole proprietor of his company, Pattison can, like Asian consortium builders—who also tend to eschew the public markets—take the long view. While pursuing an objective, he avoids the hectoring of shareholders, financial analysts or the financial press if a particular tactic doesn't produce instant success. Private ownership also keeps a company more agile, an entrepreneurial ideal.

KNOW WHEN TO HOLD 'EM

Every great organization has a great leader with the power and authority to make the necessary decisions. A central mind ensures the organization will think as one. If you can, maintain control by staying private to avoid outside interference from the market.

Pattison can operate this way because of the flat structure immediately below him. No legions of bureaucrats are working on endless analytical reports and submitting them through a hierarchy at the Jim Pattison Group. Instead, he maintains a structure that is almost unique in its simplicity among businesses of its size. Only eight key executives oversee the entire operations of the holding company. But, although the inside eight may come in contact with a division, or a company within that division, occasionally, the heads of the divisions—Automotive, Packaging, Entertainment, etc.—report directly to Pattison. In turn, individual companies within a division report to the division heads. However, most companies within the Jim Pattison Group function as if they were stand-alone companies operating under general principles laid down by Pattison.

A GOOD COACH ALLOWS PLAYERS TO PLAY

Having too many people tackling too many tasks is a recipe for anarchy, confusion, and, ultimately, organizational paralysis. Build a strong, not necessarily large, team to support the CEO, and keep the organizational structure relatively flat. Choose highly motivated specialists to drive the business forward.

A small network of opportunity spotters spread throughout North America look for potential companies to acquire and pass on their finds to the core group for analysis. Most of these spotters, as well as the core group, have known Pattison for years, are fiercely loyal to him, and know exactly what he is looking for. Harold Nelson, the man Pattison credits for helping him start his business, spent years as a spotter in the southern U.S. after he retired. Similarly, Pattison hired his old boss at the car dealership where he worked before he opened his first business. He spent 25 years overseeing many of the company's transactions. Division managers are cut from the same cloth. Pattison chooses people carefully to manage individual businesses within the group. He believes in searching out quality people, expecting much from them and rewarding them well for their efforts.

"It's a team," Pattison explains. "When we started, there was just Maureen (Maureen Chant, the Administrative Assistant whose title belies the fact that she has really been his right hand for more than 40 years), a bookkeeper and myself. Three of us started doing what we're doing, using the used car business as a base. We still have only a small team, and all together we've done, since I started, 399 third-party transactions, acquisitions, divestitures, mergers, startups, liquidations, whatever. All these separate company transactions we have done right here."

Some may view Pattison's stick-to-the-basics approach, with its emphasis on such homilies as work hard, persevere, roll with the punches and make money, as an indicator of some country bumpkin who got lucky. But it's difficult to argue with $5.5 billion worth of success.

As for the country bumpkin image, companies on the receiving end of Pattison's acquisitiveness quickly find out that the opposite is true. It could be disturbing to watch your business being dissected by an acquisition expert who probes every component, scrutinizing profit margins, cost of labour, financial management, future growth potential, the impact of globalization (even though the business may be merely regional). However, this "fundamental stuff," as Pattison likes to call it, is carried out with an eye to the ultimate goal—the profitability and sustainability of the particular company and its ability to add to the growth of Pattison empire.

Perhaps that is why Pattison has no shortage of potential acquisitions. In fact, his is often the go-to company for business operators who need to form a succession plan in order to sustain their companies. As Pattison's first believer, Harold Nelson, describes it, "a lot of people who founded companies and want to retire go to Jimmy because they know he'll keep the operation going like they did. But that doesn't mean they all make it."

Not if they've become over-organized and complacent, they won't.

5 THINGS YOU NEED TO KNOW

Pattison and his team focus on growing the company guided by five simple principles:

1. Avoid "Gold Watch Syndrome"

Big businesses often destroy the entrepreneurial spirit that started them. Entrepreneurs understand their objective, focus tightly on achieving their goals and react quickly to opportunities and challenges. Don't let growth hinder this mindset. Avoid the sluggishness tied to the mentality of organizations that operate on cruise control for 30 years until the gold watches are handed out.

2. Clarity is the Best Memo

Be straightforward about the organization's objectives and communicate them clearly and frequently. A muddy message confuses employees and gets in the way of achieving the desired result.

3. Prepare to Shift the Boat Slightly

A business must continually grow or it stagnates. Have a clear growth plan for the future, follow it religiously and adjust it when necessary, even if you make a mistake; complacency is a killer. Don't let ego get in the way of what the market is trying to tell you.

4. Know When to Hold 'Em

Every great organization has a great leader with the power and authority to make the necessary decisions. A central mind ensures the organization will think as one. If you can, maintain control by staying private to avoid outside interference from the market.

5. A Good Coach Allows Players to Play

Having too many people tackling too many tasks is a recipe for anarchy, confusion, and, ultimately, organizational paralysis. Build a strong, not necessarily large, team to support the CEO, and keep the organizational structure relatively flat. Choose highly motivated specialists to drive the business forward.

CHAPTER TWENTY-ONE

Declaration of Independence
The Value of Values

FEATURING THE WISDOM OF TERRY MCBRIDE

Terry McBride, CEO of Nettwerk Music Productions, has been called a brilliant strategist, and one of the most diversified music industry executives. McBride and Mark Jowett founded Nettwerk in Vancouver, B.C., in 1984. The company has since expanded worldwide with offices in Vancouver, Los Angeles, New York, Boston and London. It is notorious for taking such unknown artists as Sarah McLachlan and Dido and turning them into popular (and lasting) successes. In an industry dominated by large, vertically integrated entertainment companies, Nettwerk has truly remained an independent.

McBride, 44, has thrived in a sea of large competitors by adhering to a strong personal value system. The promotion template he refined with Sarah McLachlan was added to a belief that his artists should display values that touch large, usually ignored, segments of the buying public: those who appreciate quality over hype, genres over hits. Nettwerk's blueprint for success has been to zero in on a highly sophisticated, but hidden, market—a tactic not for the faint-hearted.

Update: *McBride continues to build Nettwerk and has expanded his business operations by recently partnering with his yoga instructor, Lara Kozan, to launch YYoga, a concept to unify yoga studios all over North America. McBride's vision for YYoga Studios is for them to evolve into mini-community centres focusing on health and wellness for the body, mind, and spirit. The first YYoga studio opened in Vancouver and they are continuing to expand all over North America.*

The secret to how and why consumers make buying decisions has always been the Holy Grail for business. That taste is difficult to define or measure hasn't stopped thousands of researchers and psychologists from trying. Think of the dollars spent by putative tastemakers continually refining how creators of products or services can "sell" them. The average North American is bombarded by 3,000-plus advertising messages daily. The list of techniques and tools to reach and influence end users is lengthy: mass or target marketing; advertising or direct selling; noisy hype or quiet buzz building. Ironically, in a consumer society, among the most consumed items are the sales tools themselves.

Yet even as this frenzy of consumerism escalated, some market observers began issuing warnings that customers were beginning to resist marketers' blandishments. Fatigued by incessant messaging, increasingly wary of buying what they don't really need, and tired of feeling as if they are being led by the nose to the cash register, people started to rebel by tuning out the noise and turning inward to be guided, consciously or not, by their inner values. In 1998, Shirley Roberts, founder of Market-Driven Solutions Inc.,[1] insisted that consumers were changing to become more individual, independent, sophisticated and self-focused. Often a better quality of life was more important to them than the cheapest price. More and more consumers, she said, were tapping into their own value system when buying. Values vary from person to person, of course, and range from the more trivial—convenience or unique experience—to deeper influences that reside in the human psyche itself—life-defining memories, believed-in causes, or perspectives on quality of life.

Consumers of goods and services aren't alone in this new kind of thinking. Businesses, which are in themselves consumers, have begun incorporating values into more of their strategic planning. In fact, several streams of decision-making theory and teaching now counsel business leaders to consult their personal mores when reaching corporate decisions. Providing equal weight to the head, the heart and the soul has become unexceptional, and smart managers now groom their operations to understand this new market order and in turn to serve it. The Body Shop chain of cosmetics stores was a phenomenon when it first began in the 1980s because it allied its operations and sales with social causes. Now, many companies at least give a passing nod to their

1   Shirley Roberts, *Harness The Future*, John Wiley and Sons Canada, 1998.

social or value-based responsibility, whether that means the coffee they supply is grown organically, or the suppliers they use undertake fair labour practices.

But does that mean that everyone is actually now following a value-based proposition? Yes and no. In industries such as manufacturing, populated by large, institutionalized companies, recognition of (or interest in) changing consumer tastes usually takes a back seat to production, margins and other traditional business concerns. In industries such as food, where consumer attitudes are continually monitored, changing values are usually noted early and eventually served. Typically, this responsiveness tends to be more common in industries or regions where value-based thinking is considered more important.

It's easy to assume that the creative industries (the arts in general), and those related to them (software and technology development, as well as other "knowledge" products and services), would be in the van-guard of this movement. Yet most of the creative sectors, such as music and film, usually target the masses, right down to the lowest common denominator. Creativity is often missing, even considered a threat to monetary success.

Take the music business as an example. It is well known that the in-dustry is currently in turmoil. For several years, almost-daily headlines have highlighted the problems: industry consolidation (or fragmenta-tion), revenue declines, lawsuits between artists and labels over distri-bution rights, legal wrangles over advancing technology, and resulting ownership issues regarding intellectual property.

This is not the first time the music industry has faced this kind of tumult, and its reaction has always been similar.[2] The first major challenge occurred in the 1920s when the advent of radio radically changed the delivery of music, which until that point had been con-fined to the phonograph. And in the 1950s, the emergence of rock and roll created the independent radio station. Until that time network-owned radio stations ruled the airwaves, broadcasting big band music live from music halls, live radio plays, and other material that we now think of as TV material. The independents came along and played the hot new music of the day. At each upheaval, the majors that dominated

---

2 Peter Tschmuck, How creative are the creative industries? A case of the music industry, *Journal of Arts Management, Law & Society*, 7/1/2003.

the industry reacted the same way: ignore, then oppose, then finally move to adopt the innovations that once plagued them.

The arrival of the Internet and peer-to-peer file sharing made it possible for the latest curve ball to be thrown at the recording industry, which, though a supposedly creative industry, had become too mechanized and too steeped in routine to respond creatively to the new challenge. Underneath, it is an institutionalized industry that operates more like a manufacturer than a creator. Like film, television and publishing, the music industry is dominated by large, usually vertically integrated, companies concerned more with unit production costs, mass marketing, weekly gross sales, profit margins and quarterly reports to shareholders than about addressing the needs of this new group of sophisticated or value-based buyers.

Satisfying such a niche market is usually left to the smaller independents. This business model has been demonstrated time and again across the landscape of the creative industries. The "best" movies of the year routinely come from film festivals that feature work by independent film companies, the best books frequently are issued by smaller independent publishers, and the most creative tunes often come from independent music producers.

One independent operator in the music industry who has succeeded amid the tumult is 44-year-old Terry McBride, CEO of Nettwerk Music Productions, headquartered in Vancouver, B.C. That city, while emerging as one of North America's arts-nurturing creative centres, is hardly the centre of the music universe. Nevertheless, since its formation in 1984, Nettwerk has steadily grown through self-determination, creative strategizing, and steady expansion into ancillary fields. Over 20 years, McBride has built a very large independent music business that is known for its ability to read the prevailing wind and adapt its methods. It is especially known for going against the prevailing wisdom—and succeeding. McBride's model for success is relatively simple: he understands his own values and then aligns them with the desires of underserved sectors of the music-buying public.

Through careful selection of artists, creative marketing and clever use of new delivery channels, McBride has grown his business to the point where he is acclaimed as a leader in an emerging Canadian music scene. Nettwerk is now a world-recognized music supplier with offices in Vancouver, Los Angeles, New York, Boston and London. It includes business arms in production, artist management, publishing, clothing design and merchandising, multimedia design, and movie and television music production.

As a youth, McBride got his start managing some musician friends as a hobby. The Vancouver scene at the time was a hotbed of alternative music, and McBride absorbed the kind of independent, almost rebellious, outlook that was in the air, an attitude symbolized by several punk bands whose sole purpose often appeared to be to tweak the noses of the traditional music industry and society in general.

At the age of 24, McBride turned his hobby into a profession by launching Nettwerk with partner Mark Jowett. They began by managing three bands that were making some noise on the local scene and started to refine the methodology that became the basis for the business over the next two decades. Those techniques included spotting unique talent, touring, and what is now known as guerrilla marketing—the use of unconventional, non-advertising methods to create interest in a product.

Nettwerk grew steadily, though not spectacularly, for more than 10 years, adding artists to its roster and producing music that was interesting to segments of the market, although not the market as a whole. Then McBride made his mark on the world music scene by launching singer Sarah McLachlan's career in the mid-1990s, leading to her breakthrough album *Surfacing* in 1997. He cemented his place with the unique all-women-artists music festival, Lilith Fair, which ran for three years between 1996 and 1999.

Very quickly, other artists joined the Nettwerk team—Dido, Sum 41, Barenaked Ladies, and Avril Lavigne, to name just a few. The common link among Nettwerk artists was lyrics that honestly portrayed everyday, very human feelings—sometimes humorous, occasionally raw, and often poignant. In its constant search for the next big win, the music industry in general had overlooked real emotions that millions of people experience and want to share, in favour of the artificial variety. Nettwerk was working with the basic building blocks of person-to-person communication.

All Nettwerk's artists produce music that is true to their own personal identity. Other artists may live in the same genre, but their music may come across as contrived if it doesn't issue from a wellspring of real feeling. The artists McBride has signed share an important characteristic with him—they stick with their core values and let the market decide. Increasingly, the market has liked what it heard.

But McBride did more than just follow his heart. Early on, he realized there were probably large numbers of people who felt about music as he did. With this nascent artistic value system, he looked at the industry around him and discovered something further. As a rule, the music industry had turned into a very large manufacturing industry. It still produced music, of course, and occasionally very good music, but generally the industry's product development appeared to be increasingly driven by bureaucratic thinking and risk management. Rather than ask the question: Is this new artist worthy of support and is there a market for his or her music, the question became: What is currently popular and do we have some on our roster?

In simple business terms, suppliers, confronted by a changing business landscape, had become steadily more focused on maintaining mass-market revenues by feeding the largest segment of the market—the middle of the road. Worse still, the industry chose to try to shape, or at least ride, the most common tastes rather than make the effort to understand emerging market segments.

This effort to understand, however, is the hallmark of the independent, since it is also the basis for adaptive behaviour. To avoid being crushed by the greater whole around them, independent operations must be nimble and quick. They must also continually employ adaptation to take advantage of opportunities that lie outside the mass view. When the mass zigs, they must zag.

Organizational behaviour theorists suggest that adaptation involves "using the right information, and using the information right."[3] Nettwerk achieved its independence by constantly adapting to aspects of its environment. It was the first music company to employ its own crude website, back when they were still called bulletin boards, to keep in touch with fans. It was the first music company to do its own graphics, not because it saw graphics as a business opportunity, but because it was a good cost-saving measure. Similarly, it was the first music company to issue an enhanced CD, a compact disc that contained video and graphics as well as music, and was the forerunner of the modern DVD.

---

3   Betsy B. Holloway, Adaptive selling behaviour revisited: an empirical examination of learning orientation, sales performance, and job satisfaction, *Journal of Personal Selling and Sales Management*, 6/22/2003.

In all these instances, Nettwerk had no particular strategy to revolutionize the business, or create new technology. It was simply the logical thing to do. "We always look at things and say 'Why not?'" McBride explains. "If it's logical, can be done, and it works, why not do it?" Although he may not have intellectually theorized about creating an independent, adaptive organization, McBride did it instinctively.

Independence requires a strong base, and in some organizations this base is an understanding and continual application of core personal values. According to Patrick E. Connor and Boris W. Becker, who studied managerial decision-making in the U.S. public sector, "Personal value systems have been shown to be related to job satisfaction, motivation, managerial success, leadership style, perceived competence, consumer choices, and both individual and organizational performance." [4]

If strong core personal beliefs permeate throughout an organization, they eventually define that organization's strategic, operational, product development, human resource and marketing systems. The personal belief system essentially becomes the company. In the music business, it happened in the 1920s when rebels who liked a particular style of music created the radio station. It happened again in the 1950s when rock and roll aficionados created the independent radio station that just played their kind of music instead of broadcasting concerts from ballrooms. It is happening now as music producers who prefer something outside the product mainstream closely held by major record labels use new techniques to deliver their creative services to like-minded listeners.

MIRROR, MIRROR ON THE WALL . . .

First, be very clear—and honest with yourself—about what your core values are. Understand your potential customers at a gut level before you start analyzing them. Ideally, they will align with your own. If you don't truly "get it," move on to another market.

In Nettwerk's case, there was a fundamental understanding of personal beliefs right from the beginning, and then a continual

---

4   *Public Personnel Management*, 4/1/2003.

application of the core values that grew out of them. It is not accidental that a bond of character exists among Nettwerk artists; it is the very reason for Nettwerk's existence. McBride never actively planned to be a music power or taste arbiter. Instead, he was simply drawn to artists whose music he liked because it touched something in him.

"Our pure intention when we started was to release music that we liked," McBride explains. "People think we had this amazing plan, but the only plan was to be true, really, really true. To this day we've gone with what we like, and only what we like. I believe music has to say something. If you sign an artist, you're signing a person, and you have to like what that person stands for. A lot of music now is smoke and mirrors, and there's no impact on the public. But all the highly regarded artists have been able to steadily sell five or 10 million albums with music that actually means something, by having a cause, or a social conscience. The industry has missed that completely."

. . . WHO'S IN THE FAIREST MARKET OF THEM ALL?

Identify the market that aligns with your core values and understand its features. You cannot manipulate a sophisticated market, so identify these consumers' common beliefs, needs and desires first, and then align your products accordingly. The failure to do this explains why hit and miss is so common in the entertainment industry.

McBride illustrates a phenomenon that has been slowly creeping into the business world: response-based marketing. Best described as part research into market segmentation, part application of new measurement systems, and part pure instinct, this kind of marketing requires an ability to read the various thought currents within the mind of the marketplace. It is a bottom-up process, as opposed to the more traditional top-down price-product-place-promotion marketing mix that emerged in the 1970s and has been a mantra among marketers ever since.

Amazon provides an example of a company using response-based marketing. The online store measures visitors' browsing habits and instantly adapts its product offerings based on those measures. Log onto Amazon.com and the website will address you by name and provide some suggested reading material based on your past browsing habits. This could hardly be said to be the ultimate in consumer mind-reading, but it does indicate how an organization can attempt to continually read the pulse of its customers, and the process will do doubt continue to be refined.

Nettwerk artists such as Sarah McLachlan, Dido and Avril Lavigne have been among the music industry' top sellers of recordings over the past several years because McBride was able to gauge the marketplace, find segments that weren't being served and align his value-based system to them.

"The industry wasn't paying attention, and there were huge segments being missed," he says. "In Sarah's case, it was a segment that was women, 18 to 40, families, mothers and daughters. That's why the three Lilith Fair tours were such a success and raised $10–$15 million for women's causes. Up to that point, there were male tours around, with the odd token female, but Lilith Fair proved that a female tour could be a success. The biggest-selling records over the past five or six years have all been targeted toward females between 18 and 40. Everybody thinks it's some hip-hop artist, or Eminem, who is the biggest, but it's not true. That's a perception based on hype and media and Hollywood glam that has nothing to do with the reality of who buys records."

Or why they buy them. McBride's intuition told him that many buyers were longing for music that spoke to them, that triggered memories, or could revive the buried emotions related to some long-forgotten moment in their lives. This is a realm of the psyche that is hard to gauge using conventional methods, so when looking at this market, McBride once again turned to his personal beliefs.

"Music is an intuitive thing," he explains. "It should have a heart and soul that touches people. Melody is the soul of a song, it's what you hum inside you; lyrics are the heart of a song, the words are quotable. If music is to have a lasting impact, those two things are important. When I meet an artist, I know I'm going to have to represent them as people, so we have conversations. My first conversation with Avril Lavigne, who produces emotionally charged music that speaks to young females, was 'Who are you, what do you do, what would you like to do, where do you come from, how did you grow up, what do you like to think about?' Most record companies don't do this and miss because they only want to do photo shoots and videos and all that advertising stuff. They don't listen to the lyrics or understand that if they can strike a chord with like-minded people it will catch fire."

Not only did McBride better align his artists' (and his own) tastes with the tastes of the marketplace, he also used another adaptive response to ensure that alignment would continue. Rather than take the view that music was trend-driven and disposable, he perceived a desire for music—and artists—that could last. He therefore elected to represent only people he calls "heritage artists."

"Heritage artists will have a great touring career ten years from now," he says. "Artists who are literate, mean something, have causes, and can be influential for those causes, will always draw people to concerts."

Central to this kind of independent strategy is a proper definition of success. From a business point of view, artist concert tours bring in far more revenue, in total, than record sales, especially if tours continue for years. Nettwerk doesn't (and can't) throw all its resources into turning out quick hits. Instead, it relentlessly keeps its artists on the road, playing in concerts to like-minded fans who are quite willing to hear them restate their beliefs over and over again, largely because they share them. It's a game of patience, able to be played, probably, only by a private operation like Nettwerk that doesn't have to answer to shareholders every quarter and can take a longer view of revenue streams.

This patience and independent mindset has also helped Nettwerk turn the traditional industry product rollout process on its head. Typically, companies release a single piece of music from an upcoming album to radio stations and television video channels like MTV about six weeks before the album comes out. They spend huge amounts on this marketing blitz, but it's worth it to create a buzz that will peak at the time of the album release. It's a cozy system that has worked, to a point, not only for the record companies, but also for the radio and television stations that get to air the singles early (and so contribute to the hit machine).

However, this system only works because of its sheer mass. It does not allow artists to grow and be nurtured over several albums, while their music matures. It creates the disposable artist, who is gone tomorrow, as soon as he or she fades from fashion. A disposable artist leads to a disposable product that caters to those with disposable tastes. But what about those with more sophisticated tastes, the market that Nettwerk serves? Is it a new market? Probably not, but it certainly has been a hidden one.

> **BE THE LAST LEMMING STANDING**
>
> You're unlikely to find a blueprint for how to access a hidden market. Don't be afraid to develop and adopt strategies specific to this market, regardless of what your competitors are doing. This is the leap of faith that niche entrepreneurs must take.

The music video has become a staple of the business for the past two decades. However, because of age or style, some of Nettwerk's artists don't suit that format, especially for play on MTV. Music that emphasizes lyrics and melody rarely results in widely played videos, where the formula usually comprises dancing, sexual imagery and other attention-grabbing images. Recognizing this, McBride adapted his rollout strategies to serve this hidden market of people with sophisticated tastes. So when Sarah McLachlan had a new album upcoming, he researched the marketplace for alternatives, knowing that her video was unlikely to receive much airtime on MTV. His solution: release the video on the Internet through iTunes, the first of the new for-pay downloading sites. It was a first for both Nettwerk and iTunes. The idea paid off spectacularly, drawing some five million "strings," or downloads. "The industry went crazy," says McBride. "MTV went, 'Holy Crap!' because they were left out of it."

Similarly, when Avril Lavigne was about to release her second album, McBride studied the marketplace and realized it was unlikely to generate the typical Top-40 hit. The charts were dominated by ersatz rock music and so-called "urban" music devoted to the teen hip-hop culture, and Lavigne's song appealed more to young women. McBride also had to figure out how to generate more than one hit from the album, reasoning that if he did release a single to radio and television stations through the usual route, it might sell a few million units, but the album was unlikely to keep going for long.

> **FAITH AND COURAGE TRUMP LOGIC AND REASON**
>
> You will be challenged, and possibly ridiculed, by your peers for going it alone. But if you understand what you stand for and it aligns with your target market, then stick with the program. You will succeed—it just might take longer than you expect.

So Nettwerk wrote its own marketing plan. Instead of opting for the traditional six-week Top-10 radio runup-to-market system, Nettwerk released a single and organized a 24-week tour of free concerts in local shopping malls to promote the album. Traditional radio stations hated it because they feared the single's popularity would taper off after a few weeks; MTV took a long time to sign on because the plan was so unconventional. But the mall concert tour drew hundreds of thousands of young women, produced a Top-10 hit within the first week, and then built steady, and at times spectacular, interest over the 24-week period. By the time the mall tour was over, the album had produced several hits, and three of the Top 10 singles on the charts were pop singles by young women like Lavigne. Nettwerk had tapped an entirely new market by sticking to its plan. Similarly, Nettwerk has been known to release a piece of music to public radio instead of the usual Top-40 channels.

"There are a lot of people in the business of music, but they're not in the music business, and it costs them," McBride observes. "With Avril, we knew the market was there; we just had to figure out how to access it. All we wanted to do was get to our audience over a longer time period to tell them this album was coming. We also knew the single would never get past Top 10, and we would have to get two or three hits off the album. This had never been done before and everybody told us it wouldn't work, but we decided to stick to what we were doing and it worked. It was just so logical."

FORM A COMPANY OF FRIENDS

Build your organization with like-minded people who "get" you and "get" the market. Then encourage their independent thinking and unbridle their passion.

McBride isn't alone in this kind of independent thinking, however. His entire organization thinks the same way. For example: the head of Nettwerk's graphics arm, who started with the organization more than a decade ago by packing boxes, noticed that the crude computer used to print box labels also provided fertile ground for his artistic ambitions. Soon, he was using it to design covers and posters. Similarly, several assistants to managers have gone on to become managers themselves. Why? Because they found a particular type of music rang some bells in their own psyches and started planning how it could be delivered to a wider audience.

It's the kind of independent thought McBride encourages. Within the Nettwerk operation there is a common ethos of exploration, the expansion of personal boundaries and a go-for-it attitude. The thread that weaves itself through daily thinking on the job is echoed in McBride's most commonly issued statement—"Why Not?" A loose structure allows Nettwerk's 120 employees to act with passion on what they personally like, to study it, form a concept to implement it, defend it, and then do it. This is the essence of personal growth.

McBride's assistant, Penny Nightingale, has watched this process and expects to one day join it. "People learn from him and pass it on," she says. "Assistants who have gone on to become managers learn by teaming up with a more senior manager and gaining knowledge right from the source. A huge part of Nettwerk is the teaching that goes on. Managers want other managers to grow and learn and be successful."

McBride describes his "organizational plan" this way: "We believe that whatever makes common sense should be done. You go with your intuition. We're not a corporation with boundaries and rules—we try to see everything with creative eyes. This provides a lot of freedom, lets people be more freethinking. Mostly, we try to get across that you have to learn and grow every day."

In a shop where independence is the operating axiom, a "human resource" system is almost non-existent. Nettwerk employees aren't studied and interviewed extensively when applying for jobs. Instead, current employees often refer them, or they come over from larger labels because they like the independent spirit at Nettwerk. Rae Cline, Nettwerk's director of promotions, spent five years at a major before joining the team. "I felt like I was going back to more of a grass-roots situation, where every record isn't do-or-die or must be a gigantic radio hit," she says. "It can be fun. Sometimes it feels like we're putting out the high school yearbook." [5]

When Nettwerk hires, it hires a personality, not an employee. Says McBride: "You can't run a personality. You can only say 'Look, be passionate about what you're doing.' Then if someone is growing or shows a particular talent, you note it, keep an eye on it and eventually find a place for it."

5   David L. Coddon, "Music, not money, is the motivator for rock label Nettwerk," *San Diego Union-Tribune*, 27/6/ 2004.

"I think the key thing that makes Nettwerk so unique is that there is not a set path," Nightingale adds. "So you end up with offices full of people who are different. Each person is exposed to different aspects of the company and people are naturally drawn to different things. Terry watches people, sees where they succeed and struggle and then guides them to where they can go within the company."

Such independent thinking is not always rewarded, in the music industry or elsewhere. For example, various Internet chat groups have commented on the fact that although Nettwerk has grown larger than most U.S. independents, the American press has yet to discover its success. However, it is being recognized in Canada. In 2003, Terry McBride was inducted into the Canadian Music Hall of Fame and honoured with a special achievement Juno award by the Canadian music industry. That same year, McBride and partners Ric Arboit, Dan Fraser, and Mark Jowett were nominated for the annual Ernst & Young Canadian Entrepreneur of the Year award.

But recognition from industry is not the goal of this company that defines the term "indie." It is kudos from music buyers that count. Nettwerk will simply continue to produce music that it wants to produce. McBride, who admits the record production arm of the company doesn't make much money, jokes about Nettwerk's unusual business "plan": "Break even. Don't lose money, please."

His credo is to find the music and the artists he likes and then get it to the people who see it the same way.

The true path to independence.

5 THINGS YOU NEED TO KNOW

Terry McBride and the Nettwerk team follow these principles when accessing a highly targeted, sophisticated, hidden market:

1. Mirror, Mirror on the Wall...

First, be very clear—and honest with yourself—about what your core values are. Understand your potential customers at a gut level before you start analyzing them. Ideally, they will align with your own. If you don't truly "get it," move on to another market.

2. ...Who's in the Fairest Market of Them All?

Identify the market that aligns with your core values and understand its features. You cannot manipulate a sophisticated market, so identify these consumers' common beliefs, needs and desires first, and then align your products accordingly. The failure to do this explains why hit and miss is so common in the entertainment industry.

3. Be the Last Lemming Standing

You're unlikely to find a blueprint for how to access a hidden market. Don't be afraid to develop and adopt strategies specific to this market, regardless of what your competitors are doing. This is the leap of faith niche entrepreneurs must take.

4. Faith and Courage Trump Logic and Reason

You will be challenged, and possibly ridiculed, by your peers for going it alone. But if you understand what you stand for and it aligns with your target market, then stick with the program. You will succeed—it just might take longer than you expect.

5. Form a Company of Friends

Build your organization with like-minded people who "get" you and "get" the market. Then encourage their independent thinking and unbridle their passion.

CHAPTER TWENTY-TWO

Teach Them to Fish

The Critical and Timely Rise
of Social Entrepreneurship

FEATURING THE WISDOM OF JEFF SKOLL

*In 1995, University of Toronto graduate Jeff Skoll became the first employee
and President of an unheard-of startup called eBay, which he remained
involved with until 2001.*

*One of the most important communities on the Internet today,
eBay offers the largest online auction system in the world and has some
95 million people buying and selling on its site regularly. Together, these
traders produced 2004 revenues of US$3.27 billion and net income of
US$778.2 million, making the company the most profitable of the herd of
Internet-based businesses that launched in the '90s. In fact, eBay is often
cited as one of the most innovative and successful businesses ever launched
on the Internet—period. Skoll now heads the Skoll Foundation, which backs
social entrepreneurs in a pioneering way that it calls "the new philanthropy."
While similar to social venture philanthropy, which involves active operational
input by the philanthropists, the style used by the Skoll Foundation offers a
more hands-off role.*

*Here we examine social entrepreneurship and this new philanthropy as
a discipline, explaining its close parallel, by nature and by design, to the conventional entrepreneurial universe.*

—⁓—

Update: *In 2005, Jeff Skoll's socially responsible production company
Participant Production, debuted their first slate of films, including* North
Country, Syriana, Good Night and Good Luck, *and* Murderball. *These films*

netted a total of 11 Academy Award nominations and one Oscar win (for George Cloony's supporting role in Syriana).

And 2006 proved to be an even bigger year for Jeff, as the company released the highly acclaimed documentary An Inconvenient Truth. *Al Gore's presentation on the growing climate crisis became a world-wide phenomenon and won two Academy Awards (for Best Documentary and Best Original Song). Jeff was included in* Time *magazine's 100 People of the Year in 2006, and won* Wired *magazine's Rave Award in the same year.*

For too long, corporate existence centered solely on profitability. Communal responsibility and connection were a distraction that ended up being the purview of PR departments and socialites—something corporations did to exonerate themselves from their demons. It was rarely about meaningful and sustainable change.

Thankfully, the rise of the new millennium has seen a dramatic shift in the very fabric that connects the business world to its surrounding community. Something very different is going on. To no one's surprise, this new movement is being led not by the boardrooms of established corporations, but by entrepreneurs.

Social entrepreneurship is a concept that is growing rapidly throughout the world and, according to some enthusiasts displays a potential to define the twenty-first century as traditional entrepreneurship defined the twentieth. Over the last 20 years, the growth of employment in the social sector within the developed world has been two and one-half times faster than it has been for the economy as a whole. The non-profit world has been the fastest growing sector of employment all over the world. In the US, the number of non-profits has doubled over 10 years to 1 million. In the developing world, in a country like Brazil, it has gone from about a thousand non-profits to 1 million in a span of 20 years.[3]

Certainly, as increasing numbers of bright and talented people like Jeff Skoll turn their energies to improving the lot of the disadvantaged through entrepreneurial techniques, the concept is gaining in popularity. Socially responsible investing, MBA-level management training for non-profit organizations, a swelling army of consultants and even thousands of references on Google—a handy modern measure of an idea's popularity—are all responses to a spreading interest in social entrepreneurship.

---

1   *Business Strategy Review*, Summer, 2004.

While some see the social entrepreneur as merely an efficient fundraiser; others favour a grander image that puts the social entrepreneur at the leading edge of a movement that will dominate society in the years to come. Perhaps the best definition lies somewhere between these two visions, in the realm of popular qualification. As Michael S. Malone, who produced a television series on social entrepreneurs, described it, a social entrepreneur is an individual who brings the techniques, tools, and most of all, the spirit of commercial entrepreneurship to the non-profit world. Social entrepreneurship is as old as Florence Nightingale and Jane Addams, but only in the last decade has it been recognized as a distinct discipline with its own processes and standards.

In its use of techniques and tools, which are increasingly being taught in universities in the U.S., the U.K. and other countries, social entrepreneurship is, in essence, no different from entrepreneurship in its standard sense. The difference is of course in purpose. Traditional entrepreneurship attempts to create an organization that engenders financial return, whereas social entrepreneurship strives to develop an organization that helps people, often to help themselves. In both scenarios, although the end game is very similar, social entrepreneurs seek a level of profit that is far grander than their corporate siblings. The reach is meant to go far beyond shareholders to communities of stakeholders.

To help distinguish these two streams of entrepreneurship, it is useful to compare them as business models: In the entrepreneurial model most refined in Silicon Valley, a venture begins with a startup, a business plan, and usually a prototype product. Then, as the startup company grows, it goes through several rounds of investment, ending (with luck) in a "liquidity event"—the sale of the company or going public with an initial public offering. With the former, the startup is now typically owned by a much larger company, to be subsumed within that behemoth. With the latter, the startup is now a widely held corporation and a public company.

In the social entrepreneurial model, the social entrepreneur begins with an idea for a product or service, creates a business plan and starts work on building an enterprise with the largest possible impact. For the social entrepreneur, this means systemic change in society—"not a soup kitchen, but a way to build a thousand self-supporting soup kitchens in 25 countries," is the way Malone puts it.[2] He states: "This kind of ambition requires . . . a very astute and forward-looking business plan, a strong start-up team and good business discipline—the same thing investors look for in commercial startups."

There is no liquidity event for the social entrepreneur—instead, the comparable milestone is producing a self-sustaining organization. However, just as venture capital financing has been used to fund traditional entrepreneurship, a similar—albeit, differently purposed—funding system has emerged for social enterprise. This system has gone by various names—social venture philanthropy, new philanthropy and creative philanthropy. It tends to parallel the entrepreneur's universe of seed-round, secondary-round and mezzanine financing. A growing number of foundations have begun to specialize in this style of funding.

The goal is to nurture an enterprise until it pays off in a "big win." Like traditional funders, some may get actively involved in how the venture operates, providing leadership, guidance and mentoring. Others, like the Skoll Foundation, invest in the social entrepreneur but take a hands-off approach to the investment. For a traditional venture capital firm, a big win is a return that surpasses the ten-times (the vernacular is 10X) investment range. However, for the social entrepreneur, the big win is not return on investment (ROI), but sustainability and social impact.

This new philanthropy grew out of the explosion of entrepreneurial activity, primarily in the technology sector, that developed on the west coast of the United States during the 1990s. There were plenty of new-technology millionaires. (In June 2000, *Newsweek* reported that Silicon Valley had already become home to 250,000 millionaires and was adding 64 new ones every day. Despite the tech downturn, many survived with their wealth relatively intact.) A lot of them believed that they should help social causes, but they wanted to do it in a way with which they were familiar—through an entrepreneurial model. Too often, in the tailspin that Silicon Valley suffered in the late '90s, people forget the enormous foot forward that many of the winners of that era undertook. Without the entrepreneurs of that era, arguably, social entrepreneurship would still be a good idea and not a ball that has been put into play.

They weren't the first to think of the concept of funding community change: As far back as 1988, Wall Street investor Paul Tudor Jones created the Robin Hood Foundation in New York to help low-income families in the city. The foundation, which was considered quite innovative at the time, emphasized results-oriented philanthropy and sought to measure philanthropic outcomes much the same as a company measures profits.

However, by the end of the century, newly rich tech entrepreneurs had collectively formed a group of entrepreneurial-oriented philanthropists whose sheer numbers created a critical mass that began to change the face of giving. The Foundation Center, based in New York City, reported in 2000 that since 1980 the number of U.S. foundations had more than doubled to nearly 47,000, and that more than 5,200 had climbed aboard during the last two years of the twentieth century.

Traditional philanthropy involved the doling out of funds by a foundation funded by the estate of someone who died. The new way featured donations by living people, many of them looking to the venture capital model.

Much of the thought leadership for this social philanthropy movement came from one of the first, and still best-known, philanthropic organizations emphasizing social entrepreneurship, the Ashoka Foundation (ashoka.org). This group was founded in 1980 by Bill Drayton, a former McKinsey & Co. consultant in New York and a former assistant administrator of policy, budget and management at the U.S. Environmental Protection Agency. Ashoka describes itself as a global non-profit organization that finds and funds 1,400 leading social entrepreneurs in 48 countries who implement innovative ideas for change in their communities, regions, countries and continents. Ashoka elects emerging social entrepreneurs to an international "fellowship" of their peers, providing significant financial support and an array of *pro bono* strategies and professional services. Ashoka's direct investment and leadership in promoting social entrepreneurship results in substantial "social returns" through pattern-changing solutions to major social problems. Ashoka does not accept government funding; business entrepreneurs, individuals, volunteer chapters, corporations and foundations privately finance the foundation's work.

Says Drayton: "We need fundamental, structural change in educational and human rights, every bit as much as in the hotel and steel [industries]. Fundamental change comes from entrepreneurs—people who see over the horizons and lead society to take the next step. We have had many institutions to support business entrepreneurs, but only in the last decade have people begun to recognize and support social entrepreneurs. Ashoka does two things: We help to launch [innovative] ideas for social change on a global scale and the social entrepreneurs behind them, the institutions necessary to support both the ideas and the person. In essence, we are like a venture capital firm but focused on social innovation. And the second major thing we do is build the institutions that make our new field [of social entrepreneurship] work better."[3]

Another new philanthropist is the Entrepreneur's Foundation (EF), of Menlo Park, California. Gib Myers, EF's chairman, established the foundation to encourage community reinvestment as an integral part of the entrepreneurial culture in the Silicon Valley and Bay area. Nancy Glaser, EF's director of venture philanthropy, describes the foundation's philanthropic model as typically venture capitalist. "The recipient organization has to be ready to be our partner. We bring a lot of resources—*pro bono* marketing expertise; help with organizational strategies; technical assistance, and so on."[4]

Of course, back in the mid-'90s it was unlikely that Skoll would have been able to articulate that he was to become a change agent, in the business or social sphere. A recent MBA grad from Stanford holding a job at Knight-Ridder Information and living off his credit cards, he had graduated previously as an engineer from the University of Toronto and had a couple of small computer-related businesses behind him in Canada. In Palo Alto, where he shared a house with some college buddies, Skoll was really searching for a job that would pay the bills.

As a teenager, Skoll had imagined becoming a crusading writer who would explore society's problems and find solutions for them. That dream was born when his father, who owned an industrial chemical sales business, told him and the rest of his family that he had been diagnosed with cancer. Such announcements can be devastating for any family, but to a young Jeff Skoll, what was as profound was the regret his father expressed as he faced the possibility of his life ending. "The thing he was most upset about wasn't so much that he was sick and that it was looking really bad, but that he'd never done what he wanted to do with his life," says Skoll. "You know, he wanted to sail around the

---

3   *Washington Times.* 2002.
4   Carole Schweitzer, Association Management, *Building on New Foundations*, 10/1/2000.

world and other various things, and to me, as a teenager, it very much brought home a lesson that life is a short thing and you never know."[5]

His father survived the cancer and went on to spend the next decade living out his wishes. Skoll built eBay and continued to harbour a desire to act on his internal value system. At the end of the century, he faced the reality that he had become one of the richest men in the world through a business that, while clinging to his values about community and social enhancement, wasn't quite what he had been aiming for. So Jeff Skoll, multibillionaire, only 35 years old, and still a man of simple tastes (he continued to share the house in Palo Alto with four roommates) became a philanthropist. He had earlier created the eBay Foundation, which was seeded by pre-IPO eBay stock, but now he wanted to focus on what he believed to be his true calling.

First, he made several quick, dramatic moves in the educational field. He donated Cdn $7.5 million to his alma mater, the University of Toronto, to fund two chairs in the school's electrical and computer engineering department; a third at U of T's Rotman School of Management led to the creation of a joint engineering BASc/MBA program, called the Skoll Program. It was the largest gift ever given to a Canadian University by someone under 40. This was followed by a US$2-million donation to Stanford's Graduate School of Business for a professorship in entrepreneurial studies. More recently, he founded the Skoll Centre for Social Entrepreneurship at Oxford University's Saïd Business School.

Meanwhile, Skoll had a grander vision—he was working on a plan for the Skoll Foundation, an organization that has launched him as one of the leaders of this new group of social enterprise nurturers. Says Skoll: "The turning point for me probably came about two, two-and-a-half years after eBay had gone public in 1998. The company had reached the point where I felt comfortable that the management team could handle the company without me being there. Because of my involvement in the genesis of the company, until that point there was always something, some value or some knowledge that I had of the way that this all worked. So I was very reluctant to let go. But once I felt that the values had been infused in the management team (and it is a superb group of senior managers, much more experienced than

I was), once I felt that they had grasped the incredible importance of that community/company synergy and the values that held it together, at that point I felt comfortable moving on to start to pursue the dream I had of making a difference in the equation of inequities."[6]

Using the mantra "Uncommon Heroes, Common Good," the Skoll Foundation dreams of a world where all people, regardless of geography, background, or economic status, "enjoy and employ the full range of their talents and abilities." It believes that social entrepreneurship, which Skoll says is becoming a distinct business discipline, is the best way to achieve that dream.

Says Skoll: "Our best hope for the future is this group of dedicated people who are working to solve many of the social problems, the ills, around the world. I think of the parallel to 100 years ago when the field of business was starting to take root. Back then it was kind of a groundswell, a lot of activity, but nobody was formally examining the principles and underpinnings of what was going on. It was right around that time that we began to see business schools and academic institutions take an interest in that field."[7]

Earlier, he asserted in a speech that social entrepreneurship is intensifying because it allows everyone to change his or her surrounding society. "Social entrepreneurs have a unique approach that is both evolutionary and revolutionary. Social entrepreneurs create self-sustainable models that operate in a free market where success is measured not just in financial profit, but also in the improvement of the quality of people's lives. Social entrepreneurs take workable business models and adapt them for the benefit of all our communities."[8]

The Skoll Foundation invests in social entrepreneurs through three award programs: the Skoll Awards for Social Entrepreneurship, which honour established social entrepreneurs around the world; the Skoll Awards for Innovation in Silicon Valley, which fund innovative, entrepreneurial non-profit organizations working in and around California's Silicon Valley; and the Skoll Social Sector Capacity Investments, which help strengthen the infrastructure of the social sector. In November 2003 the Skoll Centre for Social Entrepreneurship was launched at the Saïd Business School, Oxford University, with a donation of

---

6 *Business Strategy Review.*
7 *Business Strategy Review.*
8 Social Entrepreneurship: The 21st Century Revolution, March 2004.

£4.44 million (US$7 million) by the Skoll Foundation, the largest funding ever received by a business school for an international program in social entrepreneurship.

The vision, however, does not just centre on finance. The Skoll Foundation also advances its mission to connect social change agents and build community through Social Edge, an online community it has created for social entrepreneurs and other members of the social sector who want to network, learn from one another and share resources. In both 2002 and 2003, Jeff Skoll was identified by *BusinessWeek* as one of the most innovative philanthropists of the previous decade.

The Skoll Foundation adheres to strict business criteria and principles, carefully examines business plans and measures management capability before advancing funds. Unlike some other philanthropists, however, it does not step into an operational role with the social entrepreneur. In this world of the new philanthropist, the capital supplied is used not just to create a successful enterprise, but also to serve the greater good of mankind; traditional capital is leveraged into social capital. It will be interesting to see if, as social philanthropy continues to evolve and grow, its proponents will begin to apply, or focus more effort on, some of the disciplines they use in this world to their for-profit businesses.

CREATE AN INFLECTION POINT

The new era of philanthropy is about small investments being leveraged into large returns. Teaching people to fish one person at a time is not the end game anymore. As an example, the Skoll Foundation's goal is to create systemic change—"long-term changes in whole systems that empower people to lift themselves out of poverty"—around the world. The focus has been on finding leverage in the areas of education, technology and micro enterprise.

With the myriad of social causes and projects that come across the desk of most managers these days, it is crucial to have the tools and best practices to determine which ventures will have the chance for the greatest outcome to the community. When assessing a social entrepreneurial venture, these new philanthropists approach it no differently from the way they build their for-profit businesses. They start by considering the impact of their investment. They look for the "inflection point," where a small involvement can be used to create a wide impact and therefore a large "return."

The Skoll Foundation, for example, looks for a simple tool or process that will have wide repercussions. It found one in a venture called ApproTEC, which operates in Africa and has developed a simple water pump that looks like one of those stairway exercise machines commonly found in gyms throughout North America. Attached to a drilled hole in the ground, it is operated by a farmer who walks on it and pumps water for his farm or community. This US$70 device is transforming sections of rural Africa: Some 35,000 businesses have been started because of the device, and new ones are forming at the rate of 800 a month. These businesses generate US$37 million a year in profits and wages, and new revenues are equivalent to 0.5 percent of Kenya's GDP and 0.2 percent of Tanzania's GDP.

THINK LIKE AN ENTREPRENEUR

How innovative is the idea? How much of a breakthrough is it? Is it designed to effect systemic change? Can the social entrepreneur demonstrate that he or she is driven to create measurable impact?

Many investors and savvy entrepreneurs in the technology space also place great emphasis on the entrepreneurial quality of an idea, on its innovative quotient. New philanthropists bring this business idea to the realm of the social entrepreneur and often apply the for-profit world's measurement systems to ensure the idea is working. "Like all funders, we know nonprofit outcomes are not as black and white as earnings per share," says Paul Shoemaker, Executive Director of Seattle-based Social Venture Partners (SVP)."But that doesn't mean we should abandon measurement. SVP has chosen to measure two areas: the means and the ends. Infrastructure, capacity, and sustainability—these are the means through which a nonprofit executes its mission. The ends are the ultimate behavioural, academic, social outcomes being achieved by the nonprofit's clients."[9]

To pass muster with a new philanthropist, a concept must achieve some kind of breakthrough, or, as the technology community likes to call it, disruptive innovation. Mere tweaking, or copying, of another

---

9   Responsive Philanthropy, U.S. National Committee for Responsive Philanthropy, Spring, 2001.

system will not achieve the objective, which is always wide—and measurable—impact. Indeed, copying of a successful system may weaken the original system by creating destructive competition. As with any non-social venture, copycat competition often leads to a competitive marketplace where no one is a winner.

With the traditional entrepreneurship model, where the objective is to make a profit, this may not be as important: Several competitors may survive, if not thrive, by offering relatively similar products and differentiating through price, promotion, or one of the other aspects of the marketing mix that influence Porter's competitive analysis model. However, this kind of competition cannot be allowed to exist in the social enterprise sphere where the objective is to create wide and lasting impact that changes a society. This impact becomes considerably diluted if several organizations are trying to deliver the same service.

A further factor in any investor's consideration of an enterprise involves the level of the business cycle on which it exists. Like traditional venture capital companies, new philanthropists pick their favourite investing targets or level on the cycle—concept (rare), seed, secondary or mezzanine. Like most investors, they rarely fund concepts or startups. As the Entrepreneur's Foundation's Nancy Glaser described it: "The organization must be beyond startup and mature enough to be able to handle additional resources. If they don't have the people or the infrastructure, a project may drown them. So, like a venture capitalist, we analyze the infrastructure to make sure the level of readiness is sufficient."[10]

DON'T TALK, EXECUTE

The Skoll Foundation does not generally fund startups. Rather, it looks for social enterprises that have already established that their ideas are roadworthy.

Similarly, the Skoll Foundation prefers that investees have some traction before they arrive on its doorstep. In the traditional business world, a solid customer list and growing revenues are usually evidence of this traction. But in the social enterprise sphere, where customers and revenues are not the accepted metrics of success, traction usually means that the enterprise has already had some impact, has already shown that its ideas can work.

---

10 Association Management, 10/2000.

Examples of this more mature social entrepreneur might be two of Skoll's "new heroes"—Bill Strickland and Roshaneh Zafar. Strickland, an unassuming educator in Pittsburgh, Pennsylvania, began turning around the lives of high-risk youth through his Manchester Craftsman's Guild, which provides training in arts and technology. Zafar, founder of the Kashf Foundation in Pakistan, opened micro-finance institutions that provided a means for formerly neglected Pakistani women to make an economic living through their own businesses.

SHOW CAPACITY

The Skoll Foundation looks at how the social entrepreneur is in-stituting systems that will drive their inititntive forward. Innova-tion without a base of resources, the right people and other ba-sic building blocks cannot reach its potential. "Nothing happens without individuals, but nothing lasts without institutions," says Skoll.[11]

While Strickland and Zafar are undoubtedly dynamic individuals in their own right, their organizations would not have achieved any success or received investment if they had not also addressed their capacity issues, or understood how to make visions reality. While most businesses believe that it is important to have systems and management in place to ensure that the venture can achieve its objective, it is even more critical that this be the case in the world of social entrepreneurship. That's because, for so long, non-profits really operated as receivers of government (or other) funding, who were essentially hired to perform a service. A defined objective rarely entered the picture.

Therefore, the question of capacity has become vital simply because it governs whether a venture is sustainable. When an entrepreneur is building a company, he or she must ensure that the company can carry out its visions and mission, or execute the business plan. In the social venture sphere, "investors" try to determine how the social entrepreneur is building the capacity to drive the innovation forward. In both worlds, innovation without basic organizational building blocks cannot reach its potential.

The final measure of any venture's desirability as a vehicle for investment involves an intangible with which all investors, whether

---

11 Interview: Jeff Skoll, Des Dearlove, *Business Strategy Review*, Summer, 2004.

operating in the for-profit realm or not, must struggle. This is simply a feeling about the entrepreneur and whether he or she has the right stuff to achieve *remarkable* success. In making this somewhat emotional assessment, a traditional venture investor might look at the entrepreneur's track record or education. But a backer of a social enterprise venture has to look to other measures, among them such factors as strength of conviction, a clinging to a moral base, or a desire to clearly make an impact in a community.

KNOW WHO YOU ARE

In the social entrepreneurship sphere, this would echo the venture capitalist's gut feeling about an entrepreneur. "In nearly every case it is very clear whether a person is a social entrepreneur or whether they are an effective non-profit leader but probably not a social entrepreneur," says Skoll.[12]

Most social philanthropy groups, such as SVP or Angels With Attitude (a group of angel investors who seed-fund socially responsible ventures in the Pacific Northwest), design a series of criteria that outline what they look for in a venture. But this can only act as a template of sorts: The quality that underlies such frameworks is equivalent to the entrepreneurial zeal that usually distinguishes the true entrepreneur from a good manager. Skoll calls this the "ping" factor—that indefinable understanding that the social entrepreneur "rings true." This would involve absolute dedication, conviction and an ability to mobilize and inspire other people to join them. It is the same search for greatness that preoccupies the mindshare of the for-profit world on a daily basis.

In these, the first few years of the new century, it has become clear that social entrepreneurship and the new philanthropy are a growing force. However, this new wave is not without its growing pains and still has much development ahead. There is an excessive reliance, for example, on visionary leadership in both the social entrepreneurship and the philanthropic ranks, which implies a lack of organizational depth. As Jed Emerson, Executive Director of the Roberts Enterprise Development Fund, describes it: "If the field is to benefit from both the investments that have already been made and the high level of effort

---

12 *Business Strategy Review*, Spring, 2004.

undertaken by these social entrepreneurs, more effective networking, training and other support systems will be essential.

"The field of social purpose business development is an emerging one with no formalized knowledge base. Significant attention has been paid to the role and emergence of 'New Social Entrepreneurs' and others who are guiding the shifts presently taking place in the nonprofit sector. However . . . organizations need assistance in providing targeted training opportunities to mid-level managers as well, for these are the individuals who will operationalize the business and other strategies being pursued by the nonprofit corporation."[13]

Organizations like the Skoll Foundation and Ashoka, while certainly pioneering the concept of this new philanthropy, are still for the most part isolated voices. It will be intriguing to see how quickly the considerable energies of pioneers like Jeff Skoll will result in a knowledge base for social entrepreneurship that is equivalent to that of traditional entrepreneurship. Regardless, one can only hope that the rise in the number of learned fisherman is matched by an exponential growth in the community of willing teachers. That alone would be the true measure of success.

5 THINGS YOU NEED TO KNOW

Social entrepreneurs will find these guidelines useful to help distinguish their projects and attract venture philanthropists to support their cause:

1. Create an Inflection Point

The new era of philanthropy is about small investments being leveraged into large returns. Teaching people to fish one person at a time is not the end game anymore. As an example, the Skoll Foundation's goal is to create systemic change—"long-term changes in whole systems that empower people to lift themselves out of poverty"—around the world. The focus has been on finding leverage in the areas of education, technology and micro enterprise.

---

13 Marya N. Cotton, "Contempating 'enterpris': the business and legal challenges of social entrepreneurship,", *American Business Law Journal*, 9/22/2003

2. Think Like an Entrepreneur

How innovative is the idea? How much of a breakthrough is it? Is it designed to effect systemic change? Can the social entrepreneur demonstrate that he or she is driven to create measurable impact?

3. Don't Talk, Execute

The Skoll Foundation does not generally fund startups. Rather, it looks for social enterprises that have already established that their ideas are roadworthy.

4. Show Capacity

The Skoll Foundation looks at how the social entrepreneur is instituting systems that will drive their initiative forward. Innovation without a base of resources, the right people and other basic building blocks cannot reach its potential. "Nothing happens without individuals, but nothing lasts without institutions," says Skoll.[14]

5. Know Who You Are

In the social entrepreneurship sphere, this would echo the venture capitalist's gut feeling about an entrepreneur. "In nearly every case it is very clear whether a person is a social entrepreneur or whether they are an effective non-profit leader but probably not a social entrepreneur," says Skoll.[15]

---

14 Interview: Jeff Skoll, Des Dearlove, *Business Strategy Review*, Summer, 2004.
15 *Business Strategy Review*, Spring, 2004.

CHAPTER TWENTY-THREE

Taking a Stand
The Risk of Speaking Out

FEATURING THE WISDOM OF GRAYDON CARTER

Few people in journalism have been as prolific as Vanity Fair *editor Graydon Carter. He has been a force in the industry since the late '80's, when he co-founded* Spy *magazine, a satirical publication whose influence can still be found embedded in popular culture today. He was widely credited with transforming the* New York Observer *from a sluggish community newspaper into an intimate depiction of New York's cultural, political and real estate elite.*

In July of 1992, Carter accepted the position of editor-in-chief at Vanity Fair, *a post he has held ever since. He was replacing Tina Brown, the publishing powerhouse responsible for revamping the magazine and boosting circulation to well over a million readers. He faced tremendous pressure from industry insiders, who were skeptical about his ability to outperform Brown. Carter proved worthy of the challenge.*

He infused Vanity Fair *with his own unique touches, blending celebrity cover stories with serious investigative pieces. Under Carter's tutelage,* Vanity Fair *has been awarded ten National Magazine Awards, including two for the highest honour in magazine publishing: General Excellence for magazines exceeding one million in circulation. The magazine has been home to some of the biggest talent in the world, including Annie Leibovitz, Dominick Dunne and Christopher Hitchens.*

Carter has been recognized as Advertising Age's *Editor of the Year and was the first person to be twice recognized as* Adweek *magazine's Editor of the Year.*

In 2002, Carter expanded from print journalism into film production. He produced a critically acclaimed documentary about renowned Hollywood director Robert Evans, The Kid Stays in the Picture. *He was also the executive producer of 9/11, a film about the World Trade Center attacks; it garnered him an Emmy and a Peabody Award in 2006.*

In 2008 alone, he produced three documentaries. The Chicago 10 *followed the trial of a group of defendants who faced criminal charges after the 1968 Democratic National Convention riots.* Gonzo *was an in-depth biography of author Hunter S. Thompson, and* Surfwise *followed a family who eschewed a traditional lifestyle in favour of travelling the world in search of the best waves.*

Over the past six years, Carter found himself increasingly dismayed at the actions of the Bush administration, particularly in their response to the attacks on September 11. His Editor's Letters, once pithy and irreverent introductions to the magazine's features, became scathing exposés on the realities of America's conflicts in Iraq and Afghanistan. Carter transformed his column into a platform highlighting the darker side of the war at a time when Bush enjoyed unprecedented approval ratings and the rest of the mainstream press was reluctant to provide unfavourable coverage.

He was lambasted for doing so. Critics were harsh and unyielding, branding him an unpatriotic traitor. Carter refused to back down; *Vanity Fair* continued its extensive coverage, revealing the chilling reality of a conflict most Americans were unwilling to face.

This wasn't the first time the magazine had pursued controversial topics. (Carter had allowed journalist Marie Benner to publish a story about tobacco whistleblower Jeffrey Wigand, despite the tobacco company Brown & Williamson's status as a prominent advertising partner. Carter has also remained committed to educating readers about the crisis in Africa and the impacts of climate change.) However, it was the first time he used his column to express a personal opinion. He didn't have to speak up. In fact, it would have been significantly easier for him to turn a blind eye and feign indifference, safely cocooned in Manhattan.

Decades before he would be touted as the "King of New York," Edward Graydon Carter was just another lanky twenty-one-year-old working as a railway lineman in western Canada.

The job was Carter's latest foray into the world of blue-collar labour, an experiment of sorts in the year between high school and university that had included stints as a gravedigger, stock boy and bank teller. Looking back, it was a welcome detour from what he considered an inevitable career path. "I knew I'd wind up with a white-collar job at some point," he said. "I wanted to, I don't know, I just wanted to taste life."

At the age of 25, while enrolled in the University of Ottawa, he caught wind of a small venture started by a friend. The Canadian Review was a tiny literary magazine started by a friend that immediately captured Carter's interest—and his time. Attending classes quickly became a lesser priority as he delved into the world of publishing and Carter gradually built up a solid circulation of 50,000 readers. Fortunately for the publishing world, his academic career did not flourish as nicely, and he dropped out of the University of Ottawa.

He did briefly enroll at Carleton University, but after missing a majority of his classes, he was asked not to return. It was then that he decided to forgo a university education in favour of pursuing something he loved. By the time the magazine folded in 1977, Carter was ready for a new challenge and itching for a change of scenery. He moved to New York City. He arrived with everything he could fit into an old BMW and armed with a plan: he would give himself thirty days to find paid employment or return to Ottawa. On the last day of his deadline, he landed a position as a writer with *Time*, where he would spend the next few years covering politics and entertainment.

As he honed his writing skills, Carter never forgot the thrill of managing his own publication and dreamed of one day venturing off to do just that. It was an idea he often discussed with Kurt Anderson, a fellow writer at *Time*—the two would spend hours conceptualizing their perfect magazine.

They would incubate the idea for the next two years, while Carter moved to *Life* magazine. Carter and Anderson launched *Spy* in 1986 and drew heavy inspiration from the likes of A.J. Liebling and Woolcot Gibbs, famed journalists of the '20s, '30s, and '40s. *Spy* emulated the

British satirical weekly *PrivateEye* and *MAD* through a blended mix of satire and investigative journalism. The publication probed the idiosyncrasies of the entertainment industry and exposed the darker side of celebrity culture. Carter and Anderson pursued their subjects with fervour, relentlessly airing dirty laundry. *Spy* was one of the most highly acclaimed magazines of its time.

Despite its critical success, the venture was not profitable and revenue suffered during the 1990 recession. Carter and Anderson sold the company to European investors Jean Pigozzi and Charles Saatchi in 1991.

Carter was once again on the lookout for the next challenge, and it appeared in the guise of the *New York Observer*. Founded in 1987, the unknown young paper focused on reporting local community board meetings and was in the market for a new editor. Carter took on the challenge. It didn't take him long to infuse his own personal touch into the newspaper, and the *Observer* was soon transformed into "the" place to get the inside scoop about Manhattan's corporate elite, especially those who worked in real estate, in law, in the media or on Wall Street.

As with the *Canadian Review* and *Spy*, the paper thrived under Carter's watchful eye. It was a year into his new job when Carter caught the attention of S.I. Newhouse, the publishing tycoon who lorded over the Advance Publications empire and whose portfolio included *Vogue*, *Vanity Fair*, the *New Yorker*, *Architectural Digest* and more.

Newhouse was looking to change management in both the *New Yorker* and *Vanity Fair*. Initially, Carter was offered the editorship of the *New Yorker*, a dream come true. So he was disheartened when two weeks later, Newhouse switched course and offered the position to then–*Vanity Fair* editor Tina Brown.

Newhouse instead offered Carter the opportunity to become *Vanity Fair*'s editor-in-chief, an unexpected request and a detour on a path he had yet to consider. The move would be risky, and deliciously ironic: Could he succeed at a magazine renowned for courting the very celebs he had spent years ripping to shreds? Would he bring anything new to the publication that had been recently rebuilt by publishing golden girl Tina Brown? Industry insiders scoffed at the choice, and claimed Carter would be merely upholding an empire built by Brown.

He accepted the position in 1992 and hasn't looked back. Over the last seventeen years Carter has elevated *Vanity Fair* into one of the world's most respected magazines.

Put Your Best Face Forward

On his first day as a lineman in Western Canada, Carter's boss took one look at his long hair and insisted he cut it. It was an early lesson in the importance of personal branding.

During his time at *Spy* magazine he paid special attention to his wardrobe. "Because we were small and because we were scrappy, I made a very conscious effort to wear a suit and tie to work every day," he says. "You can get away with a lot more if you look like a junior part of the establishment than if you look like a renegade."

People notice the little things; first impressions are made within seconds. Carter strives to pay attention to the smallest of details in *Vanity Fair* by ensuring that each issue comes together in a way that perfectly encapsulates the magazine's values.

He instinctively learned what career coaches have been preaching for years: the importance of the personal brand. In his article "The Brand Called You," author Tom Peters describes the importance of managing the little details: "That cross-trainer you're wearing—one look at the distinctive swoosh on the side tells everyone who's got you branded. That coffee travel mug you're carrying—ah, you're a Starbucks woman! Your T-shirt with the distinctive Champion "C" on the sleeve, the blue jeans with the prominent Levi's rivets, the watch with the hey-this-certifies-I-made-it icon on the face, your fountain pen with the maker's symbol crafted into the end . . . You're branded, branded, branded, branded." Peters adds, "It's time for me—and you—to take a lesson from the big brands, a lesson that's true for anyone who's interested in what it takes to stand out and prosper in the new world of work."

Carter knew the importance of personal brand management before the term became standard business jargon. His impeccable style isn't limited to his wardrobe, but extends into other aspects of his life, including his new restaurant, the Waverly Inn, where he personally oversees the seating chart every day. Each new venture accurately reflects how he wants to be perceived, down to the very last detail. It's a strategy that has produced a longstanding reputation for class and style. In his industry, that reputation translates into solid credibility that facilitates his role as the magazine's curator for art and culture.

LIFE IS ABOUT SEATING AND LIGHTING

On his first day as a lineman in western Canada, Carter's boss took one look at his long hair and insisted he cut it. It was an early lesson in the importance of personal branding, and Carter quickly realized that cultivating the right image was an essential step towards realizing success.

It's Never Too Late to Mend Fences

As *Vanity Fair's* new editor, Carter would have to court the same celebrities he had spent years ridiculing at *Spy*. He had been merciless in their pursuit and now faced the daunting task of making amends.

He did so with humility and grace, reaching out to reconcile with some of his former victims. Donald Trump, whom *Spy* had famously labelled a "short-fingered vulgarian," accepted Carter's apology with good nature. In fact, the two became friendly and when Trump married Marla Maples a few years later, Carter was on the invite list.

Carter also offered an apology to Liz Smith, the Grand Dame of *Dish*, and one of *Spy* magazine's favourite targets, and she accepted.

Looking back, he regrets the way he handled his relationship with Tina Brown. "I blew my relationship with Tina," he said. "What I should have done was ask her advice more."

While you might not be able to repair all broken relationships, making the attempt can result in a marked improvement in your life. Carter's willingness to accept responsibility for his past missteps, paired with his actions to rectify the situation, have had a positive effect on his relationship with old colleagues, allowing him to rekindle past friendships.

IT'S NEVER TOO LATE TO MEND FENCES

There comes a time in everyone's career when a relationship can become a casualty of a business decision. A single decision can tarnish a lifelong friendship, and while it's easier to write that relationship off, remember that we each hold some measure of accountability in the fall-out. That being said, it is never too late to try and mend those relationships. You will be surprised at how forgiving people can be.

Be Yourself; Everyone Else Is Taken

Mending fences was only half the battle. Now that he had stepped into the editor's role, the industry watched in rapt attention, awaiting his next move. The first year was a turbulent ride for Carter. Under constant stress, he quickly started gaining weight and losing sleep. Advertising pages took a hit, and the rumour mill ran wild, speculating how many more days he would last. Carter confessed that he used to glance at the building's directory in the mornings to reassure himself that his name was still listed. Staff members, many of them Brown loyalists, delighted in sharing his missteps with others, circulating rumours about falling morale and an unprepared new editor who locked himself away inside his office.

Then one day, as he neared his two-year mark at *Vanity Fair*, Carter had an epiphany. "Look, don't feel sorry for yourself," he remembers thinking. "You can make this magazine anything you want." After letting three of the troublemakers on his staff go, he decided it was an opportunity to start anew with a clean slate. He began the process that had always served him well in the past: indelibly stamping his unique brand of taste and style into the pages of the magazine.

Tina Brown's *Vanity Fair* had been characterized by glossy photography spreads, high-society crime stories and near-scandalous celebrity covers that always attracted notice. Graydon added his own touches. He devoted pages and resources to investigative pieces, political commentary, and foreign affairs, bulking up the magazine's long-form journalism. He introduced nostalgic features reminiscing about the forgotten glamour of "The American Century," profiling Marilyn Monroe and JFK, both of whom graced the cover.

BE YOURSELF; EVERYONE ELSE IS TAKEN

When inheriting a new position, it is easy to become overwhelmed by the methods used by your predecessor. There can be tremendous pressure to maintain the status quo, even if you don't agree with it. While it might result in a bumpier ride, it is essential to imprint your own unique touch and make the project your own. Following your own instincts is a critical aspect of success.

Seek New Opportunities in the Everyday

It's been seventeen years since Carter took the helm, and he continues to evolve the magazine in ways that capture and delight readers. He is constantly pushing the limits and exploring new spaces for *Vanity Fair* to play in. Carter pioneered the now famous Hollywood issue, which coincides with the Oscars and usually features spectacular group shots of many the nominees. The idea was a huge success and inspired Carter to publish more specialty issues, but this time the focus would be about real, pressing subjects.

For the last three years *Vanity Fair* has produced a Green Issue. "The environmental problems we face will not go away," Carter says. "If the rest of the world consumed energy at the same rate we do in the West, we'd need four earths to supply the resources to produce that energy."

When he announced he would be dedicating an entire issue to topics relating to Africa, many were skeptical. After all, *Vanity Fair* chronicled the pampered lives of the rich and famous, not the crisis in Darfur. But Carter had a surprising announcement: a guest editor would produce the issue. The role would fall to Bono, the famous rock star turned humanitarian who championed Africa's plight.

How would *Vanity Fair* entice readers to pick up an issue that was devoted to a topic they were usually ignorant or complacent about? The Africa issue didn't boast one cover: it had twenty, all photographed by Annie Leibowitz. Included were politicians, philanthropists and artists such as George Bush, Condoleezza Rice, Barack Obama, Queen Rania of Jordan, Jay-Z, Bono, Chris Rock, Madonna, George Clooney, Brad Pitt, Don Cheadle, Maya Angelou, Oprah Winfrey, Muhammad Ali, Warren Buffett, and Bill and Melinda Gates.

The theme of the covers was a visual chain letter, something that had never been done before. Carter wanted Leibovitz to capture the necessity of having an open dialogue about these issues, and the covers became a series with each person seen talking about Africa to the next person, who would appear in a subsequent cover passing the message along to someone else.

Carter called upon *Vanity Fair*'s impressive roster and sent some of the best writers to Africa. He also invited guest writers, including Bill Clinton, to contribute their perspectives. The issue was a big success, and Carter is proud of what he's accomplished. "If you read this issue, the first thing you come away with is that you would like to get on an airplane and go there, which, considering that none of the pieces are travel stories, is quite remarkable," he says. "And I think that you come away with an understanding of the richness of Africa after this—that it's more like the West than most of us think."

SEEK NEW OPPORTUNITIES IN THE EVERYDAY

No matter how long you've been doing something, always look for ways to change and evolve. Businesses should be constantly assessing the market, their clients and their organization to identify areas of opportunity. This constant diligence will ensure that a corporation can quickly spot latent needs before their competitors.

Know When to Take a Stand

Vanity Fair has always prided itself on its impartial and even-handed reporting. In fact, Carter has deliberately chosen to not vote or buy shares during his tenure as editor, in order to maintain a neutral perspective on the issues covered. But something changed after 9/11. The more he followed the actions of the Bush White House, the angrier he became. "This got me up again in the way I haven't felt since my early 30s," he said. "It was a sense of outrage as you went along." Particularly shocking was how the Bush administration was "doing everything in its power to cut back the benefits for veterans, both of past wars and of the troops in Iraq now."

As conditions continued to worsen, Carter turned to a platform he hadn't previously considered using to air his personal grievances:

his editor's letter. His editorials turned into scathing criticisms of the President's management of the war in Iraq and of the country.

If this doesn't sound radical, consider this: in early 2003, President Bush was enjoying an approval rate of over 80 percent, and supporting the war had become a dangerously narrowed definition of patriotism. As a battle waged against unseen terrorists, critics, afraid to voice their dissent in fear of violating Bush's "You're with us or you're against us" stance, chose silence for fear of being labelled treasonous.

Carter recalled the initial reaction to his editorials. "The mail ran three to one against me in the beginning," he said. "Reactions were polite but firm, along the lines of "We love your magazine, but please lay off the President." And now? "Now it runs about three to one in my favour." While Vanity Fair's "mailbag" is regularly on the receiving end of outraged reactions in the face of controversial pieces, this particular instance focused specifically on Graydon Carter and his personal opinions.

Each additional fact he uncovered revealed a piece of an increasingly dismal portrait. Armed with his knowledge, Carter intended to publish a short handbook, but continued to unearth information that he just couldn't leave out. The book kept growing in length. "We had meetings on the research every couple of days; we went through 30,000 reports— it was daunting, what the Bush administration had done," he recalled. "I went into this thinking I knew maybe a tenth of it; I didn't know the one-thousandth of it," he said. "I'm really crummy at deadlines—which is strange, because I'm a very punctual person usually for lunches—and a really slow writer, but I had to do this in four months and worked till 2 a.m. every morning. I was saying to my kids, the one thing this book did was use my brain cells, because I've been an editor so long. An editor rarely uses his brain; he uses his gut more than his brain." By the end of it, the book had taken its toll. "My brain was worn out, the tips of my fingers were worn out," he said.

There were people in Carter's social circle who urged him to show some caution. He was, after all, angering very powerful people, and many of them owned large stakes in media companies—an industry fact he acknowledges. "I think that increasingly large chunks of popular media are owned by fewer and fewer people. That is probably a problem," he says. "I think that the administration was very crafty in labelling any kind of dissent after September 11 as the work of the unpatriotic. A lot of journalists got into trouble for saying anything that wasn't actually in line with the Republican wishes at that time. I think now the press is slowly beginning to take a far more skeptical view of the Republican administration."

For Carter, a commitment to the ethical standards of journalism, coupled with a responsibility to provide the truth, proved far more important then the tempers of corporate titans. Fortunately he has never been pressured internally from higher-ups to soften his edges. "I don't spend a great amount of time worrying about corporate interests and how they might intrude on how I edit Vanity Fair," he says. "We've been very critical of this administration, and of their cronies in the oil and gas industry. We've reported on Monsanto, Chevron, the tobacco industry . . . The list goes on. Not once have I ever been asked by somebody at Condé Nast to tone it down. That's just not part of the culture here."

Besides, it is up to journalists to be the world's eyes and ears, to document the unfolding events of our time. It's a responsibility he takes extremely seriously. "There is the belief that journalists should remain apolitical. And for the most part, I try to follow this rule," he declares. "With the Bush administration though, I just saw something so dangerous that love of country trumped the journalistic concept of impartiality. Truth is more important than balance."

Carter wanted his readers to understand what was happening and to recognize the underlying issues behind the mistakes in order to avoid the same pitfalls in the future. "We might learn to become better neighbours. And we might turn some of our attention to problems that do not require weaponry," he said. "The huge percentage of our GNP that goes to policing the world and protecting our interests around the globe can be put to better use in creating new energy sources and repairing our infrastructure."

Carter has no regrets about the stories that were printed, or the tenacity with which he pursued the administration. "No, not one," he admits. He watched the events of the last eight years unfold and felt slightly vindicated. "On some level, absolutely," he says. "But there's certainly no joy in being right. I'm sickened by what Bush and his people have done to this country. For all of our sakes, I'd with I'd been wrong."

Conclusion

The nostalgic part of Carter that so often manifests itself in tribute pieces to glorious days gone by appears as he reflects on the evolution of the politics machine. "Society has changed a lot since the days of John F. Kennedy and his ilk—and, sadly, I think that what it takes to be a politician these days discourages a lot of smart, able young people from pursuing a career in public life," he says. And yet, he manages to remain optimistic. "There is still an abundance of vision and inspiration out there. I look at people like Barack Obama, the architect Bill McDonough, and others who are working to change the world. These are people who believe in what they're saying and aren't afraid to go forward with it. That, in turn, inspires the people around them. Given how flawed the political process is in this country, the surprise is not how few great people choose to enter politics, but how many."

As for his personal goals, Carter continues to find satisfaction and challenge as *Vanity Fair*'s editor-in-chief, a position some friends say he'll have for life. "I have fewer 'what was I thinking' moments than I did 15 years ago, but I still have them," he says.

Even as the magazine industry continues to grapple with the implications of the Internet, Carter remains confident in his product offering. He maintains that the types of long style narrative found within *Vanity Fair*'s glossy covers will thrive despite the speed and availability of the web. "The whole essence of this magazine has shifted over the last four years from just going after news-breaks to go completely towards storytelling—the great yarn-spinners," he says.

Vanity Fair has a reputation for capturing its readers and immersing them within its articles, and a large part of that fascination is thanks to Carter's inimitable touch, his instincts for mixing the perfect cocktail of hard-hitting reporting topped with the right amount of celebrity garnish. It is an addictive combination that seems to come naturally to Carter, who has come leaps and bounds from a skinny young kid in western Canada. And yet, embedded within the polish, the chauffeured cars and the VIP lifestyle, a part of that boy has remained. There's a hint of Canadiana that emerges in his Editor's letter, expressed through a desire for civility, a concern for fellow citizens, and a simple wish to be a better neighbour. And under all that is a backbone of pure steel. What could be more Canadian than that?

5 THINGS YOU NEED TO KNOW

1. Put Your Best Face Forward

On his first day as a lineman in western Canada, Carter's boss took one look at his long hair and insisted he cut it. It was an early lesson in the importance of personal branding, and Carter quickly realized that cultivating the right image was an essential step towards realizing success.

2. It's Never Too Late to Mend Fences

There comes a time in everyone's career when a relationship can become a casualty of a business decision. A single decision can tarnish a lifelong friendship, and while it's significantly easier to write that relationship off, remember that we each hold some measure of accountability in the fall-out. That being said, it is never too late to try and mend those relationships. You will be surprised at how forgiving people can be.

3. Be Yourself; Everyone Else Is Taken

When inheriting a new position, it is easy to become overwhelmed by the methods used by your predecessor. There can be tremendous pressure to maintain the status quo, even if you don't agree with it. While it might result in a bumpier ride, it is essential to imprint your own unique touch and make the project your own. Following your own instincts is a critical aspect of success.

4. Seek New Opportunities in the Everyday

No matter how long you've been doing something, always look for ways to change and evolve. Businesses should be constantly assessing the market, their clients and their organization to identify areas of opportunity. This constant diligence will ensure that a corporation can quickly spot latent needs before their competitors.

5. Know What You Stand For

We each have the ethical responsibility to speak out against people or organizations that are acting in a way detrimental to society, even if it is unpopular to do so. Carter feels that there are certain issues that are too important to blindly ignore, and that it is essential for those who have a platform (be it a newspaper/magazine column or an organization) to use it responsibly and it a way that benefits the greater good.

CHAPTER TWENTY-FOUR

What's Next:
From "Me" to "We" Through
the Guidance of "Them"

FEATURING THE WISDOM OF CRAIG KIELBURGER,
FOUNDER, FREE THE CHILDREN

In 1995, while searching for the comics buried inside the weekend edition of the *Toronto Star*, 12-year-old Craig Kielburger stumbled across the article that changed his life. Iqbal Masih, also twelve years old, was a former carpet factory labourer who had been murdered for speaking out against child labour in Pakistan. Sold by his parents into slavery at an early age, Masih was tied inside a room and forced to weave carpets for twelve hours a day. For Kielburger, the horrific circumstances were a world away from his home in Thornhill, a comfortable Toronto suburb. "For me, poverty was always somewhere over there, in some far-off place," he recalls. "It never really touched my own life."

Moved by the story, he shared it with his grade seven class, and they collectively decided to take action. "I never wanted to start a charity; we just wanted to help," he said. The small group began travelling to local schools, raising awareness about child labour, but they soon realized their ability to contribute was limited.

There was an abundance of university-led initiatives supporting various causes, but no groups for grade school children to connect with each other and become civically active. And few charities would take a group of pre-teens seriously. "If you really want to help, find out where your parents keep their credit cards," was the condescending advice he received from one representative.

Kielburger decided to do something about it. He created an organization called Free the Children. "Our mission at that point was really two-fold," he explained. "First, we wanted to free the children of the world from poverty and slavery, but we also wanted to free the children of Canada from thinking they were too young and powerless to make a difference."

And what a difference they made. Since its inception in 1995, Free the Children (FTC) has grown to become the world's largest network of children helping children through education. The organization focuses on empowering youth through leadership programs in an effort to create socially conscious global citizens who act as agents of change within their communities.

To date, the FTC network is one million strong. Over 500 schools have been built in 45 countries across the globe. Kielburger, now 25, continues to lead the organization in innovative directions that are challenging the business models of traditional charities. He has shared the podium with the likes of Bill Clinton, Queen Noor, Desmond Tutu and Nelson Mandela, and was the youngest person to be inducted into the Order of Canada.

Kielburger remains humble and committed to the cause. "It still feels a little surreal," he admits, thinking about everything he has accomplished. "And there is much more work to do."

GLOBALIZED ACTION

Kielburger credits the rise of technology, in particular the ability to effortlessly communicate and share information, with the rapid growth of Free the Children. "We don't often recognize how technology has had a social and cultural impact," he says. "It's not just about products or sales." Technology has allowed Free the Children to spread its message far beyond the capabilities of a group of grade seven students.

The world has never been more connected. Younger generations have always known about 24-hour news channels, blogs and the information-disseminating power of the simple cell phone. The six o'clock news is no longer the only way to get information. Brief network snippets, combined with one person's spin, have been replaced by a constant stream of moments captured by first-hand accounts and cell phone cameras. Kielburger remembers seeing the civilian footage during the Myanmar riots in 2007. Despite a government clampdown on media outlets and an attempt to shut down the Internet, citizens were still able to document their experiences and share them with the world.

Today's youth can be versed in global issues. Kielburger has high hopes for what his generation will do with this opportunity. "When this generation comes of age, and starts to vote and to shop and to consume, they will do it with a more globalized mindset," he explains. "Once that happens, 'globalized' won't just be for technology and commerce, but you'll see a shift around more active global citizenship."

It is citizenship that will fuel Free the Children's success. "We've globalized technology, we've globalized commerce, and we've even globalized culture, but we haven't globalized compassion. I think that's starting to change."

ACTION 2.0

Kielburger hopes that this new global awareness will percolate into the public's consciousness and affect their behaviour. "There is this perception that if you want to change the world you do so by making a donation," he says, referring to the traditional charity business model. It is time for that model to evolve by making charities an extension of a conscious lifestyle.

Instead of an isolated donation, he envisions a future with consumers educated about the impact of their choices, including their purchases. For example, he mentions that few people would know that the cotton for an average T-shirt was grown with a third of a pound of pesticides. "When we shop, are we taking the time to really be informed?" he asks. And since we are, how will that affect our buying decisions?

The Internet has provided us with an unimaginable wealth of knowledge, and it is time for consumers to follow up with action. "How do we use this technology to live a lifestyle that has a positive impact on this world?" He pauses briefly before answering his own question. "We have web 2.0; I think the action 2.0 is missing: the part where we act based on the information we've received."

CHARITY AS A LIFESTYLE

Free the Children has been a leading example of social enterprise. Kielburger wanted FTC to operate differently from a regular charity.

"Traditional charity is not the most effective model," he said. "It makes you feel good, but it doesn't help the communities lift themselves out." And charities have not, historically, been self-sustaining. They are in an endless cycle of looking for handouts. From the beginning, Kielburger has sought to change the charity model.

His first focus was to make every dollar count. Kielburger is hoping to lower FTC's administrative costs of $0.09 for every donated dollar down to zero by creating new income strategies to offset costs. He has done this by introducing services and products to generate revenues to help fund the charity.

Kielburger has created "Me to We Style," a clothing line that offers domestically produced, sweatshop-free garments made using certified organic cotton and bamboo. Fifty percent of profits go to support FTC's projects in developing countries around the world. "In an age where everyone is outsourcing clothing overseas, [creating Canadian-made clothes] seems like an impossible business model," he explains. "But it's actually lucrative."

FTC also runs its own publishing division, printing socially responsible content. Publications include Kielburger's latest book, *Me to We: Finding Meaning in a Material World*.

His most recent venture is a music line that offers only socially conscious music. "At the end of each CD there are spoken words around social justice," he says. Additionally, FTC has a small travel division for people who are looking to travel on socially conscious trips.

These ventures have been profitable and have allowed Free the Children to continue its mission of improving the working and living conditions for those less fortunate, without relying solely on donations. "We wanted to push the model of charity to be self-sustaining economically," he says.

STOCK OPTIONS IN A BETTER WORLD

This mindset is an indication of the evolution of social enterprise as an emerging space between charity and business. "Business has been teaching charity for years, but now it's the other way around. We recognize that charity has a lot to teach business when it comes to innovation, employee morale and recruiting."

He is already seeing the shift. "We're able to lure business bankers to work for us and make take a tenth of their salary, and they'll do it because they want to see a better world. They'll forgo stock options to invest in a better future," he says. "It's not just about the bottom line anymore. We're seeing a space where companies don't just put their corporate social responsibility on a shelf."

Companies who capitalize on this trend will reap tremendous rewards. Kielburger sees many tangible benefits for companies that incorporate aspects of social responsibility and volunteerism into their culture. "Volunteering becomes a form of soft team building," he says. "You feel a connection to your employer, something that goes beyond just earning a paycheck." The distinction can be invaluable to young talent seeking the right organizational fit. "Young people are looking for meaning and purpose. They've seen their parents grow up with material goods and not be happy, and they don't want to wait until they retire to do something meaningful."

Companies can use volunteering initiatives as a recruitment tool to retain top employees and to empower and energize their workforce. This isn't an idea that is accepted easily. Kielburger recalls an MBA course he took about employee rewards. "I put up my hand and said, 'What about the intrinsic value of appreciating the work they do?' There were ripples of laughter," he says. "People didn't get it."

Kielburger doesn't mind the reactions; he knows companies will eventually begin to realize the financial and cultural benefits to making these types of changes. He is trying to do his part by continuing to empower and connect youth. In May of 2007, FTC launched the O-Ambassadors program in association with Oprah Winfrey's Angel Network. The program will see 2,000 clubs in 2,000 schools, educating students about global citizenship.

As for Kielburger, his passion continues to be youth engagement. He hopes to pursue his doctorate and someday teach. He recognizes that as he gets older he will need to step aside—and let the next generation of social entrepreneurs carry the torch.

Afterword

BY GUY KAWASAKI

For the past five years, I've remained convinced that I was a Canadian trapped in a Hawaiian's body. The only rational explanation that could account for this misplaced national identity is hockey: I love hockey to the core of my being, enough to become seduced by the entirety of Canadian culture, if only to better appreciate their national sport.

But after reading *Everything I Needed to Know About Business...I Learned from a Canadian*, a new explanation for my curious alignment with the Canadian persona has come to light: there are boatloads of successful Canadian tech entrepreneurs with whom I can identify. It's possible I was head-down in the penalty box while the rest of the world was taking notice of the talent emerging out of Canada, but this book snapped my attention away from the game and back into focus on business.

If you're a hockey player looking to improve your game and ask five pros how to advance your skill level, you will likely get at least seven different answers. Entrepreneurs looking for guidance often endure similar experiences—in looking for advice and direction, it's easy to become distracted by the barrage of ideas and suggestions that will be hurled your way. A good coach will remain true to the spirit of the sport by simplifying the game plan for his players. I'll attempt to do the same by fleshing out some key points raised in *Everything I Needed to Know About Business...I Learned from a Canadian*:

Get to the next curve. The action is in getting to, or creating, the next curve—not simply incrementally improving this curve. If you want to be included in a future version of this book, start by changing the world. Terry McBride, often cited as one of the first in the music industry to embrace the on-line world, was well ahead of the curve. So was Issy Sharp, who changed the hotel world by putting tiny bottles of shampoo and little bars of soap in a small, then unheard of, hotel by the name of Four Seasons Motor Inn.

Don't worry, be crappy. When you create something cool, ship it. Don't wait until you've perfected every last detail, because the market is impatient and will pass you by. Nick Graham knew this when he was making skinny ties in his apartment for sale in the markets, as did Marcia Kilgore who started out giving facials in hers. Who knew then that those early shipped products would be the primordial soup from which the Joe Boxer and Bliss Spa brands would spring forth.

Churn, baby, churn. I said you don't have to wait until you perfect a product, but I did not say you didn't have to revise and enhance your product to the best of your ability. This is the same thing as "ugly goals" that you score by scrapping for rebounds.

Never ask a customer or employee to do something that you wouldn't do. For example, you wouldn't fill out twenty fields of personal information to register and get a password, so don't expect your customers to. Value the time of others.

Focus on cash flow. Brand awareness, market share, and paper profits are secondary compared to cash. As long as cash is flowing, you're still in the game. A lesson known only too well to Jim Pattison, who has built a billion dollar empire out of cash flow businesses.

This is all you really need to do—master these 5 basic elements of successful entrepreneurship by thinking like a Canadian. I use the term "all" loosely—just as gliding out onto the ice looks effortless when executed by a seasoned hockey player, so too does forging a successful business plan look like an easy task to aspiring entrepreneurs. But mastering the basics is a necessary precedent on that path to becoming an all-star player, as you won't get far if you're nervous on ice. It's like when my hockey buddies tell me, "All you need to do is skate better, and you'll be fine."

Index

About the Authors

LEONARD BRODY

Leonard is a highly respected entrepreneur, venture capitalist and best-selling author. He has helped in raising millions of dollars for start-up companies, been through one of the largest internet IPOs in history and has been involved in the building, financing and/or sale of five companies to date.

Much critical acclaim has followed him in his endeavours. At Onvia (where he was part of the initial executive), the company was voted Canada's number one start-up in 2000 and subsequently closed a $240 million IPO on NASDAQ.

Currently, Leonard is Co-Founder and CEO of NowPublic, which is one of the pioneers in citizen generated news and quickly becoming one of the largest news agencies in the world, with over 140,000 contributing reporters in 160 countries and 6,000 cities. In the last year, *The Guardian* in London ranked NowPublic as one of top 5 news sites in the world and *Time Magazine* named it as one of the top 50 websites of the year.

Leonard acts as an advisor to venture capital funds in the US, Europe and Asia and is currently a Senior Advisor to the Canadian Ministry of International Trade, and a Director of Canada's largest technology association, CATA.

A highly sought-after public speaker, Leonard has lectured at universities such as Stanford, the Indian Institute of Technology in Mumbai and the Gordon Business School in Johannesburg. He has spoken at conferences throughout the world such as NASSCOM, the World Newspaper Congress, CEBIT and the Monaco Media Forum. His work has been featured in such publications as *USA Today*, *Fortune*, the *Wall Street Journal*, the BBC, El Mundo and Der Spiegel.

Leonard holds an Honours Bachelor of Arts from Queens University, a law degree from Osgoode Hall and is a graduate of the Private Equity Course at the Harvard Business School.

DAVID RAFFA

David Raffa is a recently minted venture capitalist, lapsed attorney and iconoclast.

He is a much sought after advisor to emerging technology companies, and is an acknowledged corporate finance expert who has made a career out of advising boards, assisting companies in raising financing, and assisting companies in engineering exits. David has served on more than twenty corporate, industry and charity boards, often as Chairman, including the BC Technology Industry Association and the Science World Equity Committee. He also served as an advisor to the BC Securities Commission and the TSX Venture Exchange. He has been engaged on a number of occasions to lead companies in achieving successful liquidity events.

David is a founder of Lions Capital, an investment banking and fund management firm that manages two venture capital funds, and that provides corporate finance services to technology companies. He serves as Lions' Chief Operating Officer and is one of the Fund Managers.

While David has a wide variety of business interests, they pretty much all involve working with and mentoring technology entrepreneurs who believe they have founded the "next greatest technology company."

When not buried under business plans or engaged in boardroom negotiations, David devotes his time to his wife and three daughters at his home in Deep Cove, BC, Canada, and occasionally sneaks out with his dog, Chiko, to partake in a little North Shore mountain biking.